T0171443

ALSO BY FELIX ROHATYN

Bold Endeavors: How Our Government Built America, and Why It Must Rebuild Now

Deal

A Political and Financial Life

Simon & Schuster

ings

Felix Rohatyn

NEW YORK · LONDON · TORONTO · SYDNEY

Simon & Schuster
1230 Avenue of the Americas
New York, NY 10020

First Simon & Schuster hardcover edition November 2010

SIMON & SCHUSTER and colophon are registered trademarks
of Simon & Schuster, Inc.

For information about special discounts for bulk purchases,
please contact Simon & Schuster Special Sales at
1-866-506-1949 or business@simonandschuster.com.

The Simon & Schuster Speakers Bureau can bring authors
to your live event. For more information or to book an event,
contact the Simon & Schuster Speakers Bureau at
1-866-248-3049 or visit our website at www.simonspeakers.com.

Text designed by Paul Dippolito

Photo Credits appear on page 276.

Manufactured in the United States of America

1   3   5   7   9   10   8   6   4   2

Library of Congress Cataloging-in-Publication Data
Rohatyn, Felix G., 1928–
Dealings : a political and financial life / Felix Rohatyn.
p.   cm.
1. Rohatyn, Felix G., 1928–   2. Investment bankers   United States—
Biography.   3. Capitalists and financiers—United
States—Biography 4. Ambassadors—United States—Biography. I. Title.
HG2463.R64A3   2010
327.73044092—dc22
[B]   2010026519

ISBN 978-1-4391-8197-3
ISBN 978-1-4391-8198-0 (ebook)

*To my wife, our children, and grandchildren,
with love and admiration*

Dealings

Prologue

A cigarette, I will always believe, saved my life. I was twelve, the year was 1940, and my family—mother, grandmother, and our longtime Polish cook—were making our anxious and harried way south through Nazi-occupied France. With mattresses tied to the roof of our car, we had driven out of Paris with the makeshift plan of somehow getting across the Spanish border. Our entire "fortune" consisted of a handful of gas coupons and a few Kolynos toothpaste tubes that, as my mother had instructed, I had emptied and then carefully refilled with dozens of gold coins.

The road out of Paris was a nightmare. Stretching into the distance was a teeming stream of refugees, a confusion packed with automobiles, horse carts, bicycles, and those with no choice but to flee on foot. A day's progress was measured in just a few frustrating miles. Worse, there was always the fear of encountering a German checkpoint. We were Jews; and the rumors about what was happening in the Dachau "internment camp" outside Munich had left us terrorized. I had no doubts about what the Nazis had in store for my family. Returning to German-occupied Paris, we feared, would be accepting a death sentence.

And so my mother, always tenacious, pulled off the main highway and improvised a southward route along unmarked roads and hardscrabble trails. After three exhausting days, we had made our way to Biarritz—only to be informed that the

Spanish border was now closed. Just moments after receiving this disheartening news, we witnessed a spectacle that ratcheted my mother's desperation and my fears up a further notch: column after column of jackbooted German troops were parading imperiously on the city's boulevards. The sight was chilling.

We drove on; the goal was now the port city of Marseille, and the new hope was a vague plan to board a ship to Casablanca. Following a road (of sorts) that weaved through a thick forest, we made our way toward Marseille with surprising speed. With the passing of each uneventful hour, our optimism grew. We became convinced that it would be only a matter of time before we were reunited with my stepfather and sailing on a ship to North Africa.

Finally, we emerged from the forest and joined a long row of cars. It was only as we moved forward that we discovered the line of vehicles was proceeding toward a German checkpoint. Frantic, my mother tried to turn around. It was impossible; we were wedged tightly into the column.

With increasingly grim resignation, we inched toward the checkpoint. Our papers clearly identified us as Jews. We would be sent back to Paris, where, in due course, we would be handed over to the Nazis. They would ship us east to the "internment" camps. I sat helplessly in the backseat, a twelve-year-old boy knowing that with each passing moment my family was moving inexorably closer toward its doom.

When at last we reached the checkpoint, my mother, hoping to delay the inevitable demand for identity papers, displayed her driver's license. The soldier, however, ignored her gesture. Instead, he absently waved our car forward, and at the same time reached into his pocket for a cigarette. As he struck a match and lighted his smoke, we drove on. It was only after we had passed through the checkpoint that I dared to look back: the soldier had stopped the car behind us.

Dealings

We continued on to Marseille. And once again fate intervened—our family was saved by a hero, Luiz Martins de Souza Dantas, the Brazilian ambassador to France. The dictator who ran Brazil, Getúlio Dornelles Vargas, had told his diplomats to arrange entry visas for 800 European immigrants. The dictator, however, had one firm caveat: no Jews should be included. De Souza Dantas, the "Schindler of Brazil," ignored this order. He helped 800 Jews, including my family, escape the Nazis. As a result, he was removed by his government and sent back to Brazil, where he died in poverty. I was number 447 on the 800 visas he distributed.

My stepfather, meanwhile, had jumped over the fence of an internment camp in Brittany and stolen a car, and he met us in Marseille. Reunited, we traveled to Casablanca, on to Lisbon, and then to Brazil. In June 1942, after a year's stay in Brazil, to our great joy and relief we at last arrived in New York City. The two years since 1940 had been exhausting and often difficult. Our capital was only what remained of the gold coins I had stuffed into the toothpaste tubes. Still, we celebrated and congratulated ourselves on the ingenuity and daring of our escape. Yet I knew: simply because a soldier in Marseille had decided to smoke a cigarette, my Jewish family was alive, and free, and able to start life over again.

Sixty years later I was back in Marseille, and once again I had good reason to believe I was in danger because I was Jewish. But now I had been fitted with a bulletproof vest, I was flanked by armed police guards and bomb-sniffing dogs, and there were uniformed snipers on the rooftops with orders to shoot any assailant who moved menacingly toward me. I was the American ambassador to France. And on this bright October day in 2000, I had come to a tree-lined square across from the American consulate to participate in the ceremonies that would rename it Place Varian Fry.

During the same year that my family had made its way to Marseille with the hope of finding passage out of France, Fry, a young American, had also come to the city. Undeterred by threats from the Gestapo and the Vichy government, and the active opposition of the U.S. State Department, Fry arrived in Marseille determined to save hundreds of artists and intellectuals—the vast majority of them Jews—from the Nazis. As the American ambassador, and as a Jew, I was determined to give a speech that would celebrate Varian Fry's courage and memory with the honor it deserved.

The security detail assigned to me by the French Ministry of the Interior did not want me to make an address in an open square. My American security force agreed. The shared concern was that it was too dangerous for a *Jewish* American official to appear in a public forum in Marseille. After all, they argued forcefully, the Middle East peace talks had recently collapsed; as a consequence the intifada raged in Israel, and a new wave of anti-Semitic violence and hooliganism had broken out in France. In such a fierce and politicized climate, the Jewish American ambassador would be a tempting target.

I am not reckless. I agreed without debate to wear a bulletproof vest. But I also had not returned to Marseille to run for safety as I had in 1940. The world had changed. And so had I.

I made my speech without incident.

The story that follows is the story of my journey, the tale of my adventures in finance and politics that culminated when a Polish-Jewish refugee from France returned to that country as the American ambassador. It is the story of how the wisdom and instincts acquired by a young boy who secreted gold coins into toothpaste tubes helped him to become a man who would work side by side with many of the titans who changed the shape of

Dealings

American capitalism, and also energized his desire to pitch in when his new homeland was in economic crisis. It is the story of a boy who ran to freedom, and then spent a lifetime determined to take advantage of the newfound opportunities created by a soldier's decision to reach for a cigarette.

One

S uccess in business, as in life, is often largely just a matter of luck. And so it was that as a young man, I had two
seemingly unconnected bits of luck, which helped to put
me on a propitious course to becoming an investment banker at
Lazard Frères and then on the way to making my first big deal.

My first life-changing stroke of good fortune occurred because the famous chanteuse Edith Piaf broke off with her boy-
friend. I was nineteen and had met her when we were both
passengers on a ship sailing from Le Havre to New York.

Before my final term at Middlebury, a small liberal arts college in bucolic Vermont where I had spent four happy years
studying physics and skiing (although not necessarily in that
order), I had returned to France to become reacquainted with
my father. It was 1947, and I had not seen my father in the seven
years since I had escaped with my mother and stepfather from
Nazi-occupied France. A brewer, my father had spent the war
hiding near Orléans in the home of a courageous man who had
supplied his factory with barrels. Now my father had reestab-
lished himself in Paris and was once again managing a brewery.

Our reunion was a happy one; we quickly discovered that
we still enjoyed each other's company. So when my father suggested I might want to follow in his footsteps at the brewery,
I gave the offer some serious thought. After all, I was doing
poorly at Middlebury. I had flunked out of the physics program

that would have allowed me to continue my studies at MIT, and I knew that I could never earn a living skiing. I decided to skip my final term and see if I had any affinity for the brewer's life.

I didn't. It was backbreaking work. From 6 A.M. to 6 P.M. I was cleaning out fermentation vats, working in the bottling plant, loading trucks. When at the end of each long day I rode the Metro home, people kept their distance; I reeked from the stink of beer. No less disturbing was the attitude of some of my coworkers. The brewery was in one of the communist districts of Paris, and the young American son of the managing director was, in some workers' minds, a suitable target for their animosity—and too often for something more tangible. On several occasions heavy beer barrels came very close to smashing into me. I soon realized that neither beer nor France represented my future. I decided to return to Middlebury and graduate.

On the ship back to America, I met a young and intriguing Indochinese woman who was an assistant to Edith Piaf. When she introduced me to the famous singer, I was surprised to discover that Piaf was a tiny, rather homely woman. Even at first glance she seemed victimized, a lonely woman who had suffered great disappointments; perhaps, I decided, it was this natural demeanor that helped to give her songs of scorned love their searing resonance. Piaf and I became friends, of a sort, during the voyage. She was impressed with my fluency in both French and English and asked if I would be willing to tutor her. A long engagement had been scheduled in a nightclub in New York called the Versailles, it was explained, and she would need to sing at least a few songs in English. The pay, she decided after some consideration, would be $5 an hour.

After I finished the term at Middlebury with a mediocre re-cord and a BS in physics, I returned to New York and began to tutor Edith Piaf. She had rented a sprawling apartment on Park Avenue that she shared with the French singers who accompanied her in the nightclub act. I would arrive in the early afternoon, when they all would just be getting up. The apartment would be chaotic, filled with people coming and going, and in her first waking hours Piaf would look ghastly—wan and even more fragile. I soon discovered that she had little interest in learning to sing in English. Rather, she wanted my help in preparing the English dialogue for her daily telephone conversations with the Hollywood actor with whom she had recently fallen madly in love. For $5 an hour, I was more than happy to comply. However, when her long-distance romance fell apart, she decided my tutorial services were no longer needed.

Abruptly, I was out of work. And yet I still needed a job. It was, then, in the aftermath of the breakup of Piaf's romance and my subsequent dismissal, that, in June 1949, my stepfather offered his help. He could contact an acquaintance, André Meyer, the senior partner at Lazard Frères, a relatively small investment bank with roots, like our family's, in Europe. Would I be interested?

I had no idea what an investment bank did. Nor, in truth, had I much interest in finding out. But I did need a paycheck. Perhaps, I thought, I could work at Lazard for the summer; by the fall, I'd be able, I felt confident, to find employment that was more suitable for someone with a degree, however undistinguished, in physics.

And so on a June morning I paid the nickel fare and took the elevated train from Eighty-Sixth Street and Third Avenue down to Wall Street. Then I walked past the Treasury Building and the New York Stock Exchange to 44 Wall Street, a somewhat rundown building that housed several medium-size brokerage houses and, on the Sixth floor, Lazard Frères.

After only a few preliminaries, Walter Fried, a kindly Austrian immigrant who was the firm's office manager, offered me a job. I would be assigned to the small department that compiled the monthly evaluations of clients' accounts. My salary would be $37.50 per week, including Saturdays until lunchtime. Mr. Meyer, Fried explained, would see me in September when he returned from Europe. Did I want the job?

At that moment I had no alternatives to consider, and so with more philosophy than enthusiasm I accepted. As for the promised interview with Mr. Meyer, I immediately put it out of my mind. I was certain I would be long gone from Lazard and the world of investment banking by the time September came.

—

"Why have you not written to thank me?"

That was the initial question Mr. Meyer asked me when I met him for the first time in September. He was a stocky, large-featured man. He spoke the words in English with a heavy French accent accompanied by a pronounced lisp. His reputation—brilliant, autocratic, a man with a volcanic temper—had become well known to me even during my short time at the firm. I was terrified.

Founded in 1848 by two New Orleans cotton merchants originally from Alsace, Lazard Frères was one of several American investment firms with deep southern roots. As the commercial shipping trade moved to San Francisco, Lazard followed. Then at the turn of the century, additional offices were opened in New York, and next in Paris and London. It was the David-Weill family, descendants of the Lazards, who controlled the firm and, wisely, brought Meyer into its Paris branch in 1927. He quickly earned respect in European financial circles for his role in helping to guide Citroën, the French automobile giant, through the depression of the 1930s. But as the winds of war swirled in Europe, Meyer relocated to America in 1940. After a brief but intense struggle with the resident Lazard partners in New York, André Meyer won full control of the office. Immediately he embarked on a determined, often relentless, always shrewd, program to transform a mid-level banking house into one of Wall Street's most powerful players.

He did this, in part, through a network of carefully cultivated connections in business and government. His was an international circle that included President Lyndon Johnson of the United States; Jean Monnet, the father of the European Common Market; Gianni Agnelli, chairman of Fiat; Eugene Black, president of the World Bank; David Rockefeller, chairman of the Chase Manhattan Bank; General Lucius Clay, the mastermind of the Berlin airlift; David Sarnoff, the head of RCA; and Bill Paley, president of CBS.

Yet in addition to forging these new relationships with the powerful, Meyer was also intent on maintaining Lazard's heritage as a family-oriented business. Like the other investment banks, Lazard had long-standing personal relationships with certain family-run corporations that had been passed on from generation to generation. The firm handled these corporations' financing needs by underwriting their securities, as well as advising them on mergers and acquisitions. And Lazard—like Lehman Brothers, Kuhn Loeb, Dillion Read, and Goldman Sachs—was viewed as a Jewish firm. We had our own strongly established set of banker-client relationships, while the gentile firms—Morgan Stanley, Eastman Dillon—had theirs.

And standing in Mr.—throughout our decades together I would always address him as either "Mr." or "monsieur"—Meyer's office, meeting him for the first time, I immediately understood the rebuke in his question. After two months at the firm, I had received a raise to $50 a week. Yet I had not thought to write him a letter of thanks. This was not how "family" members were expected to behave.

Of course, I began to apologize. Mr. Meyer listened mutely. As I rambled on, I assumed his next words would be an announcement that I was being let go. Even before he spoke, I was already disappointed. It wasn't simply that I had failed to find a job that would make better use of my physics degree. Rather, I had grown to like working at Lazard. I was finding the world of capital, its power to build businesses and affect lives in the postwar era of new beginnings, not simply engaging but exciting. And now, as a result of my perceived rudeness and ingratitude, I was about to be fired.

When at last Mr. Meyer spoke, I learned I was wrong. I was not dismissed. Instead, he offered me the opportunity to go to Europe as part of a training program. "I realize you have other interests than finance," Mr. Meyer said. Nevertheless, he suggested that I go work at several European firms associated with Lazard to learn the basics of the business. "When you return, then you can decide what you want to do in your life."

I agreed without hesitation. And this time I made sure to thank him.

In London, I worked for the Samuel Montagu firm, where I learned about precious metals and foreign exchange. At Lazard Paris, I had my first experiences in securities arbitrage, the business of buying securities in one currency and then selling—at a profit, it was hoped—in another. And at Les Fils Dreyfus in Basel, an old private banking firm with close family ties to Lazard, I was given a job in the department dealing with foreign exchange and precious metals.

It was a propitious time for a young man's education in the world of currency and precious metal transactions. In the aftermath of World War II, the European victors were, in essence, no less bankrupt than the vanquished. Trade was at a standstill and freely convertible currencies, other than the U.S. dollar and the Swiss franc, did not exist. Therefore, to encourage the recommencement of trade, a makeshift system of barter and triangle trade developed. Blocked currencies could be bought and sold for dollars at a discount and used to finance dollar-dominated trade. In those days, the Swiss banks, which held a significant amount of Europe's remaining capital, were the main actors in these dealings with foreign exchanges. And at Les Fils Dreyfus I witnessed the inventive (and on occasion anxiously speculative) transactions as European economies and corporations struggled to find their place in the postwar world. I began to appreciate the extraordinary power of capital: I felt as if I was present at the creation of a new Europe.

But Basel, a quiet, serious German-Swiss city on the Rhine, was not an ideal home for a young bachelor. It is bourgeois, wealthy, and private. I had little to do but learn the foreign exchange business and, on the weekends, ski in the mountains. My boss was a seven-foot Swiss named Shaeffer, a devotee of French food, who died happily in his sleep after an enormous meal at a great French restaurant near Lyon. If I stayed any longer in Basel, I feared that would be my fate, too.

But in the winter of 1950 I received my draft notice. A year earlier I had become, to my immense joy and pride, an American citizen. I had wrapped my Polish passport in a pink ribbon and sent it back to the Polish embassy. The Korean War had begun, and I considered it a privilege to serve in the army of my new homeland.

After basic training at Camp Atterbury, Indiana, and the Army Intelligence School at Fort Riley, Kansas, I was assigned to the Twenty-Eighth Infantry Division. The division was sent to Germany, and our headquarters was in the small town of Goppingen, about thirty-five miles from Stuttgart. I became the "order of battle intelligence" sergeant and was responsible for identifying and locating Soviet units in East Germany. As part of these duties, I needed to interact with German civilians. But it was too soon after the war; I couldn't ignore the past. I kept these contacts to a minimum.

It was in the army, where I shared barracks with young men from all around the country and from disparate backgrounds, that I began to learn what it was to be an American, and to take an active interest in my new country's political life. While I was growing up, Franklin Roosevelt had been for me the symbol of freedom and equality. And now I supported Truman in his tough stand against communism. After what I had seen in ravaged postwar Europe, I had become a staunch Democrat, committed to the party's guiding principle that government needed to play an activist role in improving its citizens' lives.

In 1953, I was transferred back to the United States. As the troopship came into New York harbor, I stared out at the Statue of Liberty and the New York skyline and rejoiced in the realization that this was my home.

I had now been out of college for five years, and my only working experience had been with Lazard Frères. And the more I thought about it, I didn't want to work anywhere else. I decided to take Mr. Meyer up on his offer of a job. After a brief stint in Switzerland, I returned to Lazard New York in 1955. I stayed for the next forty years.

Two

In Lazard's world, risk, I quickly realized with a young man's impatience, meant taking very little risk at all. Upon my return from the army, Mr. Meyer had suggested that I continue my activities trading in foreign exchange and that I also explore ways of investing the firm's capital to get a higher return than the treasury note rate. And so my daily life was now soberly measured out in a routine of transactions that profitably yielded small upward ticks of fractions of a percentage point. I yearned to do something more dramatic, to make a killing for the firm.

After a few months in the New York office, I decided I had found my chance. The investment of our excess cash was a very conservative, short-term operation of overnight loans to other brokerage firms with high credit ratings. I, however, had come across something better. I was offered the opportunity to lend $10 million—a large sum in the 1950s—at a significantly higher interest rate to a medium-size broker. Not only was the firm respectable and the interest rate attractive, but our capital would be covered by warehouse receipts of commodity products. I was certain there was no downside for Lazard.

Eagerly, I layed this all out to Edwin Herzog, the senior partner who headed the underwriting activities and was my immediate boss. He listened, and then without a moment's pause announced, "It doesn't smell right." It was an investment, he said, that was not worth the risk.

I was bitterly disappointed. I felt I was being held back by stodgy and conservative bankers who lacked the daring to appreciate a unique opportunity.

A month later, however, my perspective was dramatically realigned. I picked up the morning paper and read that a scam had taken place at the warehouse subsidiary of American Express— the very warehouse holding the commodities that were the collateral for my "sure thing" investment. Hundreds of millions of dollars were missing in what was already being called the "salad oil scandal." Billie Sol Estes, the Texas financier, would eventually be sentenced to fifteen years in prison for his role in this fraud. And my safe investment would have been a $10 million loss.

I had escaped a career-ending disaster to learn, instead, an important lesson: if a deal seems too good to be true, it is. It is often more prudent to walk away from seemingly glittering opportunities than to chase after them. As Mr. Meyer would lecture, a small profit is still a profit.

And yet, not even thirty, I still could not help feeling trapped. A banker's life spent juggling trades for an additional fraction of a percentage point of interest loomed as a very narrow and unsatisfying prospect. Perhaps, I began to wonder, I should investigate what other opportunities existed for a young army veteran with a physics degree.

But then fortune once more intervened in my life. As when I was hired at Lazard, I stumbled into a moment of happenstance that dramatically changed the course of my entire financial career.

―

The fortunate moment occurred on a Sunday morning as I sat at a breakfast table laid with heavy silver in a palatial mansion overlooking the Hudson River in Tarrytown, New York. I had fallen in with a crowd that included Phyllis Lambert, a talented architect whose father, Samuel Bronfman, was the founder of Seagram's, the Canadian distiller. On weekends Phyllis would often invite people to stay, and these lavish Sunday breakfasts served by white-jacketed waiters were part of the house party ritual.

Mr. Sam—as Phyllis's father was known to all of us—always sat at the head of the table, a small, rotund but fiercely intimidating presence. On this particular Sunday his sons Edgar and Charles were, in addition to Phyllis and myself, seated below him. And as one of the liveried waiters poured him a fresh cup of coffee, Mr. Sam rather absently, or so it seemed at the time, turned to me and asked what I did for a living.

I responded that I worked at Lazard Frères. Rather pridefully, I went on to explain that I headed the foreign exchange trading activity.

Mr. Sam cut me off. "You're wasting your time," he said with a definitiveness that left me unnerved. "The only thing André is interested in is making deals. If you really want a future with the firm, you should get into that department."

All eyes at the table turned toward me as I struggled to formulate a response. At last I mumbled that I knew nothing about mergers and had never even taken a course in economics or accounting in college. Besides, I added, if I asked for a transfer, Mr. Meyer would undoubtedly cut my pay.

"Never mind," barked Mr. Sam. "Ask for the transfer, go to night school, and if he wants to cut your pay, so be it."

By Monday morning I was convinced that Mr. Sam was right. Still, I was very nervous as I stood in front of Mr. Meyer's large desk and recounted my breakfast conversation.

"Why are you asking Sam Bronfman for advice when you should be asking me?" Mr. Meyer exploded.

I realized at once that I had made a mistake, and I hurried to explain that I had not asked for advice. Mr. Bronfman, I insisted, had simply offered it.

This explanation, however, only seemed to add more fuel to the fire of Mr. Meyer's anger. Desperately, I suggested that we forget I had raised the issue of a transfer. I would return immediately to the foreign exchange trading desk.

With my surrender, Mr. Meyer began to achieve some calm. In a tone that was decidedly more conciliatory, he matter-of-factly remarked that I did not know anything about corporate finance or mergers. But if I wanted to learn the business, I could start by working for a partner named Howard Kniffin. My pay, he added emphatically, would be cut from $15,000 to $10,000 a year.

I met Howard Kniffin later that day. He was a kind, harassed, chain-smoking banker, Mr. Meyer's right hand in most of the firm's important deals. He was entirely devoted to Mr. Meyer, an allegiance that left poor, besieged Howard in a state of perpetual anxiety. I would work under Howard for the next few years.

I also enrolled in night courses at NYU. My bible was Graham and Dodd's textbook on security analysis (the same work, I would learn years later, that had also shaped and influenced Warren Buffett's investment instincts).

And so in 1957 I began my career as an investment banker specializing in mergers and acquisitions. It was a heady time, a decade when American capitalism was about to change and I was, as it happened, fated to be a participant in this new era of giant corporate mergers.

By 1960, I had finished my tutelage under Howard Kniffin. I was thirty-two, married, with two small sons, when Mr. Meyer summoned me to his penthouse apartment in the Carlyle Hotel on Madison Avenue. As I sat surrounded by his treasures—Picassos, Renoirs, Gauguins, and Monets glowing on the walls—he began a long lecture detailing my professional shortcomings.

Dealings

I listen without comment, wondering again if I was about to be dismissed. At last, however, Mr. Meyer revealed that he had decided to make me a partner. He made it clear that this was a kindness, done out of affection for my wife and children; on several occasions he had come to our small apartment for dinner, even, to my great astonishment, assisting my wife in our narrow kitchen as she cooked. He emphasized that my interest in the firm was to be minute. I was not, he warned sternly, to allow this partnership to go to my head. Instead, I should redouble my efforts.

And I did. I set out to make my first big deal.

Three

I plotted my first significant deal in the back of a funeral parlor. With the sounds of Hebrew prayers, heartfelt eulogies, and mourners' lamentations pouring out of the adjacent chapel, I sat hunched over a small desk in the rear office of the Riverside Funeral Home as I struggled to analyze column after column of numbers. It was an environment that in most circumstances would put the transitory nature of business and success into perspective. But day after day I plowed on undeterred. I knew I was on to something.

I had wound up at this funeral home on Riverside Drive on Manhattan's West Side because Mr. Meyer wanted to do a favor for one of the firm's biggest American clients: General David Sarnoff, the chairman of RCA. Two of the general's cousins, Steve Ross and Eddie Rosenthal, wanted our help with an acquisition. Through their company Kinney National, the Rosenthal family owned funeral parlors as well as garages, parking lots, and building service concerns. As part of their funeral business, they also operated a fleet of limousines and were now hoping to acquire Avis Rent-A-Car. The fit, the Rosenthals were convinced, would be a logical one for Kinney.

A deal involving a funeral home company was not elegant enough to require Mr. Meyer's personal participation. Nevertheless, in keeping with Lazard's family orientation, he wanted to be helpful to the relatives of our longtime client General Sarnoff. And Mr. Meyer's willingness to involve the firm was reinforced after a meeting with the two cousins.

Steve Ross, the primary Kinney executive urging the acquisition, argued that Avis, controlled by "Buck" Domaine—a Boston investor and his son-in-law—was spiraling downhill, largely owing to poor management. It wouldn't be difficult for a smart, dedicated management team, he said, to turn the company around and make it a real competitor of Hertz, the dominant player in the car rental business. Intrigued, Mr. Meyer asked me to work with Ross to see if a deal was possible.

Steve Ross was a big, jovial, energetic man, a natural salesman with a disarming, backslapping style. He also possessed one of the most nimble financial minds I have ever encountered. He was determined to turn Kinney into something much more significant—a national service company. Yet at his core he loved making deals, often, it seemed to me, simply for the pleasure of making them. His guideline, I decided, was the more complicated the deal, the better. From our initial meeting, I liked Steve enormously. For the next twenty-five years we would be friends and, on occasion, partners working together in enterprises that would change the shape and scope of American business.

But back then we were two young men working out of the back of a funeral home as we struggled to plot a course to take over an ailing car rental company. One moment Ross and Rosenthal, attired in somber cutaways and striped pants, would be solemnly directing mourners to the chapel. The next moment they would be racing to my makeshift office in the back room, peering over my shoulder as we tried to juggle the numbers with the hope of discovering a path to a sensible deal.

In the end, we failed. The synergy between an airport car rental business and a company with downtown parking garages and limousine services was more wishful than real. After thanking me for my efforts, Ross and Rosenthal withdrew from the deal.

But the research I had done and the preliminary numbers I had collected told an intriguing story. In the postwar world of jets and interstate highways, more Americans would be traveling around the country for both business and vacations. The car rental business, I was convinced, had great potential for growth. And while Avis's market share was a distant second to that of Hertz, Avis was still a national brand name. No less significant, the withdrawal of a funeral company from the negotiations had removed one decidedly unappealing aspect (at least in Mr. Meyer's mind) of any potential transaction. Mr. Meyer now decided that Lazard should proceed on its own to acquire Avis.

We obtained a ninety-day option on the Dumaine family's shares and immediately began an exhaustive study of the company. It quickly became apparent that Steve Ross had been correct: Avis's problem was management, not finance. It wasn't simply an aggressive Hertz that was defeating Avis in the marketplace. Avis was also being hindered by its own executives. If Lazard were to acquire the company, we would first need to find someone who could run it.

In those days the car rental business was still a small industry, and so after only a few preliminary calls I was directed to Donald Petrie. Petrie had been executive vice president and COO of Hertz, but had left after a dispute with its founder. In a guarded way, I explained Lazard's intentions; and although Petrie had never heard of André Meyer (a likelihood that I, no doubt naively, previously would have thought impossible for anyone involved in business), he agreed to a meeting.

I took Petrie to Mr. Meyer's apartment at the Carlyle (he would be stunned when afterward I explained to him that the "very good collection of prints" he had admired on the walls were actually the genuine paintings). After I made the introductions, Petrie, smart, well-educated, and appealingly direct, proceeded to give us a fascinating primer on the car rental business. America, he said, was moving into an era when travel would be commonplace. Airport car rentals would be a necessity for businessmen, and vacationers would be attracted by the convenience of being able to rent cars in cities throughout the country. Truck rental, too, was a growing business. In fact, Petrie told us, Hertz and Avis were among General Motors' largest customers. But despite all its potential, Petrie emphasized, the rental business would prosper only if it could provide efficient, high-quality service to its customers. And the key to service was management.

Petrie's insights reinforced many of our own. He seemed the perfect man to run Avis. But there was one problem—he didn't want the job. He preferred to remain at his Long Island law firm, where he would be able to continue his many activities in the Democratic Party. However, he did know someone whom he thought might be interested, an executive he had met when Hertz had teamed with American Express in an overseas venture.

And so Petrie introduced us to Robert A. Townsend. The timing was propitious. Howard Clark had recently become CEO of American Express and "Townie" (as I, like everyone else, took to calling Townsend) was too much the freewheeling iconoclastic Californian to work for someone he dismissively regarded as a "corporation man." He was ready for a new challenge.

After our initial discussions, it was apparent that the possibilities in running Avis intrigued Townie. And we were impressed with both him and his knowledge of the industry. However, before Townie would commit himself to the job he presented us with two demands: he would take a low salary, but in return he would want a significant stock interest; and he would need total management freedom.

Mr. Meyer agreed—as long as this "freedom" included Townsend's keeping Lazard fully informed of his actions. Townie accepted this small measure of restraint. Then—more good fortune for Lazard—with Townie on board, Petrie agreed to become chairman of the executive committee.

Meanwhile, our ninety-day option was rapidly drawing to a close. Purchasing control of the company would cost us about $5 million. Petrie insisted that another $5 million would be needed to improve Avis's deteriorating fleet of vehicles. Forty years ago $10 million was not an inconsiderable sum, particularly for a small investment bank with a stated capital of only $17 million. No less daunting, Avis had lost $1.2 million in 1961. Nevertheless, now that we had a management team ready to assume control—a team we had confidence in—we moved forward. Lazard exercised its option to acquire the Dumaine family stock.

In 1962, Avis's revenues were $24 million. Hertz's were more than five times that amount. From the start, Mr. Meyer was optimistic that we could build Avis into a genuine competitor to Hertz. Yet one of his first decisions took me by surprise: I was selected to represent Lazard on the Avis board.

In my years at the firm, I had observed that Mr. Meyer, always a conservative banker, was very particular about whom he assigned to the firm's seats on boards; usually this was the domain of senior partners. With Avis, however, a very junior (and inexperienced) partner had been selected. Perhaps, he had judged there was no one else at Lazard who would get along so well with the loose, very uncorporate personalities and management styles of both Townsend and Petrie. Whatever the reason, Avis became my first experience in management culture and in how a director representing a capital owner should go about his work. It was an enduring lesson, and a great deal of fun, to boot.

Townsend, Petrie, and I weren't simply united in the uphill battle to turn a moribund company around. We became great friends. When they moved the company's headquarters from Boston to offices on Long Island, I rented a beach cottage at nearby Sands Point so we could continue our work on weekends. The prospects were exciting, and, night and day it seemed, the business occupied our lives.

The first step in re-creating Avis, Townsend believed, was to transform it into a lean, low-overhead company staffed by highly motivated employees. He personally dramatized his own commitment to this business plan by announcing very publicly that his salary would be only $36,000 and that he'd work without a secretary to assist him. He also made Avis into one of the first public companies where all the workers would benefit from profit sharing. If the company made money, all the employees— whether they were executives or worked in a garage or behind a counter at an airport—would make money. He wanted all the Avis employees to know that they were all in this turnaround together—and all would benefit if their individual actions succeeded.

Next, we turned to marketing. We needed to spread the word that this was a new and different Avis. Our ads dully reinforced the image that we were simply another Hertz. Their ads featured a palm tree, a blonde, and a Chevy convertible; ours had a palm tree, a blonde, and a Ford convertible. The only significant difference in the two company's campaigns was that Hertz, with Chevrolet's financial support, had a budget many times that of Avis. Of course, the real disparities between Hertz and Avis were well known to experienced car renters: too often our cars were poorly maintained and our reservation systems were erratic.

It was clear we needed innovative, attention-grabbing ads that would emphasize the changes we were making in the company. And the challenge would not simply be creative. We also needed to find an advertising company that would be willing to take a chance on a weak client with a small budget—all in the hope that the ad campaign dollars would eventually grow along with the company's fortunes.

Our first choice was Bill Bernbach of Doyle, Dane, Bernbach. He was the creative genius behind the Levy's rye bread campaign: a series of very ethnic faces—Afro-Americans, Chinese, and Hispanics—biting into thick sandwiches with ravenous delight as the tagline announced, "You don't have to be Jewish to love Levy's Jewish rye." We had heard, too, that Bernbach was a bit of a gambler: he might take a chance on a small client with large potential.

Bernbach agreed to create the campaign—on one condition. We would need to run the ads exactly as he submitted them.

We gulped, and finally said yes.

The slogan he devised for Avis was "We're #2. We try harder." To illustrate this newfound commitment, his ads showed cars with broken windshield wipers and dirty ashtrays. These were unsatisfactory conditions, the ads suggested, that would never be tolerated at Avis.

As it turned out, these were failings that also wouldn't be tolerated by Ford. The automaker, which financed a substantial portion of our advertising budget, refused to have its cars associated with grim pictures of decrepit and unkempt vehicles. Ford wanted cheery, upbeat, sparkling ads with blondes and convertibles.

We, however, backed Bernbach. If we compromised on the ad campaign, I informed Ford with an adamancy that owed more to instinct than to any banker's calculus, Avis would lose its only chance to become a viable competitor to Hertz. And, I added, Ford would lose an opportunity to help create a buyer that would have a greater demand for its cars.

Dealings

Without much enthusiasm, Ford agreed to let the ads run. From the start, the campaign created a stir. In the company, employees *did* try harder. As the ads promised, a new corporate culture was being created. We advertised that Townsend would personally take customers' calls, and he did. Everyone at the reservation counters wore an Avis red blazer, and executives wore these blazers, too, when they spent the now required week dealing directly with customers every six months. Townsend and Petrie even showed up at security analyst meetings in their red Avis jackets. From the maintenance crews in the garages to the man behind the desk in the president's office, Avis was, as the ads stated, working harder as a team to become number one in the business.

Customers were paying attention, too. As Bernbach had shrewdly understood, underdogs are beloved. It was as if people were rooting for us. Business travel was up, and renters were flocking to our counters. In 1963, only two years after Lazard had taken over the company, Avis was in the black for the first time. We had a net income of $1.2 million on $34 million in revenues. A year later our net income had more than doubled, to $2.9 million.

We had turned Avis around.

And I was having some adventures. As part of the new business plan, we wanted company-owned operations in all the major markets. Up to this point, the rental counters in many cities, including Boston, Baltimore, Cleveland, and Los Angeles, were run as franchises owned by private operators. Additionally, we were also determined to expand the company's position in the lucrative truck rental market. Petrie and I would spend a large part of the next three years pursuing the acquisitions of these franchises and buying up trucking companies. The negotiations took me to some strange places.

Consider what happened when I set about to acquire the string of franchises owned by one of our largest private contractors, Frank Sawyer. It turned out that Sawyer had left Boston to go on a Mediterranean cruise with his wife. He would, however, be willing to meet me when his ship docked at its next port, Tangier.

I flew to Tangier, and boarded the ship confident that I could get the deal done in a day. I was wrong. When the boat left Tangier for Malta, I realized I would have to continue on if I wanted to hammer out an agreement with Sawyer.

When we reached Malta, the deal had still not been concluded. And now I had a real dilemma—the next port of call was Odessa. I could stay on board, and perhaps reach an understanding with Sawyer. But there also was the possibility that in Odessa, as a former Polish citizen and a capitalist banker, I would be taken off the boat by Soviet authorities and interrogated by the KGB. It was the height of the cold war, a time when the communist mind was swirling with suspicions about American espionage. I decided to leave the boat and the Sawyers in Malta. After another two years Sawyer and I finally made our deal, but for a while all I thought I'd get out of my frenetic travel was the two Moroccan rugs I had purchased as I accompanied Sawyer through the bazaars of Tangier.

Another potential acquisition took me to an Italian restaurant in the mean streets of Brooklyn. As I was shown to my table to meet my host, the owner of a fleet of trucks, I was informed that the proper etiquette was to check all guns at the door. I was rather embarrassed to admit that I was packing only a calculator. Anyway, we did not buy that particular company.

And so it happily went for the next three years. I was working with friends, and we were doing things in a way that was out of the mainstream of corporate culture. Best of all, it worked. Not only was the business providing its customers with better service, but Avis was also making money. Its stock price had increased significantly. And, therefore, Lazard's investment had also appreciated. Everyone, it seemed, was satisfied by what had been accomplished.

—

Except Townsend. The challenges that had previously energized his zeal and initiative had been conquered. Now that Avis was a successful, tightly run company, he was bored. He announced that he would promote his executive vice president to his position and would himself work only part-time.

This was, I will always believe, the excuse Mr. Meyer had been secretly waiting for to justify a long-held decision to sell the firm's interest in the company. Mr. Meyer insisted that he simply did not have confidence in Townsend's chosen successor. But I think it was the rocketing price of the stock that had him itching to sell. He had never lost his trader's instinct; if Mr. Meyer had any failing as an investment banker, it was this inclination to sell too soon. "No one ever got poor by taking profits" was his maxim. This, of course, was true; but, to my mind, it was often a shortsighted way of looking at the marketplace.

Mobil Oil had previously made inquires about Avis, and now Mr. Meyer saw his chance. After informing Townsend and Petrie that he wanted their cooperation, he arranged a meeting with Mobil's chairman.

The presentation did not go well. Townsend and Petrie opposed the sale and as a consequence were reluctant to coax Mobil to make the acquisition. Mobil passed.

But Mr. Meyer did not give up. He simply decided that Lazard would handle the sale without either Townsend's or Petrie's active participation. Now he approached Harold Geneen, the chairman of ITT.

Geneen (who would in time become my friend as well as

my mentor) had been formulating a visionary plan to expand ITT into an international service company. He hoped to use the ITT global communications services to enable hotel chains like Sheraton—which he was in the midst of acquiring—and a car rental company like Avis to create an integrated worldwide reservations system for travelers. He saw the potential synergy between hotels, rental cars, and an international communications network—and the profits such an integrated service could deliver. In very short order, a deal was made.

On January 15, 1965, ITT acquired Avis for about $35 million in ITT stock. After only five years, Lazard's $5 million investment was now worth $20 million.

The deal was a great personal success for me, both within and outside the firm. Townsend, who had made a good deal of money from his stock in the company, resigned. He went to live in California, where he wrote a best-selling book, *Up the Organization*, that was a wise and spirited attack on the business practices of most corporate conglomerates. Petrie, to my delight, became a partner in Lazard Frères. We all had profited.

Yet I could not help being disappointed. I was convinced that Avis's growth had just started. A much larger and much more valuable company would exist only a few years in the future. And I was proved correct: ITT disposed of Avis twelve years later for $174 million.

Still, in my time at Avis I had learned two essential lessons that would guide me throughout my career as an investment banker. First, at its core banking is not simply about profit, but about personal relationships. And second, the key aspect of any successful merger or acquisition lies in the ability of the new company to provide a beneficial service to its customers. The company has to deliver, or it must try harder until it does.

Four

Business was booming! It was the mid-1960s charging into the 1970s—the "go-go years," as one popular financial writer aptly named them—and at Lazard I was positioned to be in the thick of many of the era's most prominent mergers and acquisitions. Every week, or so it seemed, I was flying around the country, setting out to play a role in a potential financial marriage as one giant conglomerate after another became smitten with a new corporate conquest.

The stock market loved these acquisition-driven companies, fully embracing the theory that unrelated entities could successfully be put under the corporate umbrella of a controlling conglomerate. And CEOs loved them, too; as the company's stock price rose, so did the value of their piles of stock options. It was a time when Wall Street believed that bigger was always better—and more valuable. My contrarian view, however, was that a focused company tended in the long run to provide more value for its shareholders. And despite all the adoring attention the market focused on the galloping conglomerates of the 1960s, it seemed to me that several of them were doomed from the start. For example, I was not surprised when James Ling's LTV, an aerospace and steel giant, eventually went bankrupt. To my conservative mind, it made little business sense for a company to grow simply for the sake of growth.

Nevertheless, I did appreciate that if a conglomerate were

diverse enough, had a well thought-out, even if expansive, business plan, and prudently rolled up its sleeves to do sufficient due diligence so that it could make its acquisition at a reasonable price, then it could grow *and* prosper. And so, guided by this banker's philosophy and encouraged by the high-flying spirit of the times, I became increasingly involved with one of the leading acquirers of the era, Harold Geneen, the chairman of ITT.

It was a friendship—and a learning experience—that stretched over two decades. In the process I advised ITT on nearly a dozen takeovers, served on its board, and helped it engineer what was at the time one of largest acquisitions in U.S. history. I also became very publicly embroiled in a political controversy that put photos of my chagrined face on the front pages of newspapers around the country, embarrassed me and my family, and, not least, threatened to end my career.

In 1959, when Geneen came to ITT as president, it was a huge but struggling company. Its business and assets, largely telephone manufacturing companies, were centered in Europe and Latin America. And these overseas telephone businesses were under siege. In eastern Europe, the communist governments had summarily taken control of ITT's telephone exchanges. In Cuba, Fidel Castro had nationalized ITT's subsidiary company. In Latin America, seizures of the company's assets seemed inevitable if left-wing governments took power. Even in western Europe—France, Italy, Spain, and West Germany—the prospect of nationalization seemed genuine.

Geneen, however, had a plan that he hoped would offset the loss of ITT's overseas subsidiaries. He'd build an American base. Computer and domestic telephone companies didn't interest him; those businesses, he felt, were too competitive. Instead, he'd concentrate on acquiring a broad range of U.S. national service and technology concerns. And with the ambition of Julius Caesar, he set out to create the biggest, most profitable company in the world.

In the course of the Avis deal, Mr. Meyer had introduced me to Harold Geneen just after Geneen had received the title of ITT chairman. A former clerk on the floor of the New York Stock Exchange, Hal—as all his friends called him—had the quiet, staid demeanor of an accountant. But his energy was enormous and his focus on details was both meticulous and intense.

Perhaps Hal appreciated that I shared his commitment to long hours and hard work, and that I, too, had my fair share of ambition. But whatever the reason, he treated me, although I was nearly fifteen years his junior, with friendship. I was quickly drawn into Hal's exacting world.

It was a world totally under his own imperious control. Time of day was irrelevant. Since he spent as much of his peripatetic life in Europe as in the United States, he simply ignored local clocks. In both his New York office and the executive suite at the company's headquarters in Brussels, the curtains were always tightly drawn; neither daylight nor starlight would intrude into Geneen's realm. A meeting called for 8 P.M. might not take place till 2 A.M. Geneen's whims established the schedule, and his staff and subordinates obediently set their own clocks to coincide with his.

But regardless of when these meetings would finally take place, they were all uniformly run according to Geneen's uncompromising standards. The monthly general management meetings, for example, were legendary. About eighty managers would be seated at a long table. His questions shaped by a shrewd and demanding mind, Geneen would methodically interrogate each manager. He'd be relentless, not moving on to the next executive until he was satisfied by the responses he had received. These meetings would drag on for tense hour after hour, leaving everyone except Hal visibly drained and exhausted.

Hal set high standards for himself, and it was understood that he expected no less from those around him. He was always prepared—and woe be to the subordinate or banker or secretary who approached him without similar confidence or accuracy. Before he would agree to pursue an acquisition, he would immerse himself in learning all he could about not only the business, but also about his counterparts. He insisted on having detailed biographies—personal as well as business histories—of all the executives with whom he'd be negotiating. If a report seemed too brief or, even worse, slipshod, Hal's rage would be volcanic. Knowledge, he believed, was power—and he was determined to be the most powerful businessman in the world. It was quite a demanding time for those of us who worked closely with Hal. But it was also exciting. We were, after all, setting out to create, acquisition by acquisition, a conglomerate that lived up to Hal's ambitions.

And yet despite the careful strategy that was shaping ITT's growth, the first deal I helped put together for Hal was more a product of intuition and happenstance than a banker's well-reasoned battle plan. A partner at Lazard with a background in science, Jack Franklin, had suggested I might like to accompany him on a research trip to the area south of San Francisco that would years later become famous as Silicon Valley. I agreed, and it was an education. We visited many of the electronic start-ups that dotted the valley—companies like Hewlett Packard, Eitel-McCoullough, and Ampex—and I was impressed with the commitment of managers and scientists to using technology to create not just new businesses but also a new way of American life. My problem, however, was that I was not quite convinced this earnestness was anything more than wishful thinking on their part. I did not share their visionary confidence.

In fact, on the trip I was approached by an old friend, Arthur Rock. He had moved to San Francisco to start a venture capital firm and he now suggested I join him in helping to raise capital for these fledging companies. A technological revolution that would change the face of American business was poised to happen, Arthur predicted confidently. But I, always the conservative banker, just didn't see it.

Nevertheless, while I no doubt missed one large opportunity on that trip, I did, as fate would have it, find another one looming. Franklin took me along on a visit to Jennings Radio Manufacturing, a small high-tech company in San Jose. Founded by two brothers, Jennings made vacuum switches and vacuum capacitors for the telecomunications industry. These were powerful devices; when the switches were tested, lights through San Jose would flicker and then—poof!—the entire city would go dark. No less promising, the company's inventive engineers announced that they had other ideas, other state-of-the-art devices they hoped to put in to production—if they could find the capital necessary for expansion. The company, I realized after my first short visit, clearly needed a rich corporate partner.

When I returned to New York, I brought a thick file on Jennings Radio to Geneen. Here was an acquisition, I suggested, that made sense for ITT. Not only did it fit into his plan to build an economic core of American technological concerns, but Jennings also was a company with potential: its engineers were exploring new and profitable areas.

Geneen was intrigued. He ordered his staff to run the numbers and to investigate the science. Very quickly, they agreed: purchasing Jennings Radio made sense. It was a deal with a promising upside. And the $20 million price—a pittance for ITT—was reasonable.

It would be Geneen's first acquisition as CEO, and the first deal we had made together. But my excitement was abruptly dashed. When Hal proposed the purchase to his board of directors, he reported to me with a feisty bewilderment, they were reluctant. The board did not want ITT to make the deal.

Geneen realized at once that more was at stake than simply the acquisition of a small San Jose technology concern. The board was attempting to undermine his control—and all his large plans for the future growth of ITT. With a calm resolve, he gave the board members an ultimatum: either the deal is made, or I will resign.

The board capitulated. With the acquisition of Jennings Radio, the principle was established in the company that what Harold Geneen wanted, he would get. Hal was soon off and running on one of the largest acquisition sprees in American corporate history. And I was running with him.

Five

G eneen and I were busy. He was determined to make the strategic American acquisitions that would provide the economic core for ITT to become the most profitable company in the world, and I was determined to help him. I advised him as ITT swooped in and, one after another, bought Canteen, Grinnell, Avis, Rayonnier, Levitt and Sons, Continental Baking, Scotts Seed, Pennsylvania Glass, and Airport Parking. But this corporate shopping spree was just a prelude to the deal I presented to Hal in 1968. It would be the largest acquisition not just in ITT's history, but also, by some measurements, in U.S. business history.

I urged Hal to purchase Hartford Fire Insurance. It was one of America's oldest companies and, more significant, it had a strong, conservative, cash-heavy balance sheet. It would, I explained confidently, anchor the corporate strategy Geneen had been hoping to realize: its acquisition would make ITT an international conglomerate with a comfortable, financially sound balance between its U.S. assets and its foreign holdings.

Hal prided himself on his ability to make quick decisions; for a businessman who loved to scrutinize the details, he followed his instincts to a surprising degree. And so it didn't take Hal long to agree to my proposal that ITT should pursue Hartford.

But from the start we both knew that this would be more

difficult and more complicated than any of our previous purchases. There was, after all, one significant difference between this prospective acquisition and the others Hal and I had engineered: Hartford did not want to be acquired.

More daunting, Hartford's board had a formidable array of defenses. Hartford was a Connecticut company, a major corporate presence for generations in a small, clubby state. I had no doubt that its well-connected executives and supporting legion of blueblood investment bankers could mobilize the state political establishment to man the regulatory barricades in an attempt to hold off the horde of voracious foreign (ITT's headquarters was in Brussels) corporate raiders.

Our financial strategy, too, would create further problems with Hartford's board. To obtain the most favorable accounting and tax treatment, we had decided to make this acquisition on a stock-for-stock basis. If the board objected too vehemently, this approach, already a maze of complicated tax procedures, would very likely prove impossible.

Therefore, from the start the bottom line to our thinking was that we did not want to antagonize the Hartford board any more than was necessary. This was business, not a vendetta. Besides, ITT had never made a hostile takeover bid; and both Hal and I, by nature practical businessmen rather than street fighters, were eager to avoid doing so now.

Instead, we'd win over the shareholders. We'd make them an offer they couldn't refuse. Eventually, the board would have no reasonable choice but to follow. We hoped.

—

Our plan was to grab Hartford in a "bear hug." This is a common Wall Street carrot-and-stick approach: large blocks of stock are purchased from shareholders; and then this "carrot" is promptly followed with a decidedly more menacing offer to the board to purchase a controlling interest of the company's shares at a price substantially over the market. It's a carefully orchestrated technique: the attention-grabbing offer is made in a formal letter to the board, and next there's an immediate public disclosure of the terms. Theoretically, the announcement that the target company is "in play" will result in a huge turnover of its stock. The biggest buyers will be professional traders, or arbitrageurs, and they will greedily pressure the board either to approve the deal or to search out a richer one. Under constant attack, and with the happy prospect that their own piles of stock as well as those of their shareholders will suddenly be worth incrementally more, the board will simply throw up its hands in pragmatic surrender, resigned to suffering through an unwanted but lucrative takeover. Or at least that was how our "bear hug" strategy played out in our hopeful minds.

And so after the ITT board approved, in strict secrecy, the offer to buy up Hartford's stock at an attractive premium, Howard Aibel, the general counsel of ITT, and I drove up to Hartford to deliver the formal letter. It was a snowy New England day and the storm grew more ferocious the farther we traveled from New York. By the time our car had made its way up the slippery interstate, it was late in the afternoon. We tried to find the company's chairman or at least one of Hartford's many corporate officers, but all of the major executives had apparently left early because of the storm.

Yet we were tenacious. The ITT board had set the schedule earlier in the day and we were determined to move forward according to this timetable. The prospect, too, of explaining to Hal that I had been unable to deliver a simple letter added iron to my resolve.

Puffing myself up with a counterfeit authority, I insisted to the bewildered custodian that he summon a suitable executive. If we could travel on these icy roads, so could the executive, I argued with what I hoped was convincing logic. At last, the custodian agreed to make a call.

"What's so important that you needed to see me in the middle of a blizzard?" a harried executive vice president demanded when he at last arrived. Dutifully, we handed him the letter detailing ITT's offer to purchase Hartford Fire Insurance stock at a price well beyond the market.

As he continued reading it, I went on. We're obliged to release the details of this offer prior to the opening of the stock exchange tomorrow, I said. Embarrassed, I tried to find a tone that conveyed that I was simply another hapless victim in this whole affair and not the one aiming the revolver. I added that we at ITT were eager to work together with his company. We want to engage in a constructive dialogue with the Hartford board, I explained with what I hoped sounded like sincere conviction.

Screw you, he muttered. And then he promptly turned and headed off. I watched with mute sympathy as he disappeared into the now raging snowstorm.

When the public announcement was made the next morning, Wall Street responded with a buying frenzy. The volume of shares traded in Hartford Fire Insurance was enormous—just as we had anticipated. And also as we had anticipated, the Hartford board and the Insurance Commission of Connecticut mobilized for battle.

But in the end, too many people stood to make too much money for the deal not to get the tacit support it needed from the board. In June 1970, after more than two difficult and combative years, Hartford agreed to allow itself to be acquired by ITT for a record $1.5 billion.

But just as the merger was about to be formalized, the IRS intervened. Its commissioner sternly insisted that ITT must dispose of the thousands of Hartford shares it had bought up in the open market before the IRS could rule on the tax-free aspects of the transaction.

This last-minute glitch sent Hal (and the company's army of accountants) into a small panic. If ITT didn't obtain the favorable tax ruling it had anticipated, then the entire $1.5 billion transaction would no longer make economic sense. Rather than a transformative corporate move, the acquisition would play out as an enormously costly disaster for ITT. But to whom could ITT sell its shares? The company needed not just a fair price, but also the assurance that it wasn't strengthening a potential enemy who in time would turn on Geneen and his executive team.

Mr. Meyer found a solution. After several discreet conversations with the principals, he arranged for Mediobanca, an Italian bank with whom Lazard had a long and close relationship, to acquire the shares. The IRS was satisfied. The merger could now go forward.

———

Or could it? Now the antitrust division of the Department of Justice announced that it had problems with the deal. Its concern had been fueled, in part, by an investigation Congressman Emanuel Celler, chairman of the House Judiciary Committee, had led into the growing—and increasingly public—arena of conglomerate mergers.

The committee's interest was, in retrospect, predictable. Vast, almost incomprehensible sums of money were involved, fortunes were being made seemingly overnight, and the corporate wheeling and dealing had, at least to the uninitiated, all the intrigue of insiders' conspiracies. With those attractions, the hearings would surely be well reported in the press. And that alone, I would soon discover to my dismay, was sufficient reason to convene them.

But at the time, I was young and naive. I knew I had nothing underhanded to hide. I put my faith firmly in the truth and cavalierly ignored the damaging power of manipulated political perceptions. I was the perfect patsy.

And so when ITT's acquisition of Continental Baking was singled out for scrutiny by the committee, I very obligingly granted its investigators access to my files. I knew they held nothing incriminating. In fact, they held not very much at all: an annual report of Continental Baking, a few penciled worksheets of hasty computations, a copy of the bill to ITT for services rendered, and a congratulatory note from Harold Geneen. The reality was that the file was so thin because there had been no time to write long memos to Geneen or elaborate strategic analyses. With Hal as general, I was charging forward day after day to take one hill after another. There had been no time, or need, for battle plans. We were too busy fighting the war.

The investigators didn't believe me. They were convinced that I had destroyed vital, revelatory documents. Voluntarily, I began opening my acquisition files for other deals and gave them access. These were equally sparse. I tried to explain that this was how a banker's business was done. I was constantly on the run, flying to meetings around the country. It was all rather spontaneous. There certainly was no time to follow a carefully detailed paper trail.

They had no choice but to accept my explanation. Still, I was convinced they never truly believed me. And when in the aftermath of the Celler committee's inquiries, the Department of Justice decided to undo the ITT-Hartford merger, I was once more in the government's and the press's crosshairs—and this time it looked as if there would be no escape.

Six

As with the proverbial lull before the storm, my great crisis was preceded by a moment of personal triumph. Geneen invited me to serve on the ITT board.

It was a board filled with accomplished, even celebrated individuals. George Brown, of Texas's Brown and Root, the man who had nearly single-handedly financed the early elections of Lyndon Johnson; John McCone, who had served as director of the Atomic Energy Commission and then of the CIA; and Eugene R. Black, a former head of the World Bank—all were members of the ITT board. This was heady company for a young investment banker, and I was deeply flattered to have been chosen.

Mr. Meyer decided, however, that it was too heady company. It wasn't just that I was young or not sufficiently a member of the Wall Street establishment. Rather, he explained to me with some delicacy, a Jewish refugee like myself would never be fully accepted on the board of what was then a very Waspy, deliberately blue-blooded company. He had suggested to Geneen that rather than young Rohatyn, it would make more sense to offer the board membership to another Lazard partner. Mr. Meyer's choice was a man who had been the CEO of a large company and who, not so coincidentally, carried himself with a Protestant aristocratic grace shared by many of his fellow Brook Club members. With deep but silent disappointment, I resigned myself to Mr. Meyer's logic.

Geneen, however, refused to see things in such a narrow way.

He rejected Mr. Meyer's suggestion. In fact, he made it clear that if Lazard wanted to continue the highly profitable relationship it had since 1959 with ITT, then Rohatyn, and only young Rohatyn, would represent the firm on the board. Ever practical, Mr. Meyer agreed with a smile.

Once I had my seat on the ITT board, I discovered that, despite all the great and important men in the room, the only voice that mattered was Geneen's. There would often be five or six acquisitions before the board at a single meeting, and all the overwhelmed board would do was to bow deferentially to Geneen's better-informed will. If Hal wanted it, the board would agree to buy it. I remember Gene Black's excusing himself to go to the washroom, saying as he rose, "Don't buy anything until I get back." We all laughed.

And why not? I—all of us—admired Geneen with few reservations. He could analyze a business better than anyone else I had ever met. He would never do anything illegal. I just never anticipated his political judgment failing him so dramatically, or so disastrously—or that I, a truly innocent bystander, would be swept along in the malevolent winds of this maelstrom.

It all began, I will always be convinced, when the head of the Justice Department's antitrust division, Richard McLaren, decided to target ITT. In McLaren's wrongheaded thinking, corporate bigness was by definition always anti-competitive. He attacked conglomerate mergers even when no overlapping business existed that could be affected; his tenuous and undemocratic theory was that the merger could inhibit the "potential entry" of other corporate players. ITT, the king of the conglomerates, was, in McLaren's narrow worldview, a true corporate villain. Its behavior needed to be stopped. And the ITT-Hartford merger would be the test case.

Geneen, quite naturally, refused to surrender. As a member of the ITT board and a key participant in the acquisition, Hal chose me to be one of the many people who would speak directly to McLaren's boss, Richard Kleindienst, the deputy attorney general.

I eagerly agreed. I believed a divestiture of Hartford by ITT would have an adverse effect not just on the two companies, but on the entire stock market. And, no less consequentially, in grim short order a fragile U.S. economy whose gold reserves were already being drained by the Europeans, and whose balance of payments was already dangerously out of kilter, would break apart, a victim of the ripples created by this ill-conceived government edict. Yet my disagreement with McLaren was not merely a matter of a banker's practical concerns about the marketplace. I was an instinctive democrat, a believer in the inalienable right of capitalists to use their ingenuity to prosper. Philosophically, McLaren's position was preposterous. When the ITT general counsel informed me that a meeting had been arranged between myself and Kleindienst, I applied myself to the task of preparing my very heartfelt argument.

It never—alas!—occurred to me to ask whether this was a normal, business-as-usual procedure in Washington. I was not suspicious enough, nor perceptive enough, to wonder if there was perhaps something inherently wrong about a company's director and investment banker going over the head of the antitrust chief to meet alone with the deputy attorney general. I was about to proceed up a very dangerous trail, yet I rushed blithely forward, driven by the earnest conviction that I was doing the right thing.

My meeting with Kleindienst went, I thought, well. As I had been advised by ITT's lawyers and Washington representatives, I made the case that a nullification of the merger would cause severe damage to the U.S. economy and the nation's ability to maintain a reasonable balance of international payments. It was an easy presentation to make, since I believed every word of my disheartening predictions with complete and utter certainty.

Nearly two months after my meeting with Kleindienst, a somewhat contrite McLaren called me from the deputy attorney general's office. He wanted to share a proposal for settling the Hartford case. The terms were this: ITT would need to divest itself of several major companies, including Avis, Levitt, Canteen, and parts of Grinnell. In the future, it would not be allowed to acquire any corporation with more than $100 million in assets without government approval. But the ITT-Hartford merger could stand.

On July 31, 1971, three years after I had first suggested to Geneen that we acquire Hartford, the settlement with the government was announced. At last, our $1.5 billion merger was inviolable.

Hal rejoiced. The feeling on Wall Street was that this was a great victory for ITT, for Geneen, and for me. But I was disappointed. I thought that it was not only a terrible deal, but an unfair one. It was my conviction that we should have fought the settlement all the way to the Supreme Court. I was confident—and I remain confident—that we would have won.

But even as Hal moved on to consider new acquisitions, and my anger and frustration quietly raged, the next political shadow was slowly beginning to fall. In Washington, the past, I would learn, was never truly past.

—

It began in December 1971, with a small news story. Democrats had attacked the ITT-Hartford antitrust settlement, charging that it was connected to a $400,000 contribution by ITT-Sheraton to the Republican National Committee.

The unsubstantiated allegation was buried in most newspapers, but nevertheless it did cause me some embarrassment. I was the chief economic adviser (and practically the sole supporter in the business community) of Senator Edmund Muskie of Maine, who was running for the Democratic nomination for president. On the day the story broke, I was hosting a luncheon fund-raiser for Muskie—and my star business guest was Harold Geneen. The timing was not propitious. Yet while the circumstances made me uncomfortable, there was no mention at the lunch of the allegation that had appeared in the morning's papers.

Nevertheless, I was curious. After the luncheon I asked Hal why the pledge had been made. Was there any connection to the antitrust settlement?

Hal matter-of-factly explained that the payment—"one hundred, not four hundred thousand"—to the Republican National Committee was simply a routine promotional fee made in conjunction with the San Diego Sheraton's being selected as the official Republican Convention headquarters. No one had whispered, "If you contribute to the convention, then we will settle the Hartford suit." There was, he insisted, no conspiratorial quid pro quo. The contribution to the Republican National Committee was not related in any way to the settlement of ITT's antitrust problems.

I believed Hal then. And I still believe him. Anyway, the story seemed to have quickly died. But then in February 1972, Jack Anderson, the Washington investigative columnist, received a tantalizing document—and allegations about the ITT-Hartford settlement were once again in the news. This time, they were on the front page.

—

The document Anderson received was a memo written by ITT's lobbyist Dita Beard to her boss, the ITT vice president in charge of government relations. It had been drafted in June 1971, at a time when San Diego's selection as the convention site was in the process of being finalized and also before the ITT settlement had been worked out. Its contents were explosive.

Beard wrote that ITT would pledge $400,000 to the Republican National Committee, and she specified that the source of the money must remain confidential. Only President Nixon, Attorney General John Mitchell, Congressman Bob Wilson, and Bob Haldeman, the White House chief of staff, knew the identity of the corporate donor. Any additional revelations, she suggested, could undermine the still unannounced proposal for the ITT-Hartford settlement.

More incriminating, Beard had added that she was convinced that ITT's donation had played a role in helping to resolve the antitrust negotiations as "Hal wants them." Nixon, she explained, had told the attorney general "to see that things are worked out fairly." In fact, she went on candidly, Mitchell "is definitely helping us, but cannot let it be known."

At this point, the memo was still unknown to me. I had never heard of Dita Beard or her allegations about the behind-the-scenes machinations in the Hartford settlement. However, if I had, her narrative would have seemed preposterous. The possibility that in a company as tightly controlled as Geneen's ITT, a third-level lobbyist would be directly involved in negotiations with the attorney general regarding an antitrust settlement that so dramatically affected the company's future was ludicrous. It could never have happened. Geneen would never have allowed it. And Mitchell would never have gone along with it.

But now that Anderson had the memo (and to this day his source remains a closely guarded secret), the columnist was determined to run with it. First, though, he sent his assistant, Brit Hume, to interview Beard.

She immediately conceded that she was the author of the

memo. And she claimed that she had negotiated directly with Mitchell the previous May. But she made it clear to Hume that Geneen was ignorant of the negotiations. And despite what she had written, she now told the reporter, ITT's donation had absolutely nothing to do with the settlement.

Hume dutifully wrote all this down, and then, full of a reporter's zeal for what was shaping up as an important story, went looking for additional corroboration. A director of ITT had told Hume that I was the main negotiator of the settlement, and so he tracked me down.

On March 1, I was in the departure lounge at Kennedy airport waiting for a flight to London, when in the course of a call to my office I learned that Brit Hume, an associate of Jack Anderson's, was urgently trying to reach me. What could this be about? I innocently wondered. Curious, I called him back.

When I reached Hume, he read me Beard's memo. This was the first I had heard of its contents, and I was shocked. This is total bullshit, I replied confidently.

How can you be so sure? he challenged.

Indignantly, I explained that a campaign contribution could not have played any role in the settlement, because I had convinced Kleindienst. I had met with him and very precisely, very deliberately had made the case that a revocation of the merger would have dire economic consequences for the nation. It was my argument, I said with some pride, that had persuaded him to overrule McLaren.

Oh, said Hume pregnantly.

I hung up the phone confident that simply by telling the truth, explaining events as they had actually happened, I had defused an entirely preposterous scenario. I couldn't have been more wrong, or more naive.

The next day Hume, with understandable justification, wrote that Rohatyn had a series of "secret" meetings with Kleindienst.

It was another example, he went on without any evidence, of the access ITT had purchased in the Nixon administration, another suspicious accommodation that allowed a giant corporation to go over the head of the antitrust division. The Nixon administration, Hume charged, was hiding the truth about the relationship between the Hartford settlement and ITT's contribution. Clearly, my well-intentioned and self-righteous candor had not helped. It had only made things worse.

And my fool's role in the increasingly turgid clatter of unfolding political events was not finished. Kleindienst had been scheduled to become attorney general on March 1, replacing Mitchell, who was leaving to run Nixon's reelection campaign. The nomination had sailed easily through the Judiciary Committee, but Kleindienst decided to reopen the hearings so he could refute once and for all any Democratic attacks inspired by Anderson's columns. As part of his strategy, he asked me, a liberal Democrat, to testify on his behalf. My presence, he argued, would help temper the inevitable criticism by the Democrats on the committee—senators Ted Kennedy, Phil Hart, and John Tunney. Their inclination would be to use him to get at Nixon, but the appearance of a fellow Democrat would restrain their vitriol.

And I believed him. After all, I had done nothing wrong. I had nothing to hide. What harm could be done by my appearing before a Senate committee and responding to their questions truthfully?

The answer, I was about to learn, was plenty.

On March 2, 1972, I stepped into the hearing room. Incredibly—stupidly!—I was alone. It had not occurred to me or to anyone else at Lazard that I might need a lawyer. And not just any lawyer—I needed someone familiar with the ways of Washington who could guide me through an appearance before a hostile, high-profile evidentiary hearing.

It wasn't until I was seated at the witness table, the flash-bulbs popping like fire crackers in front of my startled face, that I realized my mistake. I was a pinstriped lamb being led to the slaughter.

The list of witnesses included such headline-making names as Mitchell, Geneen, and Jack Anderson. But Kleindienst, McLaren, and I kicked off the hearings, and it was my picture staring out uncomfortably on the front page of the next day's *New York Times*.

By the lunchtime break I had come to my senses. I hurried to a phone booth and made an urgent call to Mr. Meyer. I need a lawyer, I announced with no attempt to disguise my desperation. At once.

By mid-afternoon Judge Simon Rifkind was seated behind me. A senior partner at Paul, Weiss, Rifkind, and Garrison, Si was a legend in the legal profession. But by now there was little even he could do to help me.

The questioning was relentless. The liberal Democrats on the committee—my natural allies, I had previously thought—were unforgiving. Why would Kleindienst meet with me? Why would a deputy attorney general go over the head of his antitrust chief? Who had arranged these meetings? Who else was present? Did I truly believe it was my argument about the national economic consequences if the merger unraveled that changed Kleindienst's mind? And on and pointedly on. It was clear that the Democrats didn't believe me, and after stammering my way through their questions I couldn't blame them. My story *was* hard to believe. The fact that it was true seemed to be only an annoying irrelevancy.

The press, too, showed me no mercy. The *New York Times*, the *Washington Post*, even *Fortune* magazine—all were sav-

age. And the hearings and the editorials had immediate consequences for ITT. The IRS, which had previously granted ITT
a tax-free ruling in the merger, announced that it was reopen-
ing its deliberations. A reversal would be disastrous for ITT; it
would cost the company several hundred million dollars. Then,
the SEC jumped in. The SEC announced that it was opening an
inquiry into the disclosures made by ITT and Lazard in the various filings in the merger. Who knew what kind of trouble this
could make for me and for the firm?

It was a low point for me; my future at Lazard, as an investment banker, seemed in jeopardy. I had behaved stupidly
and naively, and now previously unimagined consequences were
raining down upon my life. And when things seemed as if they
couldn't get any worse for ITT, Geneen, or myself, they did.

Who killed Salvador Allende?

Shortly after his election as president of Chile, the socialist
Salvador Allende had been murdered in a military coup. He had
run against the incumbent centrist, Eduardo Frei. But in the aftermath of his assassination, General Augusto Pinochet and the
army had taken over the government.

It was well known that Geneen and ITT had actively and
publicly opposed Allende; after all, Allende had proposed na-
tionalizing Chile's utilities, including Chilean Telephone, a
subsidiary of ITT. To Geneen, Allende's victory would create
another situation similar to what had happened in Cuba when
Castro assumed control: more of ITT's valuable foreign assets
would be expropriated.

The United States, specifically the CIA, was assumed by
many liberals in Watergate-era Washington to have played a
role in the coup and the subsequent assassination. But when
it was learned that ITT had tried to contribute $1 million to

the Frei party, Senator Frank Church decided to concentrate his inquiries on whether ITT had been complicit in Allende's murder.

In the aftermath of the ITT-Hartford hearings, with the IRS ruling still hanging over the company, and the SEC's investigation into Lazard's role in the merger continuing, this came as an unexpected and devastating blow. I felt besieged. I had no knowledge about ITT's political contributions in Chile. Another ITT Director, John McCone, a former head of the CIA, had been the intermediary between ITT and the U.S. government. He had dealt directly with Nixon and Henry Kissinger, the national security adviser. But the Church committee insisted on calling on me to testify.

I had just a walk-on role in the proceedings; I was a bit player in hearings where starring roles were played by Geneen, McCone, the CIA director, and a number of national security officials. When Senator Church asked me whether the ITT executive committee should have known about the $1 million political donation, and whether, had I known, I would have approved the sum, I replied with terse candor. We should have known, I said. And if I had known, I probably would not have approved the contribution.

But then I rambled on. If a specific request had been made to ITT by the U.S. government in the name of national security, I volunteered that I would probably have considered it. I would not, however, I emphasized, have condoned or approved any role for ITT in connection with a political assassination.

The hearings ended inconclusively. No proof was ever established of either the U.S. government's role or ITT's complicity in the ouster and murder of Allende. The only thing that had been established, I felt with some bitterness, was my dubious character.

The *Washington Post*'s columnist Nicholas Von Hoffman

dubbed me "Felix the Fixer." My children were taunted at school about their "ITT father." And Katharine Graham, the chairman of the *Washington Post*, took me aside at a dinner party to warn me that I would never serve in a Democratic administration unless I acted quickly and resigned from the ITT board. Her advice, I have to admit, was tempting: ITT—my first big success—had brought me more trouble and heartache than I might ever have imagined. But I could not resign. My resignation, I explained to Mrs. Graham, would reinforce the impression that Hal Geneen was guilty when the reality, I knew with all my heart, was that there was no convincing evidence. Further, Hal was my friend. We had been through too much together. He had steadfastly supported me for his board when Mr. Meyer had wanted someone who was not Jewish. I could not walk away from him now that times were tough.

All I could do was hope that the situation for both ITT and myself would, with the passage of time, improve.

It didn't.

Through political logic that presumed guilt because of tangential associations, ITT became entangled in the Watergate investigation. When the charges for Nixon's impeachment were being crafted, the "ITT affair" was dutifully included among the various "crimes and misdemeanors." Additionally, a special Watergate grand jury was impaneled to deal specifically with the Hartford settlement. And I was called to testify.

Prior to my appearance, it was made clear that I was not a target but simply a witness who might be able to help elucidate the facts of the matter. But this bit of news was not entirely reassuring.

My appearance was a very intimidating experience. The reality that I had to leave my counsel, Judge Rifkind, at the door of the jury room and take the stand for questioning by the prosecution and the jury panel was chilling. The prosecutor offered up a barrage of pointed questions about my role in the ITT-Hartford merger, about the arguments I had made in my attempt to persuade Kleindienst to reverse McLaren. And as I answered each one, Judge Rifkind's warning about the prosecutor never stopped resonating through my anxious mind: "He could indict Jesus Christ if he wanted to."

And no sooner had I survived the grand jury without apparent ill consequence when the SEC inquiry began to gather steam. The investigators were focusing on Lazard's involvement in brokering the sale of ITT's Hartford shares to the Italian bank, Mediobanca. I had not been involved in this transaction; Mr. Meyer had arranged the sale of the shares on his own. But nevertheless, I, too, was deposed.

What happened was that Mr. Meyer had been taken ill. The SEC agreed to depose him at his apartment in the Carlyle, with his doctor present. With his illness, however, his memory had grown vague. The SEC decided that I would be able to fill in the missing pieces of the transaction.

I couldn't. All I could do was testify under oath that I didn't know any of the details of the deal.

This seemed to satisfy the SEC. In 1977 the firm entered into a consent decree with the SEC. It included an agreement with the SEC that Lazard would satisfy broader disclosure requirements in the future. But there was no censure.

This small victory was followed by a larger one. The IRS subsequently confirmed its tax-free ruling. Finally, almost ten years after I had come to Geneen with the bold suggestion that he acquire Hartford, the deal was completed.

Only now I wished I had never approached him.

There was, however, one coda to my involvement in the entire ITT saga. Ever since my testimony before the Senate committee I had been questioning the efficacy of my meeting with Kleindienst. Had my argument really been persuasive? Or had the fix already been in? Had Geneen or someone—Beard? another ITT executive?—manipulated events without my knowledge?

When the Nixon Watergate tapes were released, I was at last able to fill in some of the missing pieces of the story. On a Saturday in July 1977, in the back pages of the *New York Times*, a story appeared that quoted several of the newly released tapes. In one of them, Nixon tells Erlichman that he had never met Harold Geneen and had no interest in ITT. But nevertheless he was incensed over McLaren's antitrust policies. He couldn't tolerate his anti–big business bent.

But it wasn't until the complete transcripts of the Nixon tapes were made public that I finally found my smoking gun. One tape contained a conversation between Nixon and Kliendienst. The president, the transcript revealed, wanted the antitrust case against ITT dropped. Kleindienst hesitated. But Nixon, full of fury, was adamant: "The order is to leave the goddamned thing alone. I don't want McLaren prosecuting people, raising hell about conglomerates, stirring things up at this point." Kleindienst once again attempted to object, but a raging Nixon refused to back down: "You son of a bitch. Don't you understand the English language? Drop the goddamned thing. Is that clear?"

The next day, according to the date of the recording, I had appeared for my appointment with Kleindienst. And so it was now revealed: I had been window dressing. Nixon had given Kleindienst a presidential order to overrule McLaren. My appearance and my well-reasoned argument were simply rationales used by the administration to justify a decision that had already been made.

Politics, I was learning, was a much rougher business than business. And the consequences could be significantly more devastating.

Seven

At its roots, the investment banker's craft, I was beginning to learn, was very much a challenge to fit disparate pieces together. Completing the puzzle required not simply diligence and strategy, but at times an iron will. To make the deal, you had on occasion to be willing to shove square pegs into round holes. And so it was when I teamed up once again with my old friend from the back room of the Riverside Funeral parlor, Steve Ross. This time, Steve had set his sights on a much bigger prize—he was determined to conquer Hollywood.

Steve was in many ways an investment banker's dream client—he was always looking for the next big deal. Even better, he was hugely imaginative, and when he set his mind to a particular challenge, he was totally—totally!—determined to achieve it. No less a gift was his knack for seeing the "next big thing." With insight that was both intuitive and visionary, he realized that the entertainment business was about to be dramatically transformed as new methods for distributing content came into play. The undertaker in the morning coat with whom I had schemed to take over a moribund rental car company now had his sights set on becoming the mogul who would lead Hollywood into its new and prosperous future.

In the three years since my aborted collaboration with Steve on the Avis deal, I had worked with his corporation,

Kinney, as it began cautiously to dabble in the entertainment business. First, I had advised Kinney in its prescient acquisition of the National Periodical Publications, the owner of the comic strip "Superman." At the time, buying a comic book franchise seemed more a whimsy than a business strategy, but Steve astutely appreciated the true strength of a superhero's commercial potential. Next, I helped Kinney, in a corollary strategic move, acquire a talent agency, Ted Ashley's Ashley Famous.

In the process of making these and other deals, Steve had carefully assembled a team of advisers he felt he could confidently count on, men who understood how he worked and whose loyalty was beyond reproach. It was such a close-knit group, and our times together were so often fun-filled and spirited, that in many ways I felt as if were back at my college fraternity. Steve, of course, was the backslapping, high-spirited fraternity president, the man setting the pace and orchestrating the festivities. The rest of us were glad to be along with him for the frolicking ride. Of course, that we were "serious" individuals, with our own independent "serious" jobs, was a reality that made our interludes with Steve even more appreciated. The team consisted of Alan Cohen, a partner at Paul, Weiss, Rifkind; Allan Ecker, counsel for Kinney; Bert Wasserman, Kinney's CFO; Arthur Liman, the vaunted senior partner at Paul, Weiss who, when things got sticky, was summoned to rush to the rescue; and, representing Lazard, myself.

Following Steve's instructions, Kinney had quietly begun a study of the motion picture and music industry. The aim was to identify a major entertainment target that Kinney could acquire. When the research was completed, Steve convened his team of advisers for a war council. The target, he announced with an air of triumph that struck me as precipitous, was Warner-Seven Arts.

In the early 1960s, Jack Warner had sold his stake in the old

Warner Brothers Studios for about $25 million. The new owners had rather passively cobbled together a weak motion picture studio called Warner-Seven Arts that was more interested in distributing films (*Bullitt, Bonnie and Clyde*) than actually making movies. But even the new Warners still had a very profitable record business consisting of the Warner Reprise label, in which Frank Sinatra held a 20 percent interest; and Atlantic Records, a label headed by Ahmet Ertegun, a Turkish entrepreneur who was a celebrated pop music producer. By the time Kinney began to focus on the company in the late 1960s, Warner-Seven Arts stock had been bouncing about erratically and rumors were circulating through Wall Street and Hollywood that the studio was up for sale. Steve Ross quickly made up his mind that he would be the buyer.

At our first strategy meeting, however, it became clear that taking control of the studio would be a difficult process. There were several major stockholders we'd need to win over, and, to complicate the challenge, each member of this diverse group had his own unique agenda and allegiances.

Consider the cast of imposing (and, in some instances, intimidating) characters we'd need to persuade if we were ever going to make a successful deal. The studio was headed by Eliot Heyman and Alan Hirschfeld, a young investment banker from Allen and Company. But they were just figureheads for Charles Allen, the canny, longtime director of Allen and Company, a New York investment bank that had earned a fortune in the entertainment business over the past decade and still had extensive relationships on the West Coast. This bank, represented Warner-Seven Arts, and therefore any deal would be impossible without Charlie Allen's support—and winning his blessing would be, I expected, nothing less than a blood sport.

Then there was Frank Sinatra. The singer not only owned a significant 20 percent of Warner Reprise records, but had—

shrewdly? mysteriously?—obtained the right of veto on any sale of the parent company. Ratcheting up the difficulty of persuading Sinatra, his lawyer, Mickey Rudin, was not simply the singer's representative in any negotiations but—shrewdly? mysteriously?—was entitled to receive 10 percent of whatever monies Sinatra received. Clearly, a deal would not be made unless Sinatra and Rudin were on board.

The other three major Warner-Seven Arts stockholders were, at least in my stodgy New York investment banker's critical appraisal, an extraordinary group. Carroll Rosenbloom was at that time the owner of the Baltimore Colts football team; when I met him for the first time in his hotel suite he was clearly under the weather, but he tersely dismissed his condition: "I'm sorry, kid, but I get these terrible headaches when I haven't had any female company for days." Morris "Mac" Schwebel, a close friend of Rosenbloom's, was both the owner of a large block of shares and the lawyer of the third significant shareholder, Lou Chesler. Chesler, a Canadian businessman, was rumored to have ties to Meyer Lansky, the mob's financier, and allegedly earned a fortune from flourishing business relationships involving an assortment of bookmakers and gamblers. And while the charges remained legally moot, the U. S. Immigration Service was nevertheless convinced. Chesler was denied entry into the United States.

To a Lazard banker accustomed to dealing with staid executives in the corridors of blue chip corporate power, it became apparent that this deal would take me into negotiations with a somewhat disconcerting assortment of players. I could only wonder if I had the right skills—and personality—to move Kinney's bid forward. But even as I met with Steve and the others to help formulate a plan to approach the shareholders, another rather unusual participant entered the fray. Commonwealth United, a West Coast conglomerate, unexpectedly made an offer to buy Warner-Seven Arts. And, in another grim indication of the decidedly uphill battle ahead, the company announced that Charles Allen was its representative in its bid for the studio.

Yet, I moaned silently, Commonwealth United, in keeping with the general character of this entire acquisition, was not by any stretch of the imagination or the balance sheet a blue chip company. A. Bruce Rozet had put together a rather marginal conglomerate; its main asset was a jukebox company, Seeburg, and there was also an assortment of real estate, insurance, and oil interests whose value was, to my banker's eye, nebulous. Nevertheless, its stock, buoyed by the creative accounting techniques that were the rage in this optimistic era of conglomeratization, was having a good (and to me, utterly mystifying) run.

Further muddying the already murky waters, one of Commonwealth's main shareholders was Bernie Cornfeld, a colorful figure who had achieved seemingly huge success by selling mutual funds to American GI's in Europe. One part promoter to another part inventive financial services entrepreneur, Cornfeld headed a firm called Investors Overseas Services (IOS). Through IOS, he had become a major investor in both Commonwealth and Warner-Seven Arts.

Quite a cast of colorful characters! But Steve Ross's mind remained set. He wanted Warner-Seven Arts. It was decided that he should be the one to approach Schwebel and Rosenbloom, in the hope that the power of his large personality would convince them of the wisdom of selling their shares to Kinney—and the money they could make in the process. He promptly called to make an appointment with the two men, only to discover that they were enjoying the Florida sun on Schwebel's yacht. Undeterred, Ross booked a ticket to Miami.

I was assigned a no less daunting task. I needed to travel only a few blocks uptown in Manhattan, yet I had to meet with Charlie Allen, the banker who represented both Warner-Seven Arts and Commonwealth United. I had to inform him that we were in the game, too. Kinney was prepared to make a competitive offer for all the shares in Warner-Seven Arts.

I did not look forward to the meeting. Walking into Charlie Allen's office, I was anxious, even a bit scared. Allen was a legend on Wall Street, a vigorous, silver-haired deal maker who had earned his reputation and his fortune on the strength of his celebrated intelligence. And now I was about to confront him with a challenge that, I knew, was contrary to his carefully laid-out plan. Shrewdly, he was in the deal so that the assets of Warner-Seven Arts would support Commonwealth's very weak balance sheet. To turn him around, I'd need to deliver an offer that would get him to rethink his allegiance to Commonwealth. Yet I also knew that it was very likely too late in the process for our side to win Allen over. Still, I had no choice but to try. Without his support, a deal couldn't be done.

Once I was in Allen's office, there were only a few polite preliminaries before I plunged into the purpose of my visit. I told Allen that I represented Kinney and that the company was prepared to make a offer superior to Commonwealth's for Warner-Seven Arts. To reinforce my point, I handed him a copy of the Kinney annual report.

Allen did not even pretend to glance at it. Instead, he flipped it back across the desk toward me. Then, his clipped words dripping with disdain, he announced, "Don't bother. The deal with Commonwealth is all set."

With a resolute calm that was entirely feigned, I politely countered that nevertheless we would make an offer to the Warner-Seven Arts board. I hoped, I said, that he would review it objectively. But as I rose to leave I couldn't help feeling that all was lost. There was not sufficient time to win over Charles Allen.

Later in the week, I called on Bernie Cornfeld. But for this meeting, unlike the meeting with Allen, I didn't arrive unarmed. I had done a study of Commonwealth's financial statements, and what I discovered was a revelation. The company was an empty shell. All its earnings had come from the purchase and quick resale of Hawaiian real estate in the last ten days of 1968. The transaction seemed at best an accounting ploy, at worst something entirely fictitous. Either way, the company clearly had very little cash in the bank and few tangible assets.

Still, I was unsure whether Commonwealth's shaky finances would have any genuine effect on Cornfeld's support for the company. He was a notorious figure at the time, and I couldn't know for sure what his arrangements were with Commonwealth or how he saw himself and his company, IOS, profiting from the acquisition of Warner-Seven Arts. I did know, however, that he had made a fortune with IOS and was spending it with free-spirited exuberance. He lived in a mansion on the shore of Lake Geneva with his mother and a retinue of ravishing women. The house was famous for its parties, many cohosted by another retinue: glamorous American socialites he had hired with the hope that their presence would give the festivities a veneer—even if a thin one—of respectability. There were plenty of stories, too, that IOS had ties to the mob. In fact, years later the company would be taken over by Robert Vesco, a dicey financier who fled to the Dominican Republic to avoid prosecution by the U.S. Justice Department.

But in 1968, when I went to see Cornfeld, he was still very rich and riding very high. At the reception desk outside his wood-paneled offices on a floor of a sleek high-rise above Fifty-Seventh Street in Manhattan, I was welcomed by his two assistants. Each was a towering blonde, and each was dressed in an outfit of white boots and a skimpy miniskirt that provocatively showed off her long legs. Although we were indoors, for some unknown reason they also wore identical sunglasses with purple lenses and huge frames. Smiling ingratiatingly, the assistants fell in on either side of me and led me to Cornfeld's office.

I had to wait for a bit until Cornfeld joined us. He was a slight, balding man dressed in a pea-green suit with wide lapels and flared trousers. In an accent that betrayed his Brooklyn roots, he jovially asked if I wanted a cup of tea or, he added with a facetious leer, perhaps one of the two women.

Pleasantly, I rejected both offers. I then announced that I had come to talk about Warner-Seven Arts. Perhaps we could limit ourselves to that subject, I quickly added, and the words struck even me as a bit too prim.

But Cornfeld was apparently not offended. Sure, he agreed, with a jovial hail-fellow smile. And so for the next hour I shared the details of our proposal for a Kinney-Warner transaction. Strategically, I had left my revelations about the precarious state of Commonwealth United finances until the end of my presentation. I wanted him to appreciate that ours was a genuine offer with real potential for growth; Commonwealth's was, well, a decidedly more dubious proposition. But my stern appraisal of Commonwealth's balance sheet did not seem to concern Cornfeld. Either he had already known the state of the company's finances, or he simply didn't care.

The meeting ended inconclusively. But I very much doubted that I had won him over. Perhaps, I wondered forlornly, things might have gone better if I had tested the sincerity of his offer of one of the blondes.

—

But leave it to Steve Ross. A blizzard was making its fierce way to New York and all the airports had been shut down. It seemed impossible for him to keep his scheduled appointment with Rosenbloom and Schwebel. Yet Steve, always resourceful, found a charter pilot who despite the storm warnings was willing to take off for Florida, and earn an exorbitant fee in the process. Steve arrived at his meeting on the yacht just as had been arranged.

He went there armed not only with the damaging information we had collected about Commonwealth's tenuous finances, but also with another trump card to play. After brainstorming for a while, we—Kinney's lawyers and my team at Lazard—had devised a new type of security as compensation for the shares we needed to acquire to cement the purchase. This new class of stock not only would have tax and accounting advantages, but also would combine the security of a preferred stock with the upside potential of common shares. It was an opportunity to sell for a profit, benefit from any future rise in the stock's price—and at the same time protect the lion's share of the funds from the IRS. This was a prospect that Rosenbloom and Schwebel, astute investors, couldn't help but find appealing. But it was Steve Ross—with his oversize personality, his enthusiastic plans for the future of the studio, his ability to win the trust of hard-nosed players like Rosenbloom and Schwebel—who in the end won their support. By the time he left the yacht that afternoon, several bottles of whiskey had been consumed—and Steve had been assured that his two new friends would support Kinney's offer.

That brought us to a showdown in front of the Warners-Seven Arts board. Bruce Rozet, the chairman of Commonwealth United, spoke first. He seemed very confident, and who could blame him? After all, he went into the meeting with both Charles Allen's and Bernie Cornfeld's support for his bid.

When he was done, Ted Ashley and I made the presentation of the Kinney offer. At first, our discussion was a litany of numbers, the dollars and cents we would pay for the stock, and the promising financial potential we saw in the studio's future. This was a typical investment banker's strategy: stick with us; we'll make you rich, and then even richer.

But, rather untypically, after I had waved the golden carrot, I proceeded to brandish a very sharp stick. I announced that we had taken it upon ourselves to alert the SEC to Commonwealth's financial shenanigans. And, in another uncommonly aggressive tactic, we had also shared our analysis of the Commonwealth balance sheet with its large institutional shareholders. This was not the way we generally conducted business at Lazard, but the deal was not our usual sort of deal, nor were we up against the usual sort of principals. On behalf of our clients, we could, when it grew necessary, become fiercely pragmatic.

Rozet was furious. As he stormed out of the meeting, he paused to shove his face directly up against mine and shout that he would sue me. But it was too late. I knew that Charles Allen and Bernie Cornfeld were too sophisticated and too practical to tie their futures—and capital!—up in a teetering corporation. They would have no choice but to negotiate the best deal they could with Kinney. Which, in short order, they did.

—

That left Frank Sinatra. Unless we could win him over, he had the legal right to veto any deal. As we were struggling to work out the proper approach to him, we received a message: Sinatra wanted to meet André Meyer. The messenger was my friend Bennett Cerf, the chairman of Random House publishers; I had met him a few years earlier when I had arranged the sale of Random House to our longtime Lazard client, RCA.

And so a meeting was arranged at Mr. Meyer's apartment in the Carlyle. I will always believe it was the glorious array of masterpieces hanging on the walls that clinched the deal. Mr. Meyer, a gracious host, walked Sinatra through the collection, sharing loving details about each Modigliani, Picasso, or Renoir. Sinatra, a painter and a lover of great art, was enthralled. When Mr. Meyer finally began to discuss the sale of the Reprise shares to Kinney, Sinatra readily agreed that something could be worked out that would be in everyone's interest. A more cynical observer might judge that the generous sale price, too, helped to convince Sinatra. Within days his Warner-Reprise shares were bought by Kinney for $25 million. Mickey Rudin, as per his long-standing arrangement with Sinatra, received $2.5 million to boot.

—

And then there was Ahmet Ertegun. Not only did we have to take control of Atlantic Records; we also needed Ertegun, a proven manager, to stay and run the company. Since Ahmet was a social friend of mine, I accompanied Ross to the meeting at Atlantic Records.

But my presence, I soon realized, was unnecessary. Steve was masterful. Before the meeting he had huddled with his children and they had given him a crash course in pop music. And now he was talking to Ahmet with great authority about Atlantic's newest supergroup, Blind Faith, and the genius of its lead guitarist, Eric Clapton. Maybe Ahmet realized that this was all a contrivance; or maybe he simply decided that it was, however much a calculated pose, an attitude he could work comfortably with in the future. Regardless of the reason, he and Steve got along like two old rock hounds. Ahmet agreed to sign a new contract, and the merger went forward.

—

Steve Ross had done it. For $400 million Kinney had in 1969 purchased Warner-Seven Arts. He had started off in a funeral parlor and wound up running a Hollywood studio. And now that Steve had the job of his dreams, he set out to enjoy every minute of it. With style and generosity, he assumed the role of a Hollywood mogul as if it had been his natural inheritance. There was the luxurious Warner villa in Acapulco where he would wine and dine his stars; there was the fleet of private jets to ferry them wherever they wished; and there was the cadre of retainers trailing deferentially in his wake. And just because he had achieved his goal of acquiring the studio, Steve did not stop looking for more strategic deals. Warner's, for example, was the first studio to acquire a cable TV operation; and in later years, this division, under Bob Pittman, a hugely talented young executive, would develop the cable channels MTV and Nickelodeon.

But Steve's ultimate achievement would come twenty years after he took control of the studio—the $14 billion merger of Warner with Time. Sadly, before Steve could solidify his control of Time-Warner, he died of prostate cancer. He was a very young sixty-five. And in the years following his death, his corporate successors squandered the rich and inventive inheritance he had left them in an ill-advised and fabulously costly merger with AOL.

From Steve, I had learned two very important lessons. With ingenuity and perseverance, a banker could accomplish many great and transforming goals in the world of business. But in the wake of Steve's death, I also learned perspective. What we bankers do is fleeting. The work of one generation can be carelessly undone by the next.

Eight

André Meyer was worried.

True, the 1960s had started out as very good years for Wall Street. Volume on the New York Stock Exchange had increased dramatically, soaring from less than 300,000 shares traded each day to a routine daily volume of more than 1 million shares. And there seemed to be no reason to think that the trend would not continue. Investors optimistically believed in the market's rosy future, eagerly buying up the "nifty fifty" growth stocks and the aggressively expanding conglomerates.

Lazard's business, too, was growing dramatically. Mr. Meyer, private by nature, did his best to keep the firm modest in size, especially as compared to the more prominent, old-line investment banks. He wanted to present us to Wall Street as a small and rather mysterious operation. Through transactions that were fully approved by the auditors, he ensured that at year's end the firm's cash reserves were substantial but not—in his prudent mind—excessive. Lazard's annual report presented a mid-level investment bank, not rich enough to be a concern to the Wall Street powerhouses or to attract the litigious sorts who might hope to make a killing with frivolous lawsuits.

But the reality was that mergers and acquisitions were a new and glamorous and very profitable activity, and Lazard was in the forefront of this wave of corporate deal making. And so was

Dealings

I. With my continuing work for ITT, my part in the purchase of Lorillard by Tisch, and my role in Kinney's acquisition of Warners I had seen my position solidify in the firm. In the process, I had also, to my delight, become a well-known figure in the world of finance.

Yet Mr. Meyer was worried. He was worried about a marketplace that had suddenly expanded exponentially, so that firms made trades involving huge, once unimaginable sums, but still functioned as largely uncontrolled and unmonitored relics of a bygone and much simpler financial era. And he was worried about the liability of solvent firms like Lazard if some of the shakier, undercapitalized Wall Street investment firms started to crumble.

Fortunately, or so it seemed at the time, in 1969 an event occurred that would allow Mr. Meyer to assuage some of his anxieties. I was invited to join the board of governors of the New York Stock Exchange (NYSE). This was, I realized, a large honor for someone my age, and for someone who was not a typical Wall Street executive. I was very flattered.

I feared, though, that Mr. Meyer would insist that I refuse the appointment. It would require, I felt certain he would decide, too public a role for a Lazard banker.

But I was wrong. I had not sufficiently gauged the effects recent events had on his concerns, or on the depth of his anxiety.

In the aftermath of the 1964 collapse of Ira Haupt and Company, a medium-size investment firm, the NYSE had set up a $25 million special trust fund to protect the customers of insolvent member firms. The $25 million had been raised from the member firms. However, Mr. Meyer—and I, too—felt that the trust fund could very well become an open-ended liability for the solvent firms, especially if several of the big investment houses collapsed simultaneously. No less of a concern was that, because at this time all the member firms were partnerships, an open-ended liability might be extended to the individual partners. Our personal wealth and savings could be at stake.

So when the invitation came for me to join the NYSE board of governors, Mr. Meyer quickly gave his endorsement. He believed that that I would be in a position to persuade the NYSE to rethink the members' unlimited bailout exposure.

And Mr. Meyer's anxieties were prescient. It wasn't long after I was seated as a member of the board of governors that his long simmering concerns about liability would come to fruition. However, the reality was far worse than even he had anticipated. The crash of 1970, the most serious economic crisis since 1929, struck Wall Street and America.

—

But before the crash and the ensuing financial panic would spread through Wall Street, I was a witness to two incidents that, I would later come to realize, were harbingers of the larger crisis that was looming. The first was nothing less than a demand to transform the entire way the investment houses did business.

It occurred, to my utter surprise, at one of the first governors' meetings I attended. There were two classes of governors: "floor" governors, who owned their own stock exchange seats and traded on the exchange; and "upstairs" governors, who did not trade on the floor but nevertheless represented member firms. While the SEC ostensibly provided the rules and oversight under which the NYSE operated, the member firms functioned for all practical purposes as a self-regulating body. That is, the board of governors—"floor" and "upstairs" members—set the policies for the NYSE, and the NYSE staff administered the operations. And so I was sitting with my fellow governors on the plushly covered red velvet seats in the boardroom, a large, multitiered amphitheater that had been designed to evoke the legislative authority of the U.S. Senate, when Dan Lufkin, a principal in the investment firm Donaldson, Lufkin, and Jenerette (DLJ), took the floor to make an announcement: DLJ was going public. In the process, he added defiantly, it would also institute changes to the anachronistic way business was being conducted on Wall Street.

Up to this point, the Wall Street investment firms had functioned as, in effect, creaky, family-owned businesses. The institutional buyer of 100,000 shares of a stock was charged the same commission per share as a buyer of 100 shares. This made, justifiably, little economic sense to the professional traders and buyers. However, there simply wasn't the "back office" technology at the firms to handle any modifications to the commission structure, especially in light of the increased volume that in recent years had already been overwhelming management.

But DLJ, a young, aggressive firm geared to institutional research and executions, saw the future—and, more important, was determined to move creatively forward into it. Therefore, DLJ would abolish the fixed-rate commission structure and in its place would institute negotiated commissions. It would bring technology to the "back offices" and replace the rickety network of partnership with a modern, well-functioning corporate structure. And, perhaps most startling, it would raise the capital to accomplish these revolutionary changes by a no less revolutionary action—it would sell shares in the firm to the public.

The board of governors was, it is no exaggeration to say, thrown into a panic. If DLJ was allowed to make this move, then the implicit laws that drive our competitive economic system would inevitably force other firms to do the same. There was too much money to be made (or lost) for other firms not to embrace these modernizing changes. All of Wall Street would need to rethink the way it did business, and its ownership structure, if the firms hoped to keep up with the rapidly evolving times.

Yet while DLJ did not need the governors' permission to reinvent itself, the NYSE was nevertheless faced with a choice. The board of governors could vote to expel DLJ from the stock exchange; or it could change the NYSE constitution to allow the selling of shares of members firms to the public. Further, we had some strategic leverage we could apply to pressure DLJ to reconsider its bold course: if the firm lost its NYSE membership, that loss could prove costly. Investors—individuals and institutions—might be reluctant to make their trades with a nonaffliated firm. With so much at stake, a wrenching, vitriolic fight errupted among the governors.

In retrospect, the opposing positions in the hard-fought debate seem glaringly apparent: either one wanted Wall Street to plod along as a largely antediluvian enterprise, growing increasingly unable to manage the expanding volume of business and capital that was pouring into the firms; or one supported a well-capitalized future in which modern technology would help ensure that the firms functioned efficiently and with, one also hoped, a reassuring level of supervision.

It was not too difficult, therefore, to pick the objectively correct side in this showdown, or so it would seem nearly forty years later. Nevertheless, at the time I opposed DLJ's petition. I did not want any changes to the NYSE constitution that would allow a member firm's shares to be sold to the public.

How can I justify this narrow position? I can't. All I can offer up in the way of logic is that I exhibited the prideful conservatism of someone who had just been granted membership in an exclusive club. With my appointment, I became another of the insiders eager to preserve *our* historic and fraternal practices, regardless of how outdated—wrongheaded, really—these rules and traditions were.

In time, though, common sense trumped my reluctance. I realized that if Wall Street was to survive as a profitable enterprise, the old boy club would need to be opened up to the public—and its capital. I supported the changes DLJ wanted to make to the NYSE constitution and, eventually, so did a sufficient majority of the other governors. The rules governing member firms were changed, and Wall Street never looked back.

When DLJ went public in 1969, its market value was about $25 million. In 2000, the successor to DLJ was sold to Credit Suisse First Boston for $11.5 billion. The entire way of doing business on Wall Street had changed in those three decades—and it was DLJ that had first mobilized Wall Street to take those first revolutionary and modernizing steps. We on the board of governors had played a large role in making this future possible by, however reluctantly, constitutionally endorsing the era of transformation.

—

But at that time there also was another, more ominous signal of the changes that were in store for Wall Street. Pickard, a small investment firm, went bankrupt. The accounts of its 3,500 customers were dutifully protected by the trust fund. But, as Mr. Meyer had anxiously predicted, the problems that Pickard had in processing the higher volume of trading and its inability to provide credible financial statements were not unique. The crisis of 1970 had begun, and other firms, and tens of thousands of other clients and their accounts, would soon be in jeopardy, too.

Nine

As the tumultuous 1960s came to an end, so did the good times on Wall Street. When the final year of the decade began, the Dow hovered loftily at around 900. Twelve rocky months later, it had fallen to a flat 800, nearly 15 percent. And trading volume, previously on a seemingly irreversible upward course, now declined, too.

By April 1970, the Dow had sunk to a once unimaginable 724. Yet, as if out of control, the market continued to slide to further depths. President Nixon tried to restore the public's confidence by announcing that if he had the means, he'd be buying stocks. The Federal Reserve attempted to reinvigorate the market by reducing margin requirements. But nothing seemed to work. In May, after the United States invaded Cambodia, the Dow fell below 700. The negative momentum now seemed unstoppable.

Most stocks plunged, but the companies that had been the favorites of the marketplace during the high-flying 1960s were hit hardest. The ten leading conglomerates declined an astounding 86 percent. Computer stocks fared only marginally better; they had fallen by 80 percent. Meanwhile the tech companies had lost 77 percent of their share value. The losses sustained in the 1970 crisis on both exchanges and the over-the-counter market totaled about $300 billion, or more than $1.4 trillion in today's dollars.

Still, on May 25, 1970, the market plunged even lower, to 640. Nixon was persuaded to preside over a dinner for government and business leaders, in the hope that this gesture would demonstrate the administration's confidence in the economy. This bit of showmanship had some effect. The market moved up above 700. But it was a short-lived rally. Panic had taken too strong a hold of the marketplace.

For many Americans, national events exacerbated a despairing sense that not just the economy had careened out of control. It was the worst of times: the war in Vietnam raged on, and neither victory nor a negotiated resolution seemed within reach. The National Guard had inexplicably shot four student protesters at Kent State. The assassinations of Martin Luther King and then Robert F. Kennedy were stunning tragedies. The brutal attacks by the Chicago police on the protesters during the Democratic convention in that city were a national disgrace. In this swirl of momentous events, the very future of the country seemed uncertain.

And on Wall Street, the chaos continued. The Penn Central Railroad went bankrupt and had to be rescued by a government loan guarantee. Lockheed Aircraft, nearly insolvent, needed similar federal help. And battered by low trading volumes and falling stock prices, many investment firms began to teeter precariously. They had emerged from the boom years without either financial controls or adequate reserves of long-term capital and were now unprepared, victims of a national economic crisis. The only protection these poorly capitalized firms could offer their anxious clients was the promise—and a decidedly limited one, at that—of the NYSE's relatively small $25 million trust fund.

André Meyer's worst fears had become a reality.

—

Then, like cascading dominoes, the investment firms started to collapse. In a flurry, several small and medium-size firms went under and the NYSE reluctantly authorized drawing $5 million from the trust fund. Along with the other governors, I listened as the vice president of the NYSE, John Cunningham, reported on these transactions and on how the firms planned to emerge as strong, well-capitalized entities. But it was apparent that he simply did not have sufficient facts to justify his sanguine reports. More disheartening, I was beginning to suspect that the NYSE staff was cavalierly allowing member firms to disguise their financial problems. Incredibly, the staff members were acting as if the firms's capitalization problems could be solved by mere bookkeeping, by simply adjusting their records to show compliance with the rules.

But on a Friday, March 13, 1970, when McDonnell, a well-established old line firm, failed—the trust fund was invaded once again. And in the wake of this startling news, new rumors began to circulate on Wall Street involving other well-known firms and horrifying capital shortages.

It was now that Bernard J. "Bunny" Lasker, the new chairman of the NYSE, decided the time had come to intervene. The NYSE needed accurate information about the financial conditions of its member firms, and it needed to institute strong oversight controls. Lasker appointed a committee that included himself; Ralph DeNunzio, vice chairman of the NYSE and executive vice president of Kidder Peabody; and two "floor" governors: Steve Pitt and Sol Litt. He asked me to be chairman.

I was a logical choice, since I had extensive experience with corporate restructuring, but once again I assumed Mr. Meyer would veto my having such an extensive role. It would require, I was certain he would complain, that I spend too much of my time away from Lazard's business.

But once again I was mistaken. Mr. Meyer gave me his approval. He believed that it was necessary to get a strong handle on the capitalization problems that were shaking Wall Street and that I, an instinctively conservative banker, could help. And so for the next year and a half I devoted most of my energies to the NYSE. Our committee's official name was Surveillance Committee of the NYSE. Yet with chilling appropriateness, it soon became widely known as the "Crisis Committee."

The committee began slowly enough, meeting on Thursdays for a civilized lunch. To my surprise, in the process I began a close friendship with Bunny Lasker. Bunny was a tall, straight-talking stock trader and arbitrageur, the head of Lasker, Stone, and Stern, his own specialist firm. He was also a child of the Lower East Side, an observant Jew, and, as a conservative and active Republican, a supporter and close personal friend of Richard Nixon. I had been raised in a bourgeois European family, was an agnostic Jew, and was a diffident, intellectualizing Democrat. We were about as different as two men could be.

Yet in this time of crisis, our differences proved complementary rather than causes for distraction. Bunny had a deep and very insightful knowledge of the stock exchange and its members. He also had invaluable contacts within the administration, including, not insignificantly, President Nixon. And his web of friendships also extended to the Republican leadership and the incoming SEC chairman, Bill Casey. I, however, had developed strong relationships with many on the Democratic side of Congress. And while Bunny was an authority on the specialized business of buying and selling securities, my experience enabled me to speak with expertise on issues involving financial restructuring and management competence. Perhaps best of all, Bunny and I were not ideologues. We had no problem with pragmatically taking advantage of each other's contacts and business knowledge. As we worked together, our large differences in temperament and personality seemed to fade from my mind. I developed an enormous respect for Bunny, a man of boundless energy, decency, patriotism, and, an invaluable quality if one is going into battle, good sense.

From the start, Bunny and I worked as a team. The first substantive decision I made was to invite SEC representatives to all our meetings. This was not a very popular decision among the NYSE staffers who had joined us. They argued that in the past the NYSE and the SEC often had an adversarial relationship. The mere presence of these "enemies," the staffers hotly argued, would be disruptive.

But I was adamant. And Bunny supported me. We both believed that the NYSE staffers had other reasons for wanting to keep the SEC at a distance. There was little doubt in my mind that a number of member firms had routinely been violating the capital rules, that a great many accounting tricks had been used to disguise the books, that as a result customers' securities were possibly at risk—and that the NYSE staff had blithely allowed this to happen. The staff members had allowed these conditions to prevail because, foolishly, they felt they had no other choice. They needed, they believed, to protect the capital that remained in the trust fund. And they were desperately trying to avoid the panic that would break out on Wall Street if the actual situation became known.

But it wasn't just the NYSE staff that was to blame. The more I learned, the more appalled I became. The capital rules of the stock exchange were archaic and inadequate for a modern, evolving business. It was true, for example, that the ratio of total indebtedness to capital under the NYSE rules—and seconded by the SEC—could be no greater than a relatively reasonable twenty to one. But to my dismay, I discovered that the definition of what represented capital was bewilderingly flexible. Loans of securities, accounts receivables, secured demand notes—all qualified as capital under the NYSE's ludicrous standards. To make a precarious situation even more dangerous, the rules allowed that this pathetically weak capital base could be withdrawn by its owners on ninety days' notice.

I was shocked. Wall Street's entire capital structure seemed balanced on a weak, impermanent capital base. If a wave of panicky investors began to withdraw their capital, I had no doubt that many firms would collapse, customers would be ruined, and the trust fund, with its inadequate resources, would be of little help. In my reeling mind, a harrowing scenario began to play out: this was 1929 again, and the government would need to intervene to prevent a devastating blow to the national economy. But, I worried, could the government find the resources and the will this time? In my anxious mood, I began to fear that if Wall Street were pulled apart as more firms collapsed, then even capitalism itself might not survive.

In these circumstances, I could not see our committee going forward without the SEC's participation. We were now meeting twice a week at 8:30 in the morning, and two SEC senior staffers—Irving Pollack, head of the SEC's enforcement division; and his deputy, Stanley Sporkin—joined our committee. Their reputations caused fear in the member firms, and their presence seemed to intimidate many of the NYSE staffers. However, I believed that wasn't necessarily a bad thing. And so for the next six months, from June to December 1970, they were present as the committee now met nearly each day.

And soon we were facing developing crises in three significant firms. No sooner had we made some progress in tackling the large problems at one investment house then the next one came harrowingly to our attention.

⏤

Hayden Stone, a large firm with 90,000 customers and more than $100 million in revenues, had been a looming problem for some time. As the national economy faltered, investors, eager to protect their assets, began to withdraw significant amounts of capital from the firm. But its books were an inadequate record of these transactions, and the stock exchange seemed content to ignore the increasingly grave issues of noncompliance. Every month Hayden, Stone lost another 1 million. But the NYSE staffers apparently were willing to overlook the fact that the firm had inadequate cash reserves. They argued that Hayden, Stone had satisfied all the NYSE capital requirements because a group of Oklahoma businessmen had pledged to the firm their stock in some highly speculative companies that had a purported market value of $17.5 million. But when these Oklahoma companies followed the general market trend and tumbled into a precipitous decline, it became clear to the "Crisis Committee" that Hayden, Stone was in violation of the NYSE's requirements for minimum capitalization.

What should the committee do? Should we let this large firm collapse, leaving its customers' stocks to be sold out from under them or tied up in receivership? Or should we attempt to keep Hayden, Stone as a going concern? We could look for a merger, or we could contribute more capital, or we could try to engineer a combination of these two approaches.

As the crisis of 1970 rocked Wall Street, this would be a decision we would need to face time after dispiriting time. Either we come to the aid of a firm, or we do nothing—except create a panic that could undermine the entire securities market.

Unanimously, the committee decided to keep Hayden, Stone in business. We asked the NYSE governors to approve a loan of $7.5 million to the firm from the special trust fund. But to find this money, we had to be inventive. We had imperiously reached into a special NYSE building fund for an additional $30 million, and in the process we had doubled the resources of the trust fund. Whether this was legal was one concern; and whether $7.5 million would be sufficient to keep Hayden, Stone afloat was another.

And no sooner had we tried to set Hayden, Stone right then one firm after another on the brink of bankruptcy came to appeal to our "Crisis Committee" for help. It seemed that wherever we looked on Wall Street we found balance sheets that were fictions.

It quickly became clear to me that we could not save all these firms. We had to let the smaller ones, the firms that would cause the least disruption to the entire marketplace, go under. We had no choice: the trust fund was overextended.

Ten

What had I gotten myself into? That despairing thought kept echoing through my mind as my work chairing the "Crisis Committee" continued to demand more and more of my time.

Yet I had little doubt about what was at stake. If a number of the big Wall Street houses collapsed, a national economic catastrophe seemed inevitable. Clearly, the trust fund was inadequate to bail out *all* the besieged firms. And this meant that André Meyer's gnawing anxiety was suddenly a genuine possibility—the partners in the wealthy member firms might be required to use their personal capital to cover the debts of the insolvent ones. A precariously constructed house of cards might very well come tumbling down. And there I was, part of a small group trying desperately to prop it up.

For the next six months, I had trouble going to sleep. And when at last I did manage to fall into a restless sleep, I would often have nightmares and wake up. On the difficult nights when sleep was impossible, I would seek out Harold Geneen. I was on the ITT board and I would arrive at his office in the middle of the night knowing that he would be there. I would use the thin excuse that there was some pressing ITT business we needed to review. But as the hours dragged on, we'd begin, invariably, to discuss the issues I was trying to deal with at the stock exchange.

Hal loved talking about business. If you put a business problem in front of him, there was little he'd enjoy more than trying to offer a solution. He'd approach it in his insightful and objective way, eagerly turning it back and forth in his churning mind. Often we'd leave his office and walk through the dark, deserted streets of Manhattan at two o'clock in the morning, trying to come up with a strategy that would do nothing less, I sometimes genuinely felt, than ensure the future of capitalism.

Hal had two rules. Rule 1: "Give me the facts. No guesses, no assumptions. Tell me what you're sure of." But when I shared with him the facts as I knew them, they were terrifying. And, no less troubling, the reality was that the "facts" I had on hand about many of the firms' finances were a murky mix of assumptions, expectations, and deliberate lies.

That left rule 2: "In a crisis, don't wait for all the facts you would like. Get as many as you can, and then move. If you wait for all the facts, it will be too late." This was a reasonable way to acquire a medium-size business when the downside risk was limited. It was not, however, a sound way to make decisions when any of the numerous choices could trigger a systemic economic crisis. But I came to realize, in my nocturnal discussions with Hal, that I had no alternative. However inadequate the information, however dangerous the consequences, I had to deal with the "facts" that I had. No wonder I had trouble sleeping. Yet these walks across Manhattan with Hal in the wee hours of the morning were too often the best part of my days, my only respite from the sea of troubles flooding my mind.

Dealing with the press was less enjoyable. Now that the problems at the stock exchange had become headline news, I, as chairman of the "Crisis Committee," found myself the focus of considerable media attention. When the stock exchange executives were interviewed, they were resolutely optimistic. Of course, they were trying to avoid creating a panic that could have a deleterious effect on the marketplace. But as the gap between their glowing promises and the more unfortunate reality began to spread, the NYSE staffers lost all credibility. I decided to take another course with the press. I would not try to frighten anyone, but at the same time I would not paint over an increasingly darkening reality with a Panglossian brush. I walked a dangerous line, always struggling to keep my balance. I was determined to tell the truth, yet I could not help realizing that even an offhand remark to a reporter might have repercussions that could affect the entire market.

But my relationship with the media became even more difficult and my sleepless nights became more commonplace when it became clear that the problems at Hayden, Stone had not been resolved. In fact, I discovered to my despair, they had grown worse.

Hayden, Stone continued to lose money. And as it did, the group of Oklahoma businessmen who had rushed in to collateralize the firm grew more enraged. Looking at the situation with some objectivity, I thought that there was reason enough on both sides for bad feelings. Hayden, Stone had been less than candid about its financial straits when it had solicited the group's investment. However, the $17.5 million in stock that had put been up for collateral was certainly more speculative than the group had revealed.

But assigning blame was not the committee's responsibility. Our mandate was to resolve what had become an untenable situation that would, if not handled decisively, have national repercussions. Therefore, we decided to find a major business partner for Hayden, Stone.

We turned to a small, aggressive firm: Cogan, Berlind, Weill, and Levitt (CBWL). (Sandy Weill would go on to be chairman of Citigroup; Arthur Levitt would serve as SEC chairman from 1992 to 2000.) They were eager to expand, but a look at Hayden,

Stone's books convinced them that this was too dangerous a merger. In the end, however, we sweetened the deal by offering another $7.5 million from the rapidly depleting trust fund and, as a further inducement, a division of the branch offices with another firm. As a result, CBWL now agreed to take over Hayden, Stone.

But before CBWL could move forward with the merger, the Chicago Board of Trade threatened to suspend Hayden, Stone. If this occurred, then the NYSE would have no choice but to take similar action. The SEC, which had been monitoring these events, also now stepped in. They made it forcefully clear that the lingering possibility of suspension had to be resolved, or Hayden, Stone would be required to declare bankruptcy.

The "Crisis Committee" decided we had to act quickly and forcefully. We set a strict deadline for the merger; otherwise, Hayden, Stone would be suspended. But before the merger could take place, the committee would need to obtain the approval of all 108 of Hayden, Stone's subordinated lenders—including the cantankerous Oklahoma group. We had chosen, we realized, a dangerous strategy. If we failed, if Hayden, Stone went under, a national crisis would, I believe, have been triggered. But I also believed we had no realistic alternative other than to make this difficult decision. It would have been irresponsible to allow the situation simply to linger.

And so we moved forward. Miraculously, with a September 11 deadline looming, we had talked all the holders, one by difficult one, into signing—until there was only one holdout.

Jack Golsen, one of the Oklahoma investors, refused to sign. He felt that the principals at Hayden, Stone had lied to him and that the NYSE, having failed to monitor the firm diligently, was also culpable. His revenge, he insisted with unshakeable conviction, would be sweet. He would force the liquidation of Hayden, Stone, and then the NYSE would be required to pay millions in damages.

Both Lasker and I had many fruitless conversations with Golsen and his lawyer. I tried to be unemotional, simply one businessman talking to another, as I laid out the case for signing. I argued—rather reasonably, I thought—that going along with the merger would be his only real chance of recouping his investment. Forcing a crisis, I said, would not help him, or the nation. But Golsen remained adamant.

On the afternoon of September 10, as the deadline moved ominously closer, the committee met with the principals of CBWL and came up with a desperation strategy. Cogan and Berlind would charter a Lear jet and fly to Oklahoma for a last-minute face-to-face conversation with Golsen.

While their jet was in the air, Lasker and I tried again with Golsen. He could not be moved. So Bunny, tenacious and resourceful, used his connections to get some last-minute help from the White House. If all else failed, then President Nixon agreed that he would call and try to use the power of his office to persuade Golsen.

Meanwhile, Cogan and Berlind landed in Oklahoma City at about 4 A.M. and went straight to a meeting with Golsen. They talked past dawn, but got nowhere. It was time to play our final card—the White House. However, Golsen infuriatingly refused to take the call from the president.

In desperation, shortly after nine o'clock on the morning of September 11, I called Golsen for one last attempt at turning him around. We talked inconclusively until Golsen, at about 9:45, peremptorily cut me off. I'll call back in five minutes, he said mysteriously.

But he didn't call back. Instead, at precisely 9:50, the telephone rang in Lasker's office. I picked it up. It was Larry Hertzog, Golsen's lawyer. "OK, Felix," he said. "You have a deal."

When the news of the CBWL–Hayden, Stone merger appeared on the NYSE ticker later that morning, the floor of the exchange erupted in cheers. I was happy, too. But the truth was, all I could think about was at last being able to get some rest. I felt completely exhausted, as if I had not slept for weeks. And I hadn't.

———

But what little rest I got was only a brief respite. No sooner had the Hayden, Stone crisis been resolved then a new one raised its head. This time the firm in trouble was Goodbody, the country's fifth-largest investment house, with 225,000 customer accounts.

For more than a year, the SEC and the stock exchange had ignored Goodbody's mounting capitalization problems. By the time the situation was brought to the committee's attention in 1970, it had grown dire. Goodbody's accounts were a slipshod mess, and—a further cause for concern—many investors had routinely violated the NYSE's capital rules and had withdrawn their money.

The SEC now intervened. It sternly gave Goodbody a November 5 deadline to resolve its capital problems or face liquidation. Clearly, we had to find capital for the firm, and we had to do it quickly. But we didn't know how much was truly needed; we could see that Goodbody's own books had little relationship to the beleaguered state of its finances.

Hoping to get accurate information, we approached Jim Hogle, the firm's largest shareholder. But Hogle tried to put us off. First he asked for more time. Then, he pleaded that he couldn't give us an accurate accounting of Goodbody's indebtedness. If he did, he was certain we'd have no choice but to shut the firm down.

Understandably, the committee did not find this a very persuasive argument. I told Hogle that it was impossible to give him any more time. The SEC's deadline was irrevocable. Goodbody's only hope was to provide us with accurate information—*now.*

Hogle started to cry. It was that painful for him to reveal the true depths of his firm's problems. At last, he shared a number: Goodbody needed $18.5 million to cover its loses.

Armed with that information—disheartening, but accurate—we set out to find investors who would inject the necessary capital. And—another miracle—we found them. A group headed by Utilities and Industries Corporation, a financial holding company, agreed to provide the $18.5 million.

The signing was scheduled to take place a week before the deadline that had been set by the SEC. On the day of the signing, however, we couldn't locate the investors. We finally tracked them down at Madison Square Garden, where they were watching a fight. It was suddenly, chillingly clear that they had no intention of honoring their oral commitment. We had been duped.

Now only a week remained until the SEC's deadline. I felt certain we had finally run out of options—and miracles. I was still deep in this resigned mood when I made my first official visit to the White House.

The occasion was the swearing-in of the new SEC chairman, Bill Casey. As I made my way forward on the receiving line, I was approached by Peter Flanagan, an assistant to President Nixon who had been my White House contact; for months I had been routinely using him to funnel all the grim news from the stock exchange to the administration. Let me introduce you to the president, he offered when he now saw me.

As Nixon and I shook hands, Flanagan explained that I was chairman of the "Crisis Committee" and that I was working with Bunny Lasker to deal with the problems at the NYSE.

"Well," said the president, "I'm glad to hear things are looking pretty good right now."

Still reeling from the collapse of the Goodbody deal, I was beyond trying to put an encouraging spin on what I was convinced was a desperate situation. "Mr. President," I replied with what I hoped was respectful candor, "I don't know where you get this information, but I am sorry to have to tell you that right now we are in a lot of trouble. We were able to deal with

Hayden, Stone. But Goodbody is in danger. And behind Goodbody are other large firms in sad shape. I wish I could be more optimistic, Mr. President. But I have to be truthful."

Nixon turned pale. He quickly led me away from the crowded receiving line and over to a window. We could now talk in private.

The president wanted me to tell him precisely what was happening on the stock exchange, and I did. When I finished, he asked who was my liaison with the White House. I explained that Lasker or I reported regularly to Flanagan.

Nixon shook his head demonstratively; Flanagan was obviously unacceptable. "Listen," he said, "I want you to call John Mitchell every night at ten. Keep him informed. We can't allow a Wall Street catastrophe. We'd have a national panic." And with that, he immediately summoned Mitchell, the attorney general, to join us in our corner by the window. Mitchell agreed that he would be waiting for my nightly calls.

As instructed, I called him regularly. On occasion, his wife Martha would pick up the phone. It was often apparent that she had been drinking, and then I would be forced to listen with mute politeness as she raged on about Vietnam, radical students, left-wing pinkos, and the cabals in Washington that were determined to bring down her husband and the president. I had called to inform the attorney general of the latest disaster we were dealing with on the stock exchange, but I would put down the phone even more disheartened, convinced that the country was charging toward a wrenching political as well as economic crisis.

Yet we had never given up on finding a solution for Goodbody. As the days leading to the SEC's deadline ticked off, Bunny Lasker called a meeting of the entire committee. He said it was imperative that we save Goodbody and he had found, he believed, a possible solution. Merrill Lynch must take over the ailing firm.

We listened, and we quickly agreed. Lasker was given the authority to approach Don Regan, the blunt, hard-nosed boss at Merrill (later, he'd serve as Ronald Reagan's secretary of the treasury).

Regan listened to Bunny; they were, after all, old friends and fellow conservative Republicans. After a bit of Bunny's persuasion, he agreed to approach his board of directors for permission to acquire Goodbody.

The Merrill board agreed—but only after Regan assured them that he would be demanding some very tough terms. The offer he made for Goodbody was certainly, at least from Merrill's perspective, a shrewd one. Merrill would invest $15 million in Goodbody, but only if the stock exchange agreed to provide up to $30 million of indemnification for potential future liabilities.

Where would we get that money? The only solution, I sourly realized, would be to impose special assessments on the member firms if these indemnification monies were needed. An extraordinary meeting of the board of governors was called and, after much impassioned debate, a vote was taken. It was agreed that the members firms could be assessed for additional funds.

Goodbody had been rescued. But in the process, André Meyer's worst fear had been realized: the trust fund had been transformed into an open-ended liability for all the member firms. And I had done nothing to try to prevent this potentially costly outcome. Rather, to Mr. Meyer's great consternation, I had actively helped to make it happen. Nevertheless, I felt that as chairman, and as a businessman concerned about the future of the NYSE, I had no other choice.

And still we continued to reel from crisis to crisis. Francis I. du Pont and Company had been run into the ground by the du Pont family. For years the stock exchange and the SEC had chosen to overlook the obvious capital violations in the firm's accounts. And when the books looked particularly alarming, the firm, with its web of du Pont connections, had always managed to rustle up sufficient capital to achieve some semblance of compliance. But now the du Ponts approach to management threatened to take not just their firm, but the rest of Wall Street with it.

The stock exchange, finally drawing the line, decided that du Pont should find a partner. After a short search, Edmund du Pont, speaking for the rest of the family, announced with great fanfare that the firm had reached an agreement to merge with Glore Forgan.

Dutifully, the "Crisis Committee" asked to see the numbers behind this merger. We were informed that no closing audit had been performed.

I was shocked. This wasn't simply unacceptable; it was madness. It was very likely that Glore Forgan's finances were as desperate as du Pont's. A merger of two troubled investment firms would not solve the problems of either one. It would only compound them.

Enraged and concerned, the committee sent Bob Haack, a former president of the stock exchange, to meet with the du Pont family. As we had instructed, Haack was blunt. He insisted that the firm needed new capital and new management.

The du Ponts were insulted. Huffily, they rejected Haack's arguments and dismissed his concerns. They refused to consider cooperating with the committee.

—

Rebuffed, we turned to Ross Perot.

Perot was the founder of Electronic Data Systems (EDS). A former employee of IBM, he had seen an opportunity to create his own data-processing company, and he made a fortune when it became one of the glamour stocks of the 1960s.

He was also a strong financial supporter of the Republicans, helpful to conservatives and to Nixon. And so it was that in one of my nightly calls to John Mitchell, the attorney general had suggested that I meet with Perot and seek his help in the du Pont crisis.

I, of course, was not a Republican, but nevertheless this suggestion made good business sense to me. In July, EDS had taken over du Pont's data-processing operations. It was a contract that paid EDS an estimated $8 million annually, and du Pont had become the company's largest customer. No less significant, its business with du Pont accounted for as much as $500 million of EDS's highly leveraged market value and, therefore, a large chunk of Ross Perot's personal fortune to boot. It was quickly apparent to me that EDS's fortunes—and Perot's—were intricately tied to the much shakier fortunes of F. I. du Pont. Now all I had to do was convince Ross Perot of this.

A meeting was soon scheduled in Lasker's apartment at the Hotel Carlyle. Lasker, DeNunzio, and I soon realized, however, that our role was not simply to serve as objective businessmen trying to shepherd a merger that made financial sense for all the parties. Rather, we were also, in effect, psychologists who had to defuse the frequent clashes between two very different cultural mind-sets.

On one side were the imperious du Ponts. Dozens of family members had invested in the firm, but for the most part they had little involvement in or even knowledge about the workings of the company. They were represented by Edmund du Pont, a man who combined an imperious attitude with a modest intelligence. He was seconded by his cousin Henry, the founder of the Winterthur museum, a man whose interests were more artistic than financial, and by his son Anthony. All the du Ponts, however seemed to have a common trait: they resented the fact that they needed to be rescued, and that their potential savior was, in their eyes, an arriviste Texan.

On the other side were Ross Perot, the West Point graduate and self-made man, and his loyal Texan aide, Mort Meyerson. They were conscientious, hardworking people and they had nothing but disdain for the du Ponts' incompetence. To their way of looking at things, the du Ponts' custodianship of their customers' accounts was not merely careless. It was unforgivable. They came to the negotiating table determined to win a large equity position in the firm. Additionally, Perot wanted assurances that F. I. du Pont would be included in the profitable underwriting syndicates that had always been the monopoly of the bigger investment houses. And beyond these specific financial demands, Perot, it seemed to me, wanted something more—respect. He saw himself as the potential savior of Wall Street, and he wanted the gratitude that was a hero's rightful reward.

Despite this clash of personalities and ambitions, the negotiations between the du Ponts and Perot moved forward. But then two unanticipated events occurred that threatened to undo all our efforts.

The first was a speech at the Economic Club of New York. Bob Haack boldly recommended abolishing the Wall Street practice of fixed commissions and instituting instead a system of negotiated rates. This was anathema to the board of governors, as well as to most of the membership, since over time it could reduce the profitability of the entire investment industry. But more crucial, it was an immediate threat to Perot's potential investment in du Pont. Why, after all, should he invest in an industry whose prospects for future earnings were being threatened?

Then, two weeks later, the second shoe dropped, loudly. The

annual du Pont audit revealed a capital shortage of $10 million—double the amount that had been previously disclosed to Perot.

He was furious. He felt, understandably, that he had been misled. He threatened to withdraw from what only days earlier had looked like a done deal unless he could negotiate better terms.

The du Ponts, however, shrugged off his concerns. A $5 million miscalculation was, to their way of looking at things, a small and largely irrelevant mistake. They refused to re-negotiate any terms.

———

Only now, as the situation began to unravel precipitously, did I feel certain that we were moving toward a financial crisis, which would have global repercussions. For at this point I had no choice but to concede that the Goodbody merger would also very likely come undone.

Merrill Lynch had insisted on a condition for its takeover of Goodbody that, as much as we had protested, we had ultimately been unable to resist: the merger was contingent on no major stock exchange firm's being in suspension at the time when the deal was finalized.

Now it seemed inevitable that both Goodbody and du Pont would be forced into bankruptcy. And hundreds of thousands of their customers would lose their investments. Institutions and families would be wiped out. The trust fund was already committed to about $100 million, and the member firms were clamoring to get out before their liability escalated further. In the wake of the collapse of these two major firms, there would be little chance of getting the Securities Investor Protection Corporation (SPIC) legislation—a program to protect stock accounts, similar to the way the FDIC insured bank accounts—through Congress.

I wondered if the "Crisis Committee" had placed too much emphasis—had allowed too much to be contingent—on the success of both these mergers. But I also knew we really did not have much choice. What other reasonable course could we have taken? The reality was that Wall Street had been pushed to the brink—and now seemed destined to tumble into this terrifying abyss.

—

But in the end Perot wisely decided that he had more to lose if he walked away from du Pont than if he took it over. In mid-December he acquired 51 percent of the firm for $10 million; the du Pont partners also agreed to come up with $15 million of additional capital. It seemed that the disaster had been averted.

Or had it? The du Pont partners never provided additional capital. Instead, they proceeded to withdraw millions of dollars from the firm. Then two months later, in April, with Perot's anger already escalating, the latest du Pont accounting disclosed that the firm actually would require an infusion of $50 million.

With that startling revelation, a new round of torturous negotiations began, involving the du Ponts, Perot, the "Crisis Committee," and, not least, the SEC. In the course of this battle, a new review of du Pont's seemingly ever-changing books was initiated. When it was completed, the bottom line was staggering. The total losses were not the $5 million the firm had originally reported. Nor were they the revised total of $50 million. Rather, the firm was approximately $100 million in debt.

Perot cut now a deal more to his liking, and the du Ponts had no realistic choice but to acquiesce. He lent du Pont $55 million in exchange for 80 percent of the firm. He also, despite protests from many of the governors, got the NYSE to indemnify him up to the sum of $15 million.

The Goodbody deal, too, could now go through. Congress approved the SPIC legislation. Wall Street reluctantly adopted negotiated commissions. And a national economic crisis was averted.

As for Perot, working with Mort Meyerson he transformed du Pont into a respectable, even reasonably profitable firm. But he also felt that Wall Street had never given him the recognition he deserved for his role as last-minute savior. He had rushed to the rescue at a perilous time, and he thought he should have received a good deal more acclaim.

I think he had a point.

In the aftermath of the 1970–1972 crisis, the way business was done on Wall Street was changed—a bit. Legislation was enacted that protected brokerage customers' accounts. Firms were allowed to incorporate, and therefore more stable capital structures were encouraged. And the SEC and the NYSE were more diligent in monitoring member firms' books and annual reports.

As for me, my role on the "Crisis Committee" during those tense days was a cautionary experience, one that reinforced my instinctive aversion to speculation and my insistence on reliable accounting practices. It also taught me many new lessons that would permanently shape my career both in banking and in public service.

I learned that in an unraveling financial crisis most of the data you'll receive are probably wrong. But you must nevertheless act.

I learned that you must rely on people who might very well have caused the problem. You need to try to incorporate them into the solution. You need to find common ground with people of different philosophies and different views—despite your own earnest beliefs.

Dealings

I learned that you need to accept with some equanimity that solutions are never neat or even final. You need to be prepared to engage in negotiations that are messy and drawn out and seem perpetually to become undone.

And I learned that the media are an inevitable—and even necessary—part of the process. You must be truthful. Candor will breed less panic than evasion.

These were hard-won lessons. But they became principles upon which I built my career.

Eleven

Experience, I was discovering, bred ideas. My involvement in the tense struggles to resolve the crisis at the New York Stock Exchange, my missteps during the ITT investigations and hearings, and my role in helping to put together the pieces in a variety of complex mergers and acquisitions—all these aspects of my life were beginning to shape a philosophy of sorts. In a meandering way, these events were steering me toward some still very inchoate thoughts about the fundamental collaboration that was necessary between government and the marketplace, about the activist role government must increasingly play in the economic life of its citizens, and about the responsibility of government to help institutions and the public persevere through difficult times.

It was not, however, until I was brought in to advise Lockheed, the giant military aircraft and missile manufacturer, that my ideas about political economy started to coalesce. But even as they took a stronger shape in my mind, I never imagined that the opportunity would soon arise to put these theories to a real-world test, or that nothing less than the future of New York City would rest in their efficacy.

But in the beginning, I was just a banker brought in to help a company through some very rough financial times. Lockheed was one of the nation's essential defense contractors, a vital resource for the testing and development of the next generation of missiles and aircraft necessary to protect America, and now the company seemed headed for bankruptcy.

The company, I ascertained after only a brief review of the situation, was being battered by a variety of circumstances. External factors such as OPEC's oil embargo and the recession caused by the increase in oil prices had taken its toll on many aviation companies, and Lockheed was no exception.

Then, Lockheed foolishly decided to return to the commercial aviation business. It announced that it would manufacture the Tri-Star, a three-engine commercial jet. Its partner would be Rolls-Royce, which agreed to develop a new type of engine for the plane. The timing of the venture was terrible; the oil embargo and the Vietnam War had wreaked financial havoc on the airline business. Rolls-Royce went bankrupt, and in the ensuing chaos it seemed inevitable that it would drag its Tri-Star partner down, too.

The besieged Lockheed managers, already reeling from the effects of their financial miscalculations, also had to deal with the ethical and legal consequences of their shoddy business practices. Management had authorized large payments to be made to senior Japanese politicians to help guarantee orders from Japanese airlines. "Bribes," the Japanese press shouted angrily when it broke the story of these payments, and a political scandal rocked Japan. In the United States, federal prosecutors were reviewing the transactions. Indictments against important Lockheed officials were a distinct possibility.

Yet, even while the company was being brought low by some genuine problems, I also found as I spent some time touring its various divisions and met with its personnel that I had entered into a unique and appealing world. Outside the besieged executive suites, the aerospace and defense industry was still a close-knit fraternity of very competitive risk takers and achievers. The engineers at Lockheed's top-secret Skunk Works facility, under its legendary boss, Clarence "Kelly" Johnson, were still using knowledge and imagination to push technology as far it would go. They remained committed to designing the aircraft of the future. And the company's test pilots, men with strutting, shining courage, routinely took to the skies to see how fast and how inventively they could fly their visionary aircraft. Lockheed was a national resource, and its employees were an integral part of the armory that protected the country. I was determined that the company should survive.

But with so much at stake, it was a difficult and often bewildering job. I reported regularly to the deputy secretary of defense, Bill Clements, a former governor of Texas. Each day, or so it seemed, I brought Clements a bid from another dubious potential investor, knowing full well that national security issues would prohibit these suitors from taking control of the company.

The shah of Iran, for example, wanted to help Lockheed. Through an intermediary he offered to purchase a number of Tri-Star planes. It was a generous order and it would have provided the funds that could keep the company in business. However, in return for his ordering a Tri-Star fleet, the shah also wanted to be able to buy a significant portion of the company. Without even a cursory review, the Pentagon quashed that offer. Similarly, there was a somewhat astounding offer from Roger Tamraz, a Lebanese businessman who owned a trading company in the United Kingdom. Representing a group of Middle Eastern oil sheiks whose identities he refused to reveal, Tamraz grandly announced that he would invest $1 billion in Lockheed. That amount of capital would undoubtedly have saved the company. Nevertheless, the Pentagon—prudently, in my opinion— vetoed this mysterious deal, too.

Dealings

Ultimately, I helped to save Lockheed the old-fashioned banker's way—by cobbling together a group of reputable investors and creating a sensible business model for the company. The company would be forced to endure some painful restructuring, it would need to abandon its dream of the Tri-Star, the banks would need to agree to be more indulgent, and the Pentagon and the government would have to provide strong financial support and guarantees. When this was all worked out, Lockheed was saved. A national resource, I felt with pride, could continue its necessary work in protecting the country.

My work for Lockheed, my involvement in helping an important national asset struggle through a recession and an energy crisis that had a mean hold on the economy of the entire country, helped crystallize my many thoughts about government. I was no longer interested in any personal future in politics. There had been a time when the possibility of holding a public position had been appealing. However, I had hitched my political aspirations to Senator Edmund Muskie's star. When his presidential campaign faltered in the snows of New Hampshire after his teary-eyed response to heckling about his wife, I realized that any prospects I might have had of filling a post in a new administration had also melted away. Yet, prodded by my work, and by my experiences at the NYSE and at Lockheed, I still continued to focus on public policy issues.

In fact, in the aftermath of Lockheed's rescue, my interest intensified. I felt as if I were a man on an intellectual mission. Also, I was energized by an immigrant's curiosity about the history of his new homeland. I read voraciously. I devoured whatever I could find on Franklin Delano Roosevelt, the Great Depression, and the New Deal. And in time, as my ideas began to take clearer shape in my mind, I concentrated my research on two inventive and powerful New Deal agencies: the Reconstruction Finance Corporation (RFC) and the Tennessee Valley Authority (TVA).

Herbert Hoover had created the RFC in the 1930s as a federal agency to invest government funds in banks in difficulty—provided the banks' managers were willing to create viable plans for restructuring their lending and investment portfolios. It was Franklin Roosevelt, however, who transformed the RFC into a much more powerful and active development agency. In the midst of the Depression, the RFC not only refinanced banks but also reached out to the nation's beleaguered cities and industries. With great success, the RFC was used to support bold and visionary federal initiatives that helped to create better lives for many Americans. For example, the TVA and the Rural Electrification Agency brought public power and electricity to corners of the country that, even in the twentieth century, did not enjoy these basic modern necessities.

Also, still at my roots a European, I read a great deal about Jean Monnet, the Frenchman who had worked to shape a new postwar Europe. By creating the European Coal and Steel Authority, Monnet had pragmatically combined the coal and steel production of France, Germany, Italy, and the Benelux countries in order to facilitate the continent's recovery from the ravages of the war and also to ensure that these industries would not be forced to turn to armaments to survive. Driven by a philosophy that was grounded in an appealing mix of pragmatism and idealism, Monnet also proposed the Common Market, a political and economic union that he hoped would guide Europe to a new century of cooperation.

As I read on, mulling over the far-reaching effects of the agencies that these two visionary leaders had created to help nations in times of great distress, I focused on the shared intellectual roots of their economic philosophies. Both men believed that during times of crisis an activist government had a responsibility to immerse itself in the economy, in order to promote national marketplaces where citizens were employed, factories prospered, and services were delivered to all in an equitable manner. Both men believed that the federal government could—and should!—play a key role in helping businesses and municipalities move beyond their troubles.

Similarly, I came to believe that an institution like the RFC could still be used to promote the economic revitalization of such crucial national assets as Lockheed. A government agency should be formed, I felt, that would work with business and labor to supervise a national recovery program. In exchange for new capital, this agency could demand the management changes, the increased labor productivity, and the price disciplines that would be necessary to bolster American businesses and even its cities during the economic and social crisis caused by the current recession and oil embargo. I had found a disciplined and yet effective plan, I was certain, for the United States to make its way successfully through a time of financial uncertainty and emerge with confidence into a new, prosperous era.

But philosophy is one thing, and action is another. I knew full well that ideas, however reasonable and even persuasive in a debate, are ultimately valuable only if they become government policy. Therefore, when my work on the NYSE helped to get me appointed to a Washington-based committee to advise the SEC, I made it a point to visit regularly with my friend Robert Strauss.

Strauss, then chairman of the Democratic Party, was a fixture of the Washington establishment. Both Republican and Democrats respected his judgment, enjoyed his ready humor, and called on him for advice. And now I wanted him to share my ideas with lawmakers.

As it happened, I was having breakfast at the Hay-Adams Hotel with Bob one morning in June 1975. In the ornate dining room, we were surrounded by tables filled with the usual collection of lobbyists, politicians, company executives, and media personages who made it their business to begin their workday with a "power" breakfast at the hotel. The talk at our table—and no doubt at many others throughout the large room—centered on a meeting that had been held at the White House the previous day.

New York City was in trouble. The city's banks had decided that in good conscience they could not state that there was "sufficient likelihood of repayment" of its short-term notes. Therefore, the banks wouldn't underwrite the notes, and New York was left without financing—with $900 million required by the month's end to keep the city out of bankruptcy. The day before, Hugh Carey, the governor of New York, and Abe Beame, the city's mayor, had called on President Gerald Ford to ask for his help. The president had refused.

"What do you think about all this?" Strauss asked. I told him quite emphatically that the bankruptcy of New York would not simply be a local emergency. It would be the impetus for a national and international financial disaster. American banks would be severely hurt, and throughout the world the dollar would come under great pressure. Our friends and allies overseas would not understand the decision to allow the country's preeminent city to go bankrupt unless America itself—its financial institutions, its industries—was also teetering on the brink of bankruptcy. The nation had struggled through a painful recession and the outrageous hiking of oil prices. The bankruptcy of New York, I predicted with total certainty, would trigger a global economic crisis.

Strauss listened without interruption. Then, when I had finished a monologue whose impassioned tone took even me by surprise, he asked one simple question: "Would you mind if I convey your views to Governor Carey?" I told him I had no objections; and soon the conversation turned into another direction.

This seemingly casual conversation had consequences. Later that morning I was sitting in the wood-paneled office of Senator Henry "Scoop" Jackson. He was considering running for president, and I had come to convince him that there was an opportunity to reach a national audience by championing a program to help urban America. New York was not the only city in trouble. Detroit, Chicago, and Cleveland were all sinking toward bankruptcy. I was sharing my plan to create a government agency similar to the RFC that, working with business and labor, could help to restructure the finances of troubled cities when I was interrupted by a cautious knock on the senator's office door.

An aide entered, and the senator stared at her in reproof. I told you, he grumbled, I did not want to be disturbed. She nodded meekly, then pointed an accusatory finger at me. I had an important call, she announced.

Apologizing profusely, I left the room. My embarrassment was genuine. What office crisis, I wondered, could demand my immediate attention?

But it wasn't a summons from Lazard. The caller was an old friend, David Burke, chief of staff of the governor of New York. Bob Strauss, he explained, had spoken to Governor Carey. And now the governor would very much like to see you this afternoon. It was urgent.

I quickly left Senator Jackson's office and headed to the airport for the shuttle back to New York. As I waited to board, I had time to make a phone call to Strauss. "How could you have offered my services without first speaking to me?" I complained.

"Look," said Bob affably; "this will take only three or four weeks of your time. You'll meet interesting people. It will be a great experience."

Bob, I would learn in time, had been correct. I would meet interesting people—in labor, the media, and government. And, as he had also predicted, it would be a great experience. I would have the opportunity to create an institution inspired by the RFC, and in the process I would test my theory about the ability of an activist government agency to cooperate with labor and business in rescuing a financially besieged municipality. But Bob had been wrong about the duration of my service. I would spend the next eighteen years working to restructure the finances of New York City.

Twelve

Aboard the shuttle to New York, as I headed toward what David Burke had insisted was an "urgent" meeting with Governor Carey, I began to realize that I should not have been so surprised by the severity of New York City's financial problems. There had been clear warnings, and I, like nearly everyone on Wall Street, had been aware of them.

In late April 1975, for example, I had received a call from a broker I had done some business with in the past. He now was urging me to buy New York City notes. "The notes," he explained as he began his enthusiastic pitch, "are free of federal, state, and city taxes, and their 9 1/4 percent rate is the equivalent of a 17 to 18 percent return on a taxable bond." "The credit is gilt-edged," he went on. "It's the credit of New York City."

As the broker continued trying to make a sale, I realized he was correct about at least one thing. It was a good deal—too good. All his call had done was to convince me that there must be a reason why these notes would be paying such high interest. And the reason, I decided, was that they carried an equally high risk. New York City, I realized, must be in trouble. Big trouble.

A dramatic change had taken place in the city's economy during the 1960s. Suffering under the weight of high costs and high taxes, corporations and individuals had fled the city. Hundreds of thousands of private sector jobs had been lost. At the same time, the size of the municipal workforce had increased dramatically. In 1960, there were about 100,000 municipal employees; by the end of the decade, this number had tripled. Further, in the years since the mayoralty of Robert Wagner at the tail end of the 1950s, these city employees had developed strong political clout. The union leaders had made sure that the politicians knew their rank-and-file members were an essential bloc vote in any citywide election.

It was an effective electoral strategy. However, it was not as fiscally wise. The generous contracts that the municipal workers received in return for their votes left the City encumbered with a level of costs that its depleted tax base could not sustain. As a consequence, the overburdened city resorted more and more to short-term loans from the banks. Deepening the problem, the state, led by Nelson Rockefeller, its Republican governor, facilitated this increasingly dangerous borrowing strategy.

During the 1960s, the city's short-term debt was nearly zero. By 1975, the debt was nearly $6 billion—a truly astounding sum. No less astounding was the fact that all the while, the city was breezily reporting balanced budgets. Of course, one didn't need to be an accountant to realize these budgets were cool fictions. To pay its bills, the city had to borrow to pay its interest on its outstanding debt—and then in addition borrow even more to pay the current deficit. Compounding the problem, no one either in or out of government seemed to have any idea of the actual amount of the city's deficit. And now this indulgent policy of constant municipal borrowing was being pushed into a sudden financial crisis because the banks, which had routinely sold the city's short-term notes, were running out of capacity.

The desperate state and city politicians were left with one time-honored alternative. They appealed to the Federal government to get the money they needed.

Dealings

Abe Beame, the newly elected mayor, went to Washington to make the city's case. He was a decent but colorless bureaucrat, a former city comptroller who had built his campaign around a persuasive promise: "He knows where the buck is." I couldn't help sourly thinking that a slightly altered slogan would have been more accurate: "He knows where the buck went."

Accompanying Beame on this grim mission to Washington was Governor Hugh Carey, a liberal former congressman from Brooklyn who had also recently been elected. Carey was an urban Democrat who had won thanks in part to the support of the labor unions. Wall Street had blatantly ignored him. It seemed to me that he had none of the background, or the political instincts, that would have prepared him for the economic disaster he was about to face. He had no choice but to learn on the job—and to learn quickly. Within weeks of his inauguration, a major financial state crisis had erupted.

The Urban Development Corporation (UDC) was on the verge of default. The UDC was an agency established by the state to provide low-cost housing to middle- and lower-income New Yorkers. This commitment to the state's less affluent citizens was well-meaning and generous in spirit, yet it was also costly. The agency financed its new construction by selling $2 billion in long-term bonds, which were to be paid off by the revenues from these projects. However, to reassure investors, these bonds also carried the "moral obligation" of the state of New York.

"Moral obligation" bonds were the inspired invention of John Mitchell. At the time Mitchell (who would go on to be Richard Nixon's attorney general and a notorious figure in the Watergate scandal) was a partner at the well-connected Manhattan law firm Mudge, Rose and had earned a reputation (as well as a considerable fortune) as a specialist in municipal bonds. Working with Governor Rockefeller's staff, he had come up with a way that would allow the state to provide the equivalent of a guarantee for projects the state was constitutionally prohibited from guaranteeing. As specified by the shrewd mechanism Mitchell had created, the "moral obligation" construction bonds would still not be guaranteed by the state. However—and this was Mitchell's inspired idea, which allowed the circumvention of the restrictive provisions in the state constitution—the state would declare it had "a moral obligation" on an annual basis to replenish a reserve fund adequate to pay the next year's debt service. The state legislature, encouraged by Governor Rockefeller, agreed that this reserve fund was indeed a "moral obligation." And since the state now acknowledged its "moral" duty to keep sufficient moneys available, underwriters and banks were willing to accept this promise as a binding guarantee. The bonds were sold to the public as if they were a blue chip investment.

When Hugh Carey came into office, the UDC had $1.1 billion of outstanding bonds. But many of its projects had incurred unanticipated difficulties and now were unable to pay their way. The bonds couldn't be serviced. The banks, however, wanted the money that was due. Bristling with anger and impatience, they called on the state to live up to its "moral obligation" and provide sufficient revenues to cover the UDC's debt.

Carey was faced with a difficult choice. If he were to accommodate the banks, there would not be enough money to buy the time needed to navigate through the looming and much larger financial upheavals that both the state and the city would soon be facing. But could a newly elected governor defy such a powerful institutional voice in New York as the banking community?

To my mind, Carey made the right choice. He said "no" to

the banks. The UDC defaulted on its bonds. And the banks, despite their exposure and their influence, went, for all practical purposes, meekly along with the governor's decision. The sad reality was that the banks were more concerned about their exposure in the larger crisis that was coming, they suddenly recognized, to a swift boil. New York City in 1975 was moving closer and closer to bankruptcy.

New York City had three distinct financing requirements. The first was seasonal. To function effectively and provide services for its citizens, the city had to pay its expenses as they occurred throughout the calendar year. But it did not receive the bulk of its compensating payments from the state—moneys for education, welfare, transportation subsidies, etc.—until June, the end of the state fiscal year. Federal funds for these programs were also received irregularly.

The city, as a consequence, routinely had a seasonal cash shortfall. So, the city would matter-of-factly sell short-term notes, confident that these would be paid back by the proceeds of state and federal payments made later in the year. It was a logical financial strategy and one that would seemingly work without a hitch—provided the city's budgets were balanced.

However, the budgets, despite the rosy numbers in the comptroller's reports, were not even close to being balanced. Over the years, the city had amassed larger and larger deficits. As taxpayers left, the city was less and less able to pay the wages of an ever-increasing municipal workforce that, thanks to its effective unions, had negotiated extraordinary benefits.

This shortfall created the city's second financing requirement. It had regularly borrowed to cover this gap between revenues—including the state and federal payments—and its expenses. And now it had to service the debt on these loans, too.

Finally, the city needed to finance its capital program. Infrastructure is key to the economy of any modern city. Municipal physical facilities—schools, streets, transportation systems, bridges, and airports—are critical not only to its economy but also to the quality of life of its citizens. Infrastructure helps determine whether a city is deemed a place where people want to live and work, or whether people decide to move to a more comfortable, more sustaining location. Therefore, the way a city deals with its infrastructure is critical to the size of its tax base.

New York City had long recognized the importance of well-maintained and well-functioning facilities. The city had legislated that the moneys to finance these essential programs would be included in a separate capital budget, ambitious sums that would be raised by the sale of long-term city bonds.

However, the disturbing reality was that for many years New York City's actual annual investment in its physical facilities had been plummeting—yet its borrowing had remained consistently high. Whereas in previous years the city had spent between $3 billion and $4 billion annually on its infrastructure, by 1975 it was neither funding the necessary minimum maintenance of its facilities nor making needed investments in new capital projects. How, then, did its lawmakers justify spending the moneys raised by the sale of its capital project bonds? With fiscal sleight of hand that was shocking (and arguably illegal), the city had glibly transferred the salaries of thousands of its employees as well as hundreds of millions of its expenditures to the capital budget.

All these dubious financing practices came to an inevitable head in April 1975. Earlier that year New York, as it had routinely done over the years, had asked the banks to market the $1.8 billion in short-term notes it would need to cover its expenses and refund its maturing notes. It was well known in the financial community that the city was hiding a large deficit; the exact amount was a mystery, but an estimated figure of $500 million was bandied about by supposedly knowledgeable municipal bureaucrats. Still, this sizable gap had never been a problem in the past. Without a word of protest, the banks had gone to market with the nearly $2 billion short-term notes that would finance necessary municipal expenses. But 1975 was different. The banks refused to sell the bonds.

——

In the 1970s, the city's banks were the primary underwriters of—and, no less significant, the main investors in—New York City and New York state obligations. In part, this was a result of political considerations: since the city and state regulated their business, it was prudent for the banks to be supportive of city and state financing needs. And it was also good business: the interest on New York obligations was tax-free to the banks.

In their dealings with the city and state, the banks primarily operated through a group of eleven institutions that collectively were known as the "clearinghouse."

In early 1975, Bankers Trust, a maverick bank run by Charlie Sanford, an aggressive southerner, was selected to be the institution driving the sale of $620 million of short-term city notes. As the group was being formed and negotiations with the city were taking place, it became apparent that New York would have to pay very steep interest rates if these notes were to be sold (as the 9 1/4 percent promised to me by the excited broker demonstrated).

Nevertheless, Sanford, speaking for Bankers Trust, was still reluctant to go along with the sale. And the other banks supported his decision not to sign the city prospectus offering the notes. The disclosure of deficits, the banks argued, was woefully insufficient. They could not state with good conscience that there was "sufficient likelihood of repayment."

For all practical purposes, in May 1975, the city was left without financing. In June it would require $900 million. In each of the following three months, $1 billion would be needed. Default was looming, and with a grim inevitability, the bankruptcy of New York City would most likely follow.

This was the dire situation when the mayor and the governor, having seemingly run out of all other options, traveled to Washington. The meeting with President Gerald Ford was brief. His terse, unequivocal response had been an emphatic "no." And now any chance of a solution to the city's problems seemed completely hopeless.

After my plane from Washington landed, I took a cab directly to my meeting with Governor Carey. I couldn't help thinking that I was on a doomed mission. What could I do? What could anyone do? Besides, while my experiences had left me with a banker's knowledge of what must be done to steady listing corporations, I truly knew very little about the intricacies of city or state finances. I had no doubt that I was charging rather blindly into a deep and possibly all-engulfing morass.

Thirteen

When I walked into Governor Carey's dark, cave-like office on West Fifty-Fifth Street in Manhattan, I could not help feeling the anxiety that was crowding along with me into the small room. I understood too well the severity of the impending financial crisis. Yet, I feared that the governor, with a politician's typical shortsightedness, might believe that simply with some accounting sleight of hand the situation could be resolved. I had come to tell him it would take more than bookkeeping tricks if New York was to be saved.

My lecture was not necessary. I had never met the governor before, and my first impression of the middle-aged man sitting at rigid attention behind the desk was one of grim resolve. There was none of the usual hail-fellow cordiality that I had encountered in my previous meetings with politicians. Rather, the governor, a large man with a bright, engaging face, shook my hand perfunctorily, and did not even offer a welcoming smile. In his terse, no-nonsense manner, I detected a comforting determination. My first thoughts were that Carey, despite his brief time in office and his apparent lack of financial expertise, had already made up his mind. He would try to make the hard political choices that might, just might, prevent the city from filing for bankruptcy.

David Burke, the governor's chief of staff, who had arranged this meeting, was also in the room. I had known Burke for many years. He had served as Senator Ted Kennedy's chief of staff, and then had gone to work for Howard Stein at the Dreyfus Fund, the biggest player in the growing mutual funds industry. I appreciated his firsthand knowledge of both business and politics. And I knew from our previous dealings that he was a man of rock-solid integrity. He also had—no small comfort in a time of crisis—a ready, often self-mocking Irish wit. The fact that Carey had chosen Burke as his right-hand man further predisposed me to respect the governor. (And in time I would discover that the very qualities I admired in Burke—scrupulous honesty and a sense of humor—were also strong strands in Carey's makeup. But those insights would come only after we had fought many tense battles together.)

The meeting that afternoon in the governor's office began without preliminaries. From the start Carey was direct. "Would you be willing," he asked, "to work with me to prevent the bankruptcy of New York City?" Then he added, "If the city goes under, it's just about a certainty that the state will follow."

I listened with mute attention, and when he was finally done I waited a moment before speaking. Ever since I had received the call from Burke, I had been working out in my mind the preconditions that would be necessary for my volunteering to serve in what I was convinced might very well turn out to be a futile struggle. Now I shared them.

First, I explained that I could not do this alone. It was too big a job. Further, having spent my career working with corporations, I had only a cursory knowledge of city and state financial practices. I also pointed out that I was known to be a liberal Democrat. If any belt-tightening effort was to succeed, it would have to be seen by the state and city legislators as a bipartisan plan. Both Republicans and Democrats should be represented in this group.

Carey listened without interrupting me, and then, with what

I would learn was typical swiftness, agreed. Yes, he said, a bi-partisan group made sense. "What else is on your mind?"

I began to explain that I could not give him unlimited time. I had responsibilities at Lazard, and I had been away from the firm for long periods during the NYSE crisis and while I was caught up in the ITT hearings. But I had a proposal. I had recently been called for jury duty. If the governor, I suggested with a sudden embarrassment, could arrange for me to be excused, I could give him those weeks.

"Jury duty," the governor repeated. And for the first time that afternoon I saw a small grin on his face. "I think we might be able to do something about that. Don't you, David?"

"I'll handle it," agreed Burke.

And so it was finalized. As a member of a bipartisan team, I would work with Carey. Before I left his office we had decided on the others in the group. There would be two Republicans—Richard Shinn, chairman of Metropolitan Life Insurance; and Donald Smiley, chairman of Macy's. In addition to me, the other Democrat would be my valued friend and attorney from the ITT hearings, Judge Simon Rifkind.

As I prepared to leave, I was already feeling rather over-whelmed by what I had gotten myself into. The challenges seemed insurmountable. But these large fears abruptly took on an increasing urgency as David Burke took me aside.

"You realize," he reminded me, "that unless we can come up with $900 million on June 18, the city will need to file for bankruptcy."

"June 18?" I said, my voice suddenly skidding. "That's in three weeks."

My long day, which had started over a casual breakfast in Washington with Bob Strauss, was still not done. Straight from the governor's office I headed to another meeting. I had every reason to believe that this discussion would be even more complicated, and certainly more volatile, than the one I had just left. With a sense of foreboding, I went uptown to the Carlyle to inform André Meyer of what I had agreed to do.

It was, I knew, a difficult time for Lazard. Mr. Meyer was in failing health and had been searching for but had not yet found a successor. Another complication was that he had been shaken by the possible repercussions of the ITT-Hartford affairs and the potential legal and financial effects of this high-profile controversy. Although by mid-1975 Lazard had pretty much managed to get through the worst of it, my getting involved in another high-profile—and high-risk—enterprise would undoubtedly make him apprehensive.

Also, I knew he expected me to continue to be a major producer of business for the firm. For almost three years I had devoted an enormous amount of time to outside matters. After my demanding service as a governor at the New York Stock Exchange, I had quickly become immersed in the ITT hearings. And now I was about to tell Mr. Meyer that I would be taking more time off from investment banking to try to save New York City. As I played out that discussion in my mind, I could almost hear his sharp anger. And, in truth, I could understand it.

And yet I was determined to serve with the group that would try to rescue New York. On the way up to the Carlyle I went through all the arguments I would make. I would explain that a fiscally sound and well-functioning New York was integral to the national economy and even the world's economy. But there was one reason pushing my commitment to help the city that I was not prepared to share with Mr. Meyer.

The ITT affair had wounded me deeply. I had been portrayed on the front page of the *New York Times* as "Felix the Fixer." My children had been taunted at school, teased by their classmates about their dad, the unscrupulous deal maker. I wanted finally to bury the misapprehensions of the ITT affair. By helping New York, I believed I could also restore my own wrongly tarnished reputation.

When I arrived at Mr. Meyer's apartment, Judge Rifkind was already there. I had asked the attorney to join us because I knew that Mr. Meyer respected him. And I also knew I would need a wise and very persuasive ally.

We sat down in the living room, where the collection of Picassos, Renoirs, Gauguins, and Monets glittered as always on the walls. But Mr. Meyer was clearly diminished. He was no longer the overpowering force that had, with an autocratic hand, guided Lazard to its significant position in the world of investment banking. His face wore a ghostly pallor, and it was apparent that he was quite weak. I looked at him with sympathy; and at the same time I reminded myself that I was now responsible for much of the firm's important and lucrative business. Perhaps he wouldn't have either the energy or the will to challenge me.

I was wrong. Mr. Meyer was adamant that I should not serve on the governor's committee. Suppose you fail, he said. Suppose the city goes bankrupt. What would be the effects on the firm, on your reputation?

Fortunately, Judge Rifkind intervened. He made the case that neither he nor I could turn down the governor. If I refused to serve, if it seemed as if I were turning my back on the besieged city, then my indifference would be criticized. My reputation would be impugned. I would be attacked as selfish and irresponsible. And the firm, too, would suffer.

Rikfind continued on to explain that this would merely be a temporary assignment. We would be advisers to Governor Carey, working with him to try to create a financing mechanism for the city, and then we would turn things over to a permanent team.

At that point I interrupted to add that I would do this instead of jury duty. "I'll be back at the firm in three weeks," I said confidently.

Mr. Meyer listened; he no longer tried to argue. I could tell that, forever practical, he had come to realize that it was too late—or this was too large a battle—to prevent my joining the governor's crisis team. Finally, he offered a Gallic shrug of surrender, and then announced that I had his permission to serve. But before I left his apartment, he shared a last piece of wisdom.

"Three weeks, you think?" he warned. "Let me tell you that public service is like a young mistress. It's very hard to leave."

I assured him that his concern was unnecessary. But time would prove him right.

—

The next day the newly appointed team of four advisers gathered in the governor's office. We were joined by Peter Goldmark, the state budget director; Judah Gribetz, the governor's counsel; and David Burke. Very quickly the many political and economic intricacies of the crisis we were facing became apparent.

I had met Richard Shinn a few times. As chairman of Met Life, he was undeniably an important New Yorker. I did not know Don Smiley, and at first glance I decided he had a stiff, rather reserved demeanor. But I knew that as chairman of Macy's he had a huge stake in New York's future.

As the session began, Shinn made it clear that he was wary about joining a high-profile committee in a situation with a significant potential political downside. Quite pointedly, both Shinn and Smiley stated that, as leading Republican New Yorkers, they did not want to be seen as taking sides in a dispute between a Democratic governor and a Republican president.

Carey's response was forceful, and typically direct. He insisted that he had no intention of waging a political war. Nor did he want to use any of us for partisan political purposes. The reality was, the governor explained, that to make the necessary changes in the city and state, he would need the support of the Republicans in the state legislature in Albany as well as the Democrats in the New York City Council. And every New Yorker, he confided, might eventually need to look to Washington for additional help.

Our assignment, he declared, was twofold. First, it was fact-finding. We needed to assess just how bad the city's financial situation was. And—arguably an even more daunting challenge—we would also need to come up with a plan to try to fix things.

The four of us looked at one another, and I was certain we all had the same troubled thought: what had we gotten into?

Even in those first, still tentative days it grew clear to me that before any plan to rescue New York could begin to be formulated, I had to answer with objectivity a single complex and chilling question: is bankruptcy a viable option for New York City?

New York was a tale of two cities. One was a shiny city of wealth and privilege, of sprawling co-op apartments on Park and Fifth avenues, of charity galas, Broadway openings, and acclaimed private schools. The other was a city of crumbling neighborhoods, of tenements in the South Bronx and Bedford-Stuyvesant, of crime and poverty, of families dependent on public assistance and inadequate public schools. If the city went bankrupt, those who lived on Fifth and Park avenues could, if they wanted, leave. But the residents of Bed-Stuy and Crown Heights would not have this option. They would have to suffer through the inevitable scale-downs in welfare and Medicaid payments, in public housing, in public health, in the schools, and in the fire and police departments. I had no doubt that the business exodus from the city would accelerate and that New York's tax base would decline, perhaps permanently and irreparably. I also had another large fear: the painful memory of the riots of 1968 was still strong. I worried that as life in the city became harder for those who already were frustrated and disappointed, resentment would lead enraged people into the streets.

The political crisis would have more subtle, yet building consequences—and the ultimate results, I predicted, would be no less pernicious. New York City was in many real and symbolic ways the liberal capital of the nation. And as the 1976 presidential election approached, the Ford administration seemed determined to portray the city as a tangible example of the intellectual bankruptcy of both liberalism and the Democratic Party. Secretary of the Treasury Bill Simon never seemed to miss an opportunity to make this vindictive point. Ron Nessen, President Ford's press secretary, gloated that New York was like "a wayward daughter hooked on heroin." "You don't give her $100 a day to support her habit," he snarled. "You make her go cold turkey to break the habit." And President Ford and his advisers made sure the Republican platform included a harsh, unforgiving edict: "New York City must pay for its sins, and the rest of the country must learn from the city's mistakes, or be doomed by them." I had little doubt that the bankruptcy of New York would be used by the Republicans as justification for the reversal of the many essential, beneficial, and progressive social programs that had been created since the time of the New Deal. As a result, America would become a crueler, undemocratic, and less remarkable nation.

And as a banker I understood that the economic crisis in the city would have immediate national and global financial repercussions. New York City would not go into bankruptcy alone. The city, after all, represented half of the economy of New York state. If the city's tax receipts were suddenly deeply impaired, if the city could not meet its commitments to fund its social programs, then these would need to be made up by the state. Yet the state did not have sufficient reserve funds or anticipated revenues to meet this shortfall. It would create an impossible dilemma—the state would face bankruptcy, although by law states cannot go into default.

The consequences of nearly simultaneous city and state failures would be staggering. The combined indebtedness of the city and the state represented about 20 percent of the capital in the entire U.S. banking system, and New York City's big banks were the institutions most heavily exposed. If the nation's banks started teetering, no one could predict how severe the resulting national economic meltdown would be or how long it would last.

It had already become clear that the city's fiscal troubles were sending shock waves through the global marketplace. As New York appeared to move closer and closer to bankruptcy, the foreign exchange markets grew shaky and the dollar began to slip. If there was an actual bankruptcy, I could imagine the dollar sinking to a rock-bottom level, and the entire global economy spinning perilously out of control.

The more research I did, and the more I thought through the consequences, the more I found myself circling back to my initial instinctive judgment. With renewed conviction, I informed my fellow committee members that the bankruptcy of New York was totally unacceptable.

As I became more deeply involved in trying to help formulate a rescue plan during those initial weeks, I started to realize that the lessons I had learned at the NYSE were of immense value. After all, there were many similarities between the problems at the stock exchange three years earlier and those I was now trying to resolve. Both crises had involved large public institutions (although the NYSE was a private sector entity). And both were the result of general economic conditions that were initially ignored and then, when things grew worse, recklessly camouflaged by the regulators who had the responsibility to step in and make necessary changes.

I also went into this new battle fortified by some basic wisdom I had learned to value during my time at the NYSE. Geneen's rule still held true: "In a crisis, things are always worse than they appear. Don't try to get every last piece of data. Act early, and try to get out ahead. If you wait until you have 100 percent of what you think you need, you will be like someone sitting on the beach with the tide coming in."

Additionally, the NYSE had taught me that it is always wiser to be candid with the press. Initially, I had worried that open disclosure of a financial problem could help to escalate the very crisis I was trying to avoid. Yet both in the city's crisis and at the NYSE there was so much press coverage reporters seemingly never stopped calling me with pointed questions. I soon realized I was facing a very simple choice. Either I could mislead, or I could be candid. I decided on candor.

In fact, I came to believe that in those two running news stories it was crucial for me to play the role of an objective source. After all, the leadership of both institutions lacked anyone who could speak to the public without appearing either self-serving or self-protective. I was the outsider; I had no blame for what had happened and was working pro bono to fix it. I had nothing to hide. There was no reason, I decided, why I shouldn't speak with both authority and truthfulness. And Governor Carey supported me in this decision.

More significant, this policy of talking frankly about the issues had consequences that allowed us to better manage the crisis as it continued to play out over the years. Since both poli-

ticians and the public learned to believe that my grim apprais-
als were accurate, they were more willing to accept that painful
actions were necessary. And, as was also essential, my candor
helped me to win the confidence of the reporters covering the
story, as well as the editorial support of their newspapers for the
tough decisions we had to make. There are enough problems in
any crisis without having to deal with an adversarial or suspicious press, too.

Yet there were also, I came to realize, two major differences
between the crisis at the NYSE and the one I was now mired
in. First, the city's problems were pervasive, rooted in political,
social, and economic issues. It had taken years to get into such
dire straits. And it would take years to get out.

Second, whereas the crisis at the NYSE could be resolved
by a relatively small group of people who could quickly be
convinced of the benefits of working together to take decisive
actions, any solution to the city's problems would involve a
small army of individuals whose long-standing instincts were
adversarial.

We needed to get all these individuals with different responsibilities and conflicting constituencies to support our still un-
formulated plan. And if that weren't challenge enough, our plan
had to find a way to bring the city's budget into balance within
a reasonable period, create a mechanism that would keep the
budget balanced once this goal was achieved, and simultaneously revive the city's flagging economy.

But even before we could try to put together any far-reaching
plan, before we could try to get the support of all these factions,
we needed an immediate infusion of capital. The city needed
$900 million on June 18 to avoid bankruptcy. That deadline
was only three weeks away.

Fourteen

With the June 18 deadline rapidly approaching, we called a meeting over the Memorial Day weekend at Dick Shinn's large, comfortable home in Greenwich, Connecticut. Joining the committee were the chairman of the lead banks—Wriston, Patterson, Sanford, McGillicuddy, and Rockefeller—and the governor's senior staff.

Even before the meeting began, our core group of four had reached a number of key decisions. We had agreed that to have credibility and to protect its bondholders from bankruptcy, we needed a financing vehicle that was an agency of the state, rather than the city. Further, this vehicle would require a certain level of assured revenues so that it could service the bonds it would issue and pay them off in their lifetime. And we needed to deal unambiguously with the politically delicate question of how much control this new agency and the state would have over the city.

Before we could do this, we needed to get the facts. Yet wherever we turned, the numbers were soft. We tried to get a head count—but the city did not know exactly how many people it employed. The best estimate was *around* 300,000. We tried to find out the size of the outstanding short-term debt. We were authoritatively told that $3 billion would become due over the next three months—but at the last minute an additional $2.5 billion of housing notes was added to this already staggering sum.

This "oversight" struck me as incredible. Bewildered, I had asked James Cavanagh, the first deputy mayor, the reason for this omission. He matter-of-factly explained that the housing notes had been classified as long-term bonds because they had originally been sold in anticipation of selling long-term bonds in the future. For the past decade or more, the city had been rolling these notes over and over—all in the vague anticipation of someday selling long-term bonds.

I was stunned. As patiently as I could, I tried to point out to him that since the city could no longer sell bonds, the notes were coming due *now*.

"Mr. Rohatyn," the first deputy mayor replied breezily, "I see you don't know much about municipal finance."

"Mr. Cavanagh," I shot back. "True, I may not know much about municipal finance. But I know about bullshit. And what you're giving me is pure bullshit."

Undaunted, Cavanagh turned to Judge Rifkind and tried to convince him that the city was not running a deficit. Rather, he suggested, New York required seasonal loans simply because of the time lapses between its cash receipts and its disbursements.

"Mr. Cavanagh," a frustrated Rifkind countered, "if you are right, then I should be committed."

And while we knew we certainly had to reduce the deficit, we also understood that we could not accomplish this all at once. Such a radical step would produce too many cutbacks in services and, as a result, too much social chaos. But how large was the actual deficit? The city comptroller and the state budget office confidently agreed that the shortfall was about $500 million, out of a city budget of approximately $12 billion. (We were suspicious of this number and initiated an independent audit of the city. When it was completed a year later, it revealed an actual deficit that was three times the size of the supposedly authoritative number—a shortfall of $1.5 billion.)

But that Memorial Day weekend the only number that we were truly certain of was the twenty days until the June 18 deadline. I convinced the group that we had no choice but to obey "Geneen's law": "Don't wait until you get all the facts, because by then it will be too late."

So that weekend we acted. We decided to create a state agency with the initial authority to issue $3 billion in long-term bonds. And the sale of these bonds would be used to pay off the $3 billion in city notes that were due in the coming summer and fall. We agreed to call this agency the Municipal Assistance Corporation, but even on that first day we were referring to it simply as MAC.

—

Although MAC was an ingeniously designed vehicle, it was also a series of compromises. It was, quite naturally, shaped in large part by the political realities.

We assigned to the agency, as it needed, a first call on the city's sales taxes and the stock transfer tax. And, as a further guarantee that the revenues would be available, we provided that these taxes be turned into state taxes in order to shelter them from a city bankruptcy.

The agency would have a nine-member board of directors, all private citizens appointed by the governor, with the mayor having the right to recommend four of them. A cross section of city and state political entities (state senate, state assembly, Board of Estimate, City Council, comptrollers) would have non-voting observers. There would be no union representation.

While MAC had oversight power regarding the city's budget, the language establishing this authority was admittedly vague. After all, we had to try to please a variety of powerful voices who already had trouble agreeing on any issue. Governor Carey, for example, did not want to appear to be taking over the city—nor did he want the responsibility of doing so. The Republicans in the state senate wanted harsh automatic budget-balancing formulas (cheerfully "forgetting" that two of the most prominent members of their party, Governor Rockefeller and Mayor Lindsay, both shared heavy responsibility for helping to create the crisis). Meanwhile, the Democrats in the assembly wanted to protect the power and independence of the mayor, who, with the support of the City Council, wanted home rule.

And even as we were piecing MAC together, we knew there would inevitably be lawsuits challenging its constitutionality. We had to craft a structure that would scrupulously satisfy state law. But, as Judge Rifkind kept reminding me, no matter how deftly our legal experts designed this vehicle, there was still no guarantee that it would pass the scrutiny of state judges. They were political creatures, and their decisions were more often than not grounded in political rather than legal concerns.

But we had no real choice except to move quickly forward. We had to hope that the legislature would vote MAC into law, and in the meantime we had to turn out a series of financial packages that would get us through June 18.

So we did. We came up with a plan that included the following components: a $100 million loan from the banks; an agreement by the banks to extend for another year the $280 million of city notes coming immediately due; a $200 million advance by the state against further education payments; and additional financial contributions from a variety of city accounts. It wasn't a particularly deft way of covering the short-term debt, but it would work—if we could succeed in getting MAC's control over the city accepted.

As that complicated battle began to be played out, my education commenced in earnest. The purely financial restructuring questions we were trying to deal with were not unfamiliar to me. But of course these were on a much larger scale and had greater elements of uncertainty than situations I held dealt with in the past.

In the days after our Memorial Day meeting when we had agreed on the MAC structure in principle and the banks agreed to finance our June 18 requirement of $900 million, we needed to negotiate the charter of MAC with the city, the state legislature, and the unions. We had just a little over two weeks until the default date.

———

The entire city was consumed by the crisis. Mayor Beame's initial reaction was to want no part of MAC. Instead, he announced an austere budget, and the city sent layoff notices to 20,000 employees.

The union leaders held a mass demonstration in front of the City Bank headquarters on Wall Street, and as a crowd of 10,000 cheered, they predicted chaos. Victor Gotbaum, of DC37, pointedly denounced Walter Wriston, the chairman of City Bank, as the "chief villain" of the crisis. Barry Feinstein, head of the Teamsters, predicted, "Hospitals would be a mechanism to move people to the morgue." The head of the sanitation workers' union threatened that there would be "hundreds of tons of garbage in the streets." Harold Melnick, the president of the Sergeants Benevolent Association, warned that crime would rise to a "disastrous" level. And nearly all the union leaders issued the same pledge: they would not allow the city's budget to be balanced on the "backs of the workers."

The hearings at City Hall were similarly raucous, but we refused to be intimidated by the highly charged atmosphere. Rifkind, Shinn, Smiley, and I met with the mayor and the City Council to deliver a terse message. The only alternative to MAC was bankruptcy—and that was not an acceptable option.

At the same time, the leadership of the state senate in Albany was insisting on tough control measures. And time was running out.

Rifkind and I hurried around the third floor of the state capital building. We shuttled between the Democratic senators and the Republicans. We met in the north side conference room with the Democratic assemblymen; and when they left, the Republicans filed in. And we ran back and forth to the governor's second-floor office, seeking advice. I tried my best to be persuasive, and to convey the urgency of getting MAC approved.

Still, one large problem kept surfacing during these crucial discussions in Albany. I could not, in good faith, guarantee success even if everyone agreed to all that we were proposing. When I was asked directly whether MAC would solve the city's problems or whether default would still be a possibility, I answered truthfully. I said there was no certainty that MAC would entirely erase the likelihood of default; there were many issues over which the agency had no control affecting the situation. Nevertheless, I had no doubt, I said emphatically, that if we did not create MAC, default was inevitable. "I would be kidding you," I went on, "if I told you I was sure three billion dollars could be raised in the next ninety days." "But," I added, "without MAC the chances are zero."

By 6:30 on the morning of June 10, the governor's staff had completed the seventh revision of the MAC charter legislation. Immediately they faxed it to City Hall for comments. Two hours later the city's comments had been incorporated into the proposal and the four state legislative leaders met to sign off on it. By mid-morning, Hugh Carey was in the Red Room signing the bill. "Is that the Big Mac legislation?" a reporter asked. "Yes," he agreed, and added, punning: "That's the one I'm going to sign with relish."

We had cleared the first hurdle.

The next day, June 11, the board of directors of MAC met for the first time. There were nine individuals: five named by the governor, the others by the mayor. Tom Flynn, the former head of Arthur Young, a major accounting firm, would serve as chairman.

The first meeting of the board was tense. We had just barely succeeded in raising the $900 million needed to avoid default. But—incredibly, it seemed to me—three weeks down the road we would need *another* $1 billion.

I decided that we had little choice but to pursue a very risky strategy. I asked Pat Patterson, chairman of Morgan, to head an underwriting group that, together with Salomon Brothers, would bring $1 billion of MAC bonds to the market. It would be the biggest municipal sale ever. And we had only until early July—less than a month!—to get it done.

So much was riding on this first bond sale. It had to establish the public credit of MAC. This was essential because we would need to raise an additional $2 billion in the following two months. And more revenue would be required shortly after that. By September, MAC would have exhausted its $3 billion borrowing authority, and the city would need to borrow $4 billion over the following nine months on its own. It seemed clear to me that none of these future demands would be met unless we established the market viability of MAC with the success of this first unprecedented offering. I decided to throw my energy into making this sale work. But after it was over, I told the governor, I would step down.

Events quickly began jeopardizing the success of the forthcoming sale. The effort got off to a bad start—and then turned worse. In response to the necessary municipal budget cuts and layoffs, the unions went to war. And they waged a shrewd campaign. The sanitation workers struck first. Almost immediately, posters appeared at the airports and the train stations announcing, "Welcome to Stink City." The patrolmen's union then proclaimed that New York had become "Fear City." As the city struggled through a crime wave, out-of-work cops distributed leaflets ominously wondering, "Who's next?" The unions encouraged a growing sense that the reduction of municipal workers had left the city unmanageable.

In early July, just as we were coming to the market with our MAC bonds, the mayor caved in. He canceled most of the layoffs of sanitation workers. On the heels of this rash mayoral decision, the city lost a court case that would have allowed it to lengthen working hours for its employees. These ill-timed events alone would have had a detrimental effect on MAC's ability to market its bonds. But there was still another ominous complication. As our bonds began to trade publicly for the first time, the market collapsed by a staggering 10 percent. This meant not only that our underwriters had lost $100 million, but also that MAC's ability to do further significant business in such a weak marketplace would be unlikely.

Under all these pressures, our July financing collapsed.

In the aftermath of the failure of the MAC bonds in the marketplace, Governor Carey asked me to reconsider my decision to leave MAC. He wanted me to remain on the board.

I asked him for time to think about what I would do, but in my heart I knew I could not leave. I was committed to helping to save the city, and a strategy was beginning to take shape in my mind. It was still inchoate, and I knew that it would be a long shot. But I was determined to try it out.

Still, before I could inform the governor that I was staying, I needed to have a discussion with André Meyer. Now that his illness had worsened, he was spending more time in Switzerland. With some trepidation, I made an overseas phone call.

Mr. Meyer made a small pretense of arguing, but he seemed unable to find the will. When I said that I would serve for only another year, I think we both knew I was being disingenuous.

And so I went back to work at MAC. But in the weeks following our failed bond sale, I was determined to make some necessary changes. One: we had to separate MAC more clearly from the city. Two: MAC had to impose a tougher budgetary program on the city. Three: we had to restructure the leadership of MAC.

Without delay, I went to work behind the scenes to change the MAC board. The leadership was divided, more or less, into hawks and doves—that is, those who supported the tough economic choices needed to balance the city's budget, and those who were more inclined to look for compromises or stopgap measures. Bill Ellinghaus and I were the leaders of the hawkish faction. Disturbingly, Tom Flynn, the chairman of the MAC board, was one of the doves.

Carey and Burke supported my belief that Flynn, although a very likeable man who brought with him the credibility of having served as the head of a well-respected accounting firm, should not continue as chairman. He was too deferential to the mayor and to City Hall. The time had come, I felt with some conviction, to make difficult, often unpleasant economic decisions. If individual members of the MAC board were unwilling to support these actions, then I didn't want them to serve in leadership positions.

With good grace and some apparent relief, Flynn agreed to step down. Bill Ellinghaus was the perfect choice to replace him. He was an appointee of the mayor, but was also a strong supporter of the governor. And so with a new chairman, MAC began to move forward.

As we did, I began thinking for the first time about the possibility of a "social contract" with the unions and the banks. If I could engineer a compromise whereby the different factions would acknowledge their responsibilities to each other, then a long-term solution to the city's problems might be possible.

Yet long-term solutions needed to be postponed. There were immediate concerns. The threat of default was once again in the air. We had raised $1 billion for July, but now we needed another $1 billion for August. And it wasn't likely that we could count on our existing revenue sources to produce such a sizable sum.

With tensions rising, a meeting was called at City Hall. Those present included the mayor, the MAC board, and the chiefs of the municipal labor unions. This meeting represented a turning point. For the first time, the unions seemed to recognize that they needed to deal with MAC. After all, MAC represented the state and therefore had credibility. The city, they now realized, was too dependent on outside financing to enforce its will.

Therefore, when we outlined our new program, the unions, while not happy, treated it with serious consideration. Our new proposals included a wage freeze, a doubling of the bus and subway fares, increases in bridge and tunnel tolls, reforms in accounting, a $375 million reduction in the capital budget, and the opening of discussions to get the state to cover the $125 million necessary to operate the court, corrections, and probation systems.

The financial community greeted this plan with only modest support, feeling that it was not enough. Meanwhile, the mayor announced that the city would not impose layoffs beyond the 14,000 workers already fired. Still, we were buoyed when the unions gave our program some encouragement. Gotbaum, of DC37, was the first to agree to wage deferrals. Then John De-

Lury of the sanitation workers' union came on board, too. Together, they represented about 175,000 workers.

Encouraged, we went to work trying to put a budget limitation on the city. Ellinghaus and I pushed Beame and Cavanagh relentlessly. We were convinced that some form of managerial review of the city's operations was imperative. The mayor, however, was firmly opposed to a management board that would have oversight power regarding the city.

But after a five-hour secret meeting at Waldorf-Astoria Hotel, where the governor, the mayor, Ellinghaus, Shinn, and I had a frank—and sometimes combative—discussion, the mayor relented. Mayor Beame agreed to appoint Dick Shinn, one of our original group of four, to head a board that would review how the city spent its money.

It was a significant victory for MAC, but it was also one that was short-lived. We still needed to scramble to sell enough bonds to cover the $960 million needed for August.

Arthur Levitt, the state comptroller, refused to invest state pension funds in our bonds. So we turned to the unions. They agreed to invest $250 million. With a bridge loan from the banks and a $120 million advance from the state, and the banks also agreeing to extend $100 million of notes that were coming due, we then went back to try to attract institutional investors. It was a weak market, and we had to offer bonds at very high rates of interest with very short maturities. But we managed to sell $250 million of MAC bonds.

In that precarious fashion, we met our August requirement of $960 million. But no sooner had we accomplished that impossible task then we were looking at September, when another $1 billion would be due. It was like climbing sand dunes—a grueling and ultimately futile exercise. Something had to change. I knew we could not keep going on this way.

Fifteen

My life became consumed by the crisis. I was living in a rather modest residential hotel, the Alrae. The hotel had a particularly louche reputation among Wall Streeters; rakish middle-age brokers could often be found dining in the dark, secretive shadows of its restaurant, Cave Henry IV, accompanied by ladies with whom they preferred not to be seen. The Alrae, I quickly came to realize, was neither a suitable nor a practical place for me to try to resolve nothing less than the future of New York City. I decided I would work out of my offices at Lazard, and even after MAC had its own headquarters at the World Trade Center, Lazard remained my base of operations.

Yet, while I still had my old Lazard office, I spent practically all my time—days and nights—in the company of my new colleagues in MAC. I developed close friendships with Bill Ellinghaus, Hugh Carey, and David Burke. And I became, both by necessity and by inclination, friendly with many people in the media.

This had unforeseen consequences. The *New York Times*, for example, ran a flattering profile with the headline "Fiscal Relief Pitcher." I was compared to Hugh Casey of the Brooklyn Dodgers, a pitcher who "when all seemed lost, came in and saved the game." That assessment seemed a bit optimistic to me; after all, the ninth inning was still a long way off, and the outcome of this nail-biting game was still very much up in the air. Yet I enjoyed the attention.

My friend Clay Felker, the publisher of *New York Magazine*, made his evening headquarters at Elaine's. This Upper East Side restaurant was always quite a scene, an expensive hangout for movie and media stars, authors and reporters, moguls and models. It was the sort of trendy place that personified for many what making it in New York was all about. I was introduced to this unofficial club by Felker and, thanks to my newfound celebrity, welcomed into it by the restaurant's big, boisterous owner, Elaine Kauffman. I would spend many a happy evening there—and some evenings I regretted.

There was the time, for example, when, after a particularly testy session with Jim Cavanagh and a few other recalcitrant city officials, I met Felker and his wife, the writer Gail Sheehy, for dinner at Elaine's. They had brought along Jack Newfield, a tenacious reporter for the *Village Voice*.

It was a long, pleasant meal. After my combative day, I was glad to have a beer and vent about Cavanagh and the dysfunctional Beame administration.

After dinner, I asked for the check, but Newfield insisted on paying. I went back to the Alrae and quickly fell asleep. But at 6 A.M. I was awoken by the ringing phone. It was the governor's press secretary. As I struggled to keep my eyes open, he began to read Newfield's column. In a moment I was wide awake. Newfield had recounted our conversation last evening verbatim, including my frank, uncensored criticism of many of the principals in the Beame administration. These were the men with whom I would need to negotiate. I was livid. It was an outrageous breach of trust.

I called Newfield and expressed my anger. Very coolly, he explained that since he had paid the check, that made everything on the record. It was a professional dinner. I should have realized I was being interviewed.

Dealings

After that, I watched what I said, even on my social nights on the town. And I was very careful about who picked up the check.

But I didn't stop going to Elaine's. I remember the time when I was at the restaurant having dinner with Carey and Burke and the governor's security man approached with a message. The mayor wanted to talk with him right away. Elaine's was, as usual, buzzing with a crowded, happy noise, so we decided to go to the bar across the street to make the call.

We entered a dingy, down-at-the-heels establishment and the governor asked for the phone. One of the hard-core drinkers at the bar looked up from his shot glass, stared at us for a moment, and then spoke. "Say," he said slowly and with a bit of a slur, "You look like Hugh Carey."

"Are you kidding?" Carey shot back. "What would the governor be doing in a dump like this?"

The man considered the question, nodded in mute agreement, and then returned his attention to his drink. After the call to the mayor had ironed out the latest wrinkle in this round of MAC negotiations, we went back to our table across the street. The next day the story went around that the governor and I were running the city from Elaine's. This was, of course, an exaggeration; but it was, I should concede in retrospect, an assessment that was grounded in some truth.

Over time, I also became friendly with some of the labor leaders I had been meeting. However, negotiating with the unions, I learned, had its own unique rules. The leaders insisted that our discussions be conducted with a bit of theater; they wanted their rank-and-file members to appreciate how tenaciously they were battling. So, although tentative agreements would be reached in secret discussions, we would nevertheless schedule a high-profile meeting in one of the big hotels. Television cameras would be in the lobby to record the union leaders marching in with looks of steadfast determination. But in the suite upstairs, they would join Ellinghaus and me for hours of television or poker. After sufficient time had passed to suggest the intensity of the debate, we all, looking genuinely exhausted, would trundle back down to the lobby. It would be about 4 A.M. And now with the television cameras once again rolling, we would announce the tentative agreement that had been worked out as much as a day earlier.

Victor Gotbaum and I became close friends. At the time, we were both single fathers, and after hard-fought meetings we would sometimes meet up with our children and go as a group to Chinese restaurants. And since both Victor and I had summer cottages on Long Island, we would also occasionally meet on weekends. I began to think more and more of the possibility of someday restructuring the city's political base into a sort of partnership between business and labor.

But that kind of long-term vision, of course, was wishful thinking. There were still large and pressing problems that needed to be resolved without delay.

By August 1975, after all the problems we had in finally raising the nearly $1 billion required at the beginning of the month, it became clear that MAC bonds could no longer be sold in the public markets. There were simply no buyers for them. And once again the talk of a possible default intensified.

In the middle of the month, *Business Week* captured the increasingly gloomy mood with its cover story headline: "Why New York City Won't Make It Financially. There Seems to Be No Way the City Can Avoid Default." "New York City is again poised on the brink of a financial abyss," the story reported. "And this time the question is not whether it will tumble in, but when."

I had to concede that this might very well be correct. As the end of the month loomed, we were looking anxiously for the next $1 billion we would need by the middle of September. And, no less daunting, an additional $2 billion would be required over the following three months.

I decided the time had come to throw a Hail Mary pass.

I met with the governor and outlined a decidedly desperate strategy. At the end of the road, it would, if successful, lead us to federal assistance. But there was no guarantee of success, and it certainly would be a rickety road.

The key element of my plan was to create a fiscal supervisory board for the city. In conjunction with the state, this board would set the amount of revenues available to the city, control all borrowing and labor contracts, and on a quarterly basis make sure that the city's finances remained within the framework of its financial plan.

Carey agreed to this strategy. Of course, it really wasn't a strategy. It was the only choice we had left. And so this new supervisory board came into being. It was called the Emergency Financial Control Board (EFCB), and its members were the governor, the mayor, the state and city comptrollers, and three businessmen appointed by Carey. It was decided that John Zuccotti would replace the discredited Jim Cavanagh as the city's first deputy mayor and that he would work closely with the EFCB's executive director, Steve Berger. I would replace Ellinghaus as chairman of MAC.

The banks supported this approach. They agreed that maintaining strict control over the city's spending was essential. And after some negotiating, the unions came on board, too. They agreed to an annual 6 percent reduction through either early retirement or attrition in the workforce over the next four years; this would cut 50,000 workers from the payroll. When this number was added to the 14,000 layoffs that had already occurred, the municipal workforce would be reduced by a total of more than 60,000 people, or 20 percent.

Now we turned to the state. Through the EFCB the state was clearly increasing its direct control over the city, and I thought it was now suitable that the state give something back in return. We proposed that the state make a direct investment in what would be a new $2.3 billion financing plan.

This plan had two unique elements. One: this was the first time MAC had suggested a program that would extend over several months. Two: it was also the first plan that involved the state directly.

This desperation financial package was like a supplicant's going hat in hand to all his acquaintances. It would—at least as I optimistically explained it in my conversations with the governor and the MAC board—raise this $2.3 billion from a wide number of sources. It would require the state to borrow $750 million on behalf of the city. The state comptroller, despite his previous refusals, would be mandated to invest several hundred million dollars from the state pension funds. City pension funds would add $500 million to their previous investments. Prepayment of real estate taxes would add further millions. And the banks would invest another $250 million and agree to extend the payment date of $150 million of notes that would soon be due.

It was unquestionably the weakest financial plan I had ever put together. But it was the best I could come up with under the circumstances. And the situation was growing graver each month. As a consequence of the latest fears about the city's default, the state was now having difficulty raising money.

And, I realized, there was still another complication. It would be impossible to conduct the negotiations for this new plan in any kind of secrecy. We didn't have the time for quietly arranged meetings. Besides, the press coverage was relentless. I had no doubt the specifics would inevitably be leaked and become front-page news. Therefore, I told the governor we might as well announce our proposed $2.3 billion plan designed to take us until the beginning of December. Carey agreed.

It was a very tentative announcement. We made it clear that there were no commitments other than the state's acceptance of the EFCB. Further, as the package was contingent on our getting all the principals' support, no individual commitment was firm until all were on board. And after the announcement had been made came the truly hard part: we had to go to work to make it a reality.

The negotiations with the state legislature were agonizing. There was heated debate about allowing the EFCB to have such strict control over the city, about the imposition of new taxes, and about the state's investment of its pension funds in MAC bonds. However, the legislature finally agreed to the package.

But then Arthur Levitt, the state comptroller, went to court to challenge the mandated investment of state pension moneys. I was furious. I thought that Levitt was once again avoiding his responsibilities to the city. The court, however, agreed with Levitt.

This decision affected only $125 million. Still, the larger concern was that it would unravel the other commitments to the plan, particularly the city pension fund moneys. After a series of frantic negotiations, though, we managed to keep the other parts of the puzzle in place. And the situation began to look more promising after we succeeded in selling $150 million of MAC bonds to a variety of state entities. By early October, we believed that the city would be in good shape until December 5. So, we turned our attention to Washington.

The unarticulated part of my plan—at least in the public announcement—had always been the hope that if we pulled off this $2.3 billion rescue, the next step would be a federally assisted three-year or even four-year strategy. It was hoped that by December the Ford administration would realize that the city and state were inextricably intertwined. A default by the city would inevitably be followed by a default of the state. And no administration, not even the hard-hearted Republicans who now controlled Washington, would take that risk. Or so I hoped.

In October, Senator William Proxmire, Democrat of Wisconsin, held hearings of the Banking Committee on the formal plan Carey had submitted, the Municipal Emergency Act of 1975. Most of the Washington lawmakers focused on the proposed federal guarantees of securities issued by the state or a specifically created state agency (in this case MAC) to finance local governments when it was clear that the private capital market had closed. This was precisely the idea I had discussed with Senator Jackson six months earlier, and the possibility that it could soon become law was very gratifying. There was, of course, some Republican opposition on the Banking Committee, but Proxmire was sympathetic and even Senator Richard Lugar, a Republican, struck a positive note. I was encouraged, guardedly optimistic, in fact, when I returned from the hearings to New York.

Then once again, the situation began to unravel.

Sixteen

It all had been going so smoothly. Since September, all the parties in our $2.3 billion financing plan for the city had made their investments on schedule.

But on Thursday, October 16, the trustees of the Teachers Pension Fund balked. The fund had earlier agreed to purchase $150 million of MAC bonds as part of a $450 million package that would provide the city with the money to pay off notes maturing on October 17. Now the trustees of the teachers' fund wanted us to find another source for the $150 million they had pledged. They were enraged because a week earlier the EFCB had refused to approve a contract with New York's teachers unless the teachers agreed to a three-year deferral of a wage increase similar to the deferrals that the other municipal unions had accepted. Despite their previous promise, the trustees now had decided that if the state comptroller could refuse to buy MAC bonds and get away with it, they could too.

That Thursday night, only twenty-four hours before the payment was due, the trustees agreed to attend an emergency meeting at the governor's office. The governor, dressed in white tie and tails, arrived later, directly from the Waldorf-Astoria Hotel, where the annual Alfred E. Smith memorial dinner was being held.

It was a heated session. Back and forth went the angry arguments. The trustees were adamant. They would not approve the payment of $150 million to purchase MAC bonds unless Albert Shanker, the head of the teachers' union, gave them his authorization. But Shanker did not want the teachers' contract to include the three-year deferral of wage increases, although we had made the other municipal unions accept it. At 1 A.M. we told the trustees they might as well go home and get at least a few hours of sleep. We asked them to return at 7 A.M. They left, making their way through a horde of reporters. It was now Friday, October 17. The notes were due today.

So much was at stake. If the Teachers Pension Fund refused to invest the $150 million it had promised, the city would default at the close of business today. But if we gave in to Shanker, then we'd have to modify the contracts of all the city unions. And that, too, would mean certain bankruptcy.

What was sustaining us, as we waited for the negotiations to begin at 7 A.M., was our belief that ultimately Shanker would realize it would not be in his union's (or, in fact, anyone's) best interest if the city were forced into bankruptcy. Bankruptcy would cause tens of thousands of layoffs, and an even greater exposure of the unions to the underfunding of their pensions. If the city's pension contributions were interrupted, these funds would be depleted in a few years. Employees' benefits would be terminated. It was a situation no union leader would want for his members, and no city worker would want for his family.

Yet I had a very bad feeling about how the negotiations might wind up. I knew that Shanker, like most union leaders, was accustomed to pushing bargaining sessions to the brink. Last-minute agreements at 3 or 4 A.M. were routine. However, we needed the funds to be on deposit with a New York bank by 3 P.M. Friday if we were to be able to pay off the notes. My concern was that Shanker might not be aware of the technical requirements, or would ignore them. My nightmare was that Shanker would inadvertently lead us into default.

I decided we needed to put some safeguards into place quickly. First, we should discover whether the other city pension funds would, if it became necessary, provide the moneys the teachers had pledged. I called Victor Gotbaum of DC37 and then Jack Bigel, a financial and negotiating adviser to several municipal unions, informed them of the dire outlook and asked them to reflect on it. This was the most I could request. I knew they could not give me a commitment that would undermine a fellow union leader's bargaining position. Neither would they be willing to make a pledge that might possibly leak to the press before they had spoken to their officers. All I could do was inform them that before 3 P.M. Friday I might very well be reaching out to them.

Next, I contacted both the Ford administration and the Federal Reserve Bank (the Fed) to inform them that MAC might request an emergency loan from the Fed within the next 24 hours. When I reached Bill Seidman at the White House shortly after 7 A.M. on Friday, he told me that not only was the administration aware of events, but its level of concern was rising. Like all of us, the administration had observed the volatility of the financial markets on Thursday, with stocks weak, bond trading all but evaporated, currency trading in Europe at a standstill, and gold prices rising sharply. A bankrupt New York would have consequences for the entire global marketplace. As the likelihood of a default increased, the administration—at last!—was realizing this.

I also told the governor that we should instruct the New York bank superintendent to keep one bank open beyond the normal 3 P.M. closing time. My thought was that if Shanker waited until the last minute to agree, we'd need to have a bank ready to receive the funds. After a conversation with Carey, the state bank superintendent, John Heimann, instructed Manufacturers Hanover to remain open until midnight. To make sure that this "after hours" strategy was actually practical, I called Judge Rifkind and asked for a legal opinion. Did New York have until midnight to pay off its notes rather than the usual bank closing time at 3 P.M.? Rifkind, to my great satisfaction, concurred that default for nonpayment would not occur until the end of the entire day.

At 7 A.M. the teachers' trustees walked through the scrum of press and television cameras on the street outside the governor's office and dutifully returned for the scheduled meeting. But it was futile. They continued to insist that they would obey Shanker's instructions; they would not accept a contract with deferred wage increases.

As this meeting began, Carey and Rifkind were meeting with Shanker at the apartment of the realtor Richard Ravitch, who was one of New York's prominent business leaders. This location had been chosen because it was "common ground;" Ravitch was a friend of both the governor and the union leader, and my friend as well.

As for me, I had walked the city streets with David Burke and George Gould after the first session with the trustees had ended at one o'clock that morning. We had tried to think of something else we might do, some other compromise we could offer Shanker, but none came to our minds. Whatever we gave Shanker we would need to give to the other unions—and those modifications would cause the entire financial structure we had built to come tumbling down. There was, I concluded with frustrated resignation, nothing we could tell him, no argument we could make, that he had not heard in our initial discussions. Either he would believe keeping our plan in place was better for his members than a bankrupt city, or he would not. We had come to the precipice.

All we could do now was wait. While we paced anxiously, we received reports that Carey was standing firm in his meeting

O. A. Fialho
E
F. S. Mirsky

TRADUTORES
JURAMENTADOS

Eu, traductor publico abaixo-assignado
e interprete commercial juramentado desta
praça do Rio de Janeiro:
C E R T I F I C O que me foi apresentado
um documento exarado em idioma _francez_,
afim de traduzil-o para o vernaculo, o
que cumpri em razão do meu officio e cu-
ja traducção é a seguinte:(Doc. 11.447/41)

T R A D U C Ç Ã O: Ser. I Nº 734915 – Nº 7315/III/37
República da Polonia – PASSPORTE expedido a favor do
cidadão polonez Feliks Jerzy ROHATYN, domiciliado na
França – Local e data do nascimento: Wielun, 21 de
Maio de 1928 – Rosto redondo – Olhos azues – Cabel-
los castanhos – Havia a photographia do portador au-
thenticada por carimbo do Consulado da Polonia em Paris. – Assignatura do portador: (a) F. Rohatyn – O pre-
sente passaporte é valido para todos os paizes e ex-
pira em 23 de Março de 1939, salvo renovação. Expedi-
do em Paris, aos 23 de Março de 1937 – Pelo Consul Ge-
ral (a) W. Kzerowski – Havia o carimbo do Consulado
Geral da Policia em Paris. – Havia a prorogação do
passaporte até 27 de Agosto de 1941, concedida pelo
Consulado da Polonia em Nice (a) Z. Szubert – Vice-
Consul Carimbo do Consulado Polonez em Nice. ———
———Havia o Visto Diplomatico nº 447 da Embaixada do
Brasil em Vichy – Valido para viajar para o Brasil.
Vichy, 28 de Outubro de 1940 (a) L. de Souza Dantas
Havia o carimbo da Embaixada do Brasil em Paris. ———
———Havia o carimbo do Serviço de Immigração no por-

The visa that allowed me to flee Nazi-occupied France at age twelve, issued in Marseille by Luis Martins de Souza Dantas, the Brazilian ambassador to France who defied his government's orders and provided visas that saved my family and eight hundred other Jews.

My mother, Edith Plessner. Ingenio[us], fearless, and tenacious, she led our fa[m]ily from Paris to Marseille and a boa[t to] Casablanca. Hiding gold coins in too[th]paste tubes, she improvised our esc[ape] south on unmarked roads and bywa[ys,] eluding Nazi troops and a death s[en]tence if we were discovered.

My father, Alexander Rohatyn. After World War II we reunited in Paris, where he had re-established himself as a brewer. Thinking I might follow in his footsteps, I worked in his brewery but soon decided neither beer nor France would be my future.

Family snapshots from the seventies. Top, from left to right, my son Michael Rohatyn, my stepdaughter Nina Griscom, my wife, Elizabeth, and my son Pierre Rohatyn. Middle, Michael and Pierre. Bottom, my sons, Nicholas, left, and Michael Rohatyn.

André Meyer, my teacher and men[tor].
Shrewd, autocratic, and known for his vol[ca]-
nic temper, Mr. Meyer used his genius, rele[nt]-
less determination, and a carefully cultiva[ted]
network of business and government c[on]-
nections to transform Lazard Frères into [one]
of the most powerful players on Wall Str[eet]
while maintaining the investment bank's [her]-
itage as a family-oriented business.

Michel David-Weill, who succeeded André
Meyer as chairman of Lazard Frères. Mr.
Meyer had asked me to take over but I
wanted to remain a banker and suggested
he name Michel. An heir of Lazard's founders, unfailingly courteous and affable, Michel had a penetrating intelligence and as
chairman clashed with Mr. Meyer, but once
he took full control, Michel ran the bank as
André Meyer had shaped it.

The legendary Harold Geneen, chairman of ITT. I advised Geneen on his first acquisition as ITT's CEO and eventually became a company director. The ITT-Hartford merger drew Geneen and me into a political quagmire that threatened my banking career and taught me that politics was a much rougher business than business.

Then attorney general-designate Richard Kleindienst and me in 1972, preparing to testify before the Senate Judiciary Committee about allegations that the Justice Department had settled a suit against ITT in exchange for political gifts to the GOP. Confident that I'd done nothing wrong and had nothing to fear, I was a pin-striped lamb being led to the slaughter.

Steven J. Ross, the jovial, back-slapping young president of Kinney National whom I met in the back of a funeral parlor to plot my first major deal, Kinney's takeover of Avis Rent-A-Car. Steve and I would be friends and occasional partners for twenty-five years and I would help him become a Hollywood mogul with Kinney's 1969 purchase of Warner-Seven Arts.

My friend, Lew Wasserman, chairman of the Music Corporation of America. Despite misgivings, I helped him arrange the sale of MCA to the Japanese firm Matsushita. The relationship between the companies never worked and Matsushita sold MCA to Seagram's without ever discussing it with Lew.

General Electric CEO Jack Welch, center, with Bob Frederick and Thornton Bradshaw, announcing GE's 1985 merger with RCA. Along with Hal Geneen, Jack was the most impressive CEO I ever worked with in my long career, an especially brilliant manager of people.

A caricature of Ross Johnson, the CEO of RJR Nabisco whose management group brazenly attempted the largest leveraged buyout in history and became symbols of the boundless greed that drove financial markets in the 1980s. I came to regret my involvement in the RJR deal, and it changed the way I thought about investment banking and American business.

15

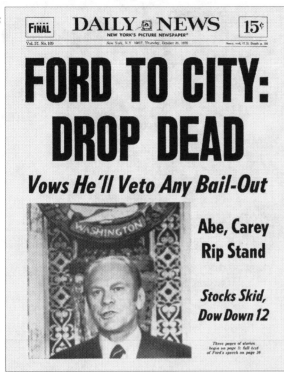

After President Ford vowed to vet any bill that would provide fundin to avoid a bankruptcy of New Yor City, the *Daily News* ran this famou headline. When New York governc Hugh Carey saw it he shouted, "No we're going to win!"

16

Newsweek magazine exaggerates my height.

With Governor Hugh Carey in 1977. Forceful, direct, a politician who put the public interest above partisanship or personal ambition, Hugh Carey was the leader we needed to save New York City from catastrophic bankruptcy. He gave me unconditional support when I chaired MAC, and we became lifelong friends.

At a press conference with Governor Carey, center, and New York mayor Abe Beame after we met with President-elect Jimmy Carter. President Ford had recanted his 1975 refusal to help New York avoid default but Carter still carried New York City, which enabled him to win the state and defeat Ford in the 1976 election.

Albert Shanker, center, president of New York City's teachers' union, at a 1968 rally. During its fiscal crisis, the city was an hour away from bankruptcy when Shanker agreed to his union's purchase of $150 million in municipal bonds that kept New York solvent.

With my friends, Betsy and Victor Gotbaum, in Southampton, N.Y. I met Victor when he led DC37, the huge municipal hospital workers union, and agreed to collective bargaining concessions that helped stabilize New York City's finances. We were both single fathers and would wrap up a day of grueling negotiations by taking our kids out for Chinese food together.

With Jack Bigel, far right, the financial advisor to New York City unions, after a MAC meeting. He was a tough, cynical labor leader but also a smart, practical man. Despite his distrust of bankers, Bigel knew the city must avoid default and we had to work together.

From left, British prime minister Harold Wilson, President Gerald Ford, French president Valery Giscard d'Estaing, and German chancellor Helmut Schmidt at a 1975 meeting in Helsinki. Giscard and Schmidt publicly warned Federal Reserve chairman Arthur Burns that a bankruptcy of New York City would bring global economic catastrophe, prompting Ford to end his opposition to federal aid for the city.

With Brooke Astor, circa 1980.

Paul LeClerc, president of the New York Public Library, and Brooke Astor with my wife, Elizabeth (right). Elizabeth served as chairman of the Library's board until we left New York for the U.S. embassy in Paris.

French president François Mitterrand presents me with the Legion of Honor. Jean Riboud, the CEO of the oil service company Schlumberger, introduced me to Mitterrand, whose election as president would worry the Reagan administration. We became friends and I visited Mitterrand at his modest Left Bank apartment, which he preferred to the Elysée Palace. He told me, "You must do for France what you did for New York."

With President Clinton in 1999. Bill Clinton had asked me to consider serving as ambassador to Japan but I was able to convince him that I would be more useful to his administration in France.

This painting of Elizabeth and our dogs, Nobu and Noodles, in the garden of the residence of the American ambassador to France, was presented to us by our friend Liliane de Rothschild when we completed our diplomatic service. The ambassador lives in the third floor apartment of this historic mansion in the heart of Paris; its grand salons are used for official functions, and special visitors, including the president and first lady, stay in elegant guest rooms on the second floor.

Elizabeth and I greet former French prime minister Edouard Balladur at a 1998 U.S. embassy reception in Paris. My predecessor as ambassador, Pamela Harriman, had introduced me to Balladur so I might help convince him that America was not driving down the dollar in order to subvert the introduction of the euro.

Elizabeth and I walk in the garden of the U.S. embassy residence in 1999.

In my office at the American embassy in Paris, 1999.

with Shanker. The union leader was no less intransigent. I gave up all hope. Bankruptcy seemed unavoidable, just hours away.

Then at 2 P.M. Shanker emerged from the meeting at Ravitch's apartment. He appeared totally drained, like a man who had spent all his resources in the course of a grueling battle. As the television cameras rolled, he announced that he would recommend to the trustees that they vote to make the $150 million investment.

At 3 P.M. the trustees voted as the union leader had recommended. Fortunately, we had made the necessary arrangements to keep Manufacturers Hanover open. Just before midnight the $150 million transaction was concluded. Bankruptcy had been averted.

Like Shanker, I was completely drained too. For two days, uncertainty and tension had kept building. There had been no time to sleep, and I doubted whether I could have slept anyway. That night, restored a bit, I joined Carey and Burke for a celebratory dinner at Elaine's. Woody Allen was at an adjacent table. When he came by to say hello, I reminded him of his movie *Sleeper*. According to a line in the film, "The world came to an end when a man named Albert Shanker got ahold of the atom bomb." Last night, I told Woody, it had almost happened.

—

Once again we had managed to avoid disaster. But we could not continue to lurch from crisis to crisis. The time had come, I realized, to formalize a long-term solution. In fact, it was a necessity.

After New York state had committed $750 million to the city's plan in September, the bankers became less willing to underwrite the sale of the state bonds required to cement the package. And the bankers' position was understandable. Six months earlier, state notes had been trading at 5.37 percent interest;

now they traded at a significantly higher rate. It became clear to me that unless we could resolve the city's needs for the next three to four years, the state would also soon no longer be creditworthy.

So, we tried to get a handle on the size of the problem we were facing. As best we could estimate, the city's cumulative deficit was $3.3 billion. It was an enormous figure, but nevertheless we began working on a plan that would allow us to pay off this deficit over three years. It would involve using pension fund assets, investments from banks and insurance companies, and federal assistance. Ultimately, we would need to raise $6 billion.

Yet we had already cut back on services and infrastructure investments as much as was tolerable. We were committed to reducing the city's workforce by 20 percent; that was 60,000 jobs. We had doubled mass transit fares. We had raised taxes. We had for the first time imposed tuition at City University. To make further cuts, to raise additional taxes, would, I felt, jeopardize the quality of daily life in the city. Living in New York City would become too much of a struggle for its citizens.

There was only one alternative. Carey, Burke, and I agreed that we would need to confront the Ford administration and the Proxmire committee. We would make it clear to Washington that these federal guarantees would become one of the defining issues in the coming 1976 presidential campaign.

At last, I was beginning to see a way out of the crisis. I put together my "endgame" strategy. It was a three- or four-year plan entirely financed by the unions and banks, but conditional on a federal short-term loan program that would help us get through the initial financial rough spots.

Early in October I sat down for breakfast at the Regency Hotel on Park Avenue with Jack Bigel, a tough, brilliant adviser to several unions. The Regency is famous in New York as the meeting place for "power breakfasts," the room where many of the city's corporate and financial movers and shakers first discuss their latest big deals. That morning I had asked Bigel to join me to discuss the biggest "deal" of my career: a plan to put New York back on its feet permanently.

Bigel was one of the smartest, toughest, most cynical labor leaders I had to deal with. He was committed to New York, but I don't believe he ever trusted me. He worked with me, and with the bankers as well, because he was a practical man. He understood that the survival of union benefits depended on a robust and economically viable New York. If the city went into bankruptcy, pensions would be jeopardized. If he had to work with me to ensure that municipal workers continued to receive what they were entitled to, he was willing to collaborate. Therefore, when I told him that my long-term plan required a significant investment from the municipal union pension funds, Bigel listened carefully.

After a moment, he began to write some numbers on a napkin. Then he passed it to me. The numbers represented, he explained, the reserves of the five municipal union pension funds. Their total capital, according to the sums he had added on the napkin, amounted to $8.8 billion. Bigel looked me straight in the eye and said that the unions might be willing to commit a total of $4 billion to my plan. I was elated. With the union's commitment, my plan might very well become a reality. But my conservative banker's nature made me advise Bigel that it would be more prudent for the union funds not to invest half their reserves. Perhaps, I suggested, we should begin with an investment of just $2.5 billion.

And so with the unions on board, we began to put together the final financial construct. It would be a package of investments and loan extensions that would amount to $6.6 billion.

There were several key elements: The unions would, as I had worked out with Bigel at the Regency, invest $2.5 billion of new funds; the banks and the unions would cooperate to extend $2.8 billion of maturing notes; and, arguably most significant, a three-year moratorium would be declared on the repayment of $1.6 billion of maturing publicly held city notes.

This moratorium turned out to be the most controversial action we took during the entire crisis. That reaction, of course, did not take us entirely by surprise. Before we decided to take such a step, we had struggled with the decision. After all, a moratorium is, in many ways, a default by another name. It would be a serious blot on the state's credit. But we had no choice. We simply were not able to raise the funds to pay off these notes. Our only alternative, we reluctantly decided, was to ask the legislature to declare a moratorium for three years, during which we would pay interest but not principal. At the end of the third year, we felt confident we would have the funds to pay the notes back. But until then, repayment was an impossibility.

The banks argued strenuously against this deferral. I remember being in a fiery meeting in the governor's office as one after another of the city's leading bankers—Wriston, Rockefeller, and Patterson—went on the attack, insisting that we were doing something meretricious. I answered them politely. Yes, I agreed, a deferral was a terrible thing. But, I went on pointedly, the consequences of the city's default would be worse. And, I added, they had it in their power to create a situation where a moratorium would be unnecessary. All they needed to do was lend us the $1.6 billion required to pay off the notes that were coming due. After all, I said, the union pension funds were buying $2.5 billion of MAC bonds.

As I had expected, the bankers refused to come up with an additional $1.6 billion; their banks, they reminded me, had already made significant investments in city and state paper.

Then the time had come, I said firmly, for the banks to make a choice. We had a legal opinion written by Judge Rifkind citing precedents during the Depression that had authorized deferring bond payoffs. We had already presented this opinion to the state lawmakers. Additionally, we would offer the holders of maturing notes the opportunity to exchange them for ten-year MAC bonds carrying 8 percent interest and having a liquid market. If the legislature voted to authorize the moratorium and the exchange, I challenged the bankers, would the banks go along with it? Or, did they want the city to file for bankruptcy?

Carey's stand was no less relentless. He told the bankers that if they were willing to accept the moratorium, he would expect nothing less than their public support. He would want their endorsements when we announced the new long-term package.

The bankers did not immediately reply. We waited anxiously. Without the moratorium, the entire package would be doomed. And without their support, it would be very nearly impossible to get the legislature's approval.

At last, the bankers spoke. One after another they made it clear that in principle they were against a deferral. But one after another they finally came to the same conclusion: they would support the moratorium; it was the only way to avoid bankruptcy.

—

Yet as we made progress putting the final pieces of this plan together, we were once again shaken. At the end of October, President Ford gave a speech at the National Press Club, directed at New York. It was harsh, a mean-spirited recitation of many of the complaints his administration had previously made about the city's wanton spending practices. All the city's many recent acts of fiscal belt-tightening and the Herculean efforts by the unions, the banks, and officials to reduce the deficit were deliberately ignored. "I can tell you now," the president vowed, "that I am prepared now to veto any bill that has as its purpose a federal bailout of New York City to prevent a default."

I had watched the president's speech with the governor in his office, and our spirits skidded. If Ford was reelected, we knew the city would be cut loose. The federal government would shrug, and then watch, uninterested, as New York filed for bankruptcy.

When I met Carey and Burke later that evening at Elaine's, we were a morose group. It seemed to each of us that the federal guarantees, which were the linchpin of our long-term rescue plan, would never become a reality. And, therefore, our entire plan was doomed.

It was about 10 P.M. when the newsboy, as he did every night, came into the restaurant hawking the early edition of the *Daily News*. Absently, I bought a copy. It was only as the paper was passed to me that I glanced at the front page. The headline that filled the front page was: "Ford to City: Drop Dead." Excited, I quickly passed the paper to the governor.

Carey scanned the headline, then he let out a shout. "Now we're going to win!" he rejoiced.

And the governor was right. True, the president had not said those actual words. But every New Yorker knew that was what he had meant. His narrow-minded dismissal of the city would cost him the presidency. And the election of a Democrat would ensure federal participation in an economic plan to revitalize New York.

By November 28 most of the pieces in the long-term package had fallen into place. The last commitments by the pension funds and banks had been obtained. The legislature had raised a variety of taxes that would bring in an additional $200 million in revenues, but, as we had requested, had avoided increasing the sales tax. And it approved the moratorium on the remaining city notes, as well as the exchange for MAC bonds. All that remained was for President Ford to sign the bill before him that mandated federal assistance.

In the meantime, our cause received international support. At the first Western Economic Summit in Rambouillet, France, Arthur Burns, chairman of the Federal Reserve, raised the issue of New York City's fiscal crisis with President Giscard d'Estaing of France and Chancellor Helmut Schmidt of Germany. They declared that the possibility of the city's declaring bankruptcy would be "unthinkable." From abroad, they told Burns, it would be seen as if America was filing for bankruptcy, too. The dollar would be devalued, and a global economic crisis would follow. Dutifully, Burns informed President Ford of the concern expressed by these European leaders.

As for myself, I told the governor that there was nothing more I could do. I had not spent a weekend or a holiday with my children since before the crisis had erupted on Memorial Day. I was now going to spend the Thanksgiving weekend skiing in Utah with my son Michael. If President Ford signed our assistance legislation, I said to the governor as I walked out of his office, I would be back after the holiday. If not, I would just stay on my mountain.

"If he doesn't sign," Carey replied with a small laugh, "I might have to join you."

But neither of us needed to stay on the mountain. On December 2, Ford signed the New York Emergency Finance Act of 1975. It provided New York with $2.3 billion of seasonal financing and gave the city three years to pay down the deficit and balance its budget.

This marked the end of New York City's fiscal crisis—almost. Nearly a year later, in November 1976, the New York State Court of Appeals declared that the moratorium on maturing notes was unconstitutional. Payment had been suspended on $1.1 billion of notes, and unless New York could now come up with the money to cover this sum, the city would once again be facing bankruptcy.

The banks quickly tried to turn this latest crisis to their advantage. They had never approved of the EFCB's having such strict control over the city, and they offered us a solution that would also change the EFCB. They would provide the necessary $1.1 billion—but only if a new, permanent control board was created. However, to me and the other members of MAC, the prospect of a board regulating the city's spending that would be controlled by individuals selected by the bankers was untenable. It would mean the end of democracy—and the end of democratic, public-spirited decision making—for the city.

Fortunately, we managed to come up with another strategy. With the help of Salomon Brothers, we offered the holders of the remaining city notes a new issue of MAC bonds. These carried a high interest rate and traded in an active market. The vast majority of note holders accepted the exchange, and we had no trouble raising the funds for the few who decided to redeem their bonds.

New York City could now begin to rebuild.

Jimmy Carter was elected president of the United States in 1976. New York state made the difference, and the vote in New York City allowed Carter to carry the state. Ed Koch was elected mayor in 1977 on a platform of fiscal controls. In 1978 Congress approved a federal long-term guarantee program for New York. In 1980 the city submitted a balanced budget. In 1981 the city successfully reentered the bond market. Four years later, MAC no longer had any need to sell bonds; the city was able to sell its own. By 2008, all the outstanding MAC bonds had been paid off. And MAC surpluses enabled the city under Mayor Giuliani to increase its police force by 11,000 officers.

Today, New York City has full access to the financial markets and can borrow to accommodate all its needs. In the ensuing decades of balanced budgets—even frequent surpluses—New York and its residents have prospered. The revitalized city has become preeminent, acclaimed as the economic and cultural capital of the world. Yet, there are still serious economic problems looming for the city and the state. The consequences of the financial crisis of 2008 will necessitate municipal and state fiscal belt-tightening. And politicians will need to find the courage to make difficult budgetary accommodations and decisions. Or else, history could grimly repeat itself.

As for me, after eigteen years, in 1993, I stepped down as chairman of MAC. This chairmanship had been the most rewarding experience of my professional life.

Seventeen

I had been summoned to Switzerland. André Meyer was dying, and he insisted that I come to his mountaintop chalet in Grans-sur-Sierre and speak with him face-to-face. I had no doubt about what he wanted. And I also was certain what my response would be.

It was 1977. My responsibilities at MAC still kept me busy, but now that New York City was on its way to firmer financial ground, I could devote more of my time and energy to my work at Lazard. I returned to a firm that was bursting with capital, active in dozens of important deals—and in a state of transition.

For more than thirty years Mr. Meyer had run Lazard with absolute authority. He was in charge of daily operations, generated most of the firm's income and prestige, hand-selected the partners, and personally decided on the percentage interest a partner would receive each year that would determine his compensation. Mr. Meyer had established the firm's culture. He had indoctrinated a generation of the firm's investment bankers with the belief that Lazard stood for quality rather than quantity in its activities, and that we were gentlemen, not hucksters. And now, as his health deteriorated, as the remnants of the firm's entanglement in the ITT affair continued to be a distraction and an embarrassment, the time had come for a change of leadership.

Over the past few years, Mr. Meyer had realized this—to a

degree. On several occasions he had reached outside the firm to hire an accomplished businessman, in the hope of training him to be his designated successor. Invariably, however, he would soon turn against this supposed heir, pay him off, and then start the process all over again.

He had also on many occasions tried to persuade me to take over the leadership of the firm. I didn't want the job. Authority at Lazard, I believed, could come from only two sources: either you were a member of the controlling family, or you generated significant and prestigious business. I fulfilled one of these criteria. Despite the demanding hours I spent as chairman of the MAC board, I continued to bring a great deal of business into the firm. But I also felt that it would be impossible to manage the firm and still function as an active and aggressive investment banker. Therefore, each time Mr. Meyer tried to persuade me to take his place, I turned him down.

Yet, as requested, I arrived in Switzerland to speak with him. The view from his chalet was magnificent—towering snow-capped mountains, an ice-blue dome of sky. And Mr. Meyer was dying. He nevertheless found a bit of his old strength and indomitable will and tried to convince me that I should change my mind and agree to succeed him. To this day, I'm not sure if he really wanted me to take the job, or if his persistence was largely driven by irritation over my refusal. At one point he even threatened to liquidate the firm if I did not agree. He couldn't seem to understand why someone would not want to run Lazard. But I didn't. And I had come to the mountaintop with an alternative plan. I suggested that he appoint Michel David-Weill.

Michel was the grandson of David David-Weill and the son of Pierre David-Weill, members of the Lazard family. It was Pierre David-Weill, the senior partner in Paris, who had brought Mr. Meyer into the firm in 1926, had recognized his talent, and had ceded the operating authority to him by the start of the Depression. Yet Mr. Meyer always had a complicated, often antagonistic, relationship with Pierre David-Weill. In Europe, the David-Weills were seen as second only to the Rothschilds as the leading Jewish banking family. Mr. Meyer, the son of bourgeois Jews, was both fascinated by and resentful of the David-Weills' aristocratic pedigree.

In time, he came to agree that Michel David-Weill was the logical choice. But even as he turned more authority over to Michel, he repeated his threat to liquidate the firm, and continued to ask me to be his replacement.

But by the end of 1978, Michel seemed more or less firmly in control of the firm; and within six months, Mr. Meyer, at age eighty-one had died in a hospital in Lausanne. I was asked by his family to speak at his memorial service, and keeping my composure proved difficult. We had shared a powerful relationship—friend, mentor, demanding boss—for the more than forty years I had worked with him. He had shaped my life, and also my career. He was buried in Paris, in the Jewish section of the Montparnasse cemetery, and as I left his grave I knew someone unique had gone out of my life.

Shortly after I returned from the funeral in France, Michel and I met at my small summer cottage on Long Island. I had known Michel since we had first worked together in New York in the 1950s; in 1961 we had both become partners. We were never intimates, but we had an easy, comfortable relationship. He was a cherubic-looking man, often with a large Cuban cigar in his mouth and seemingly always with a smile on his face, a man of unfailing courtesy. Yet I also knew that beneath the affable exterior, Michel had a mind that considered ideas and events with a penetrating intelligence. No less valuable in a banker, he had his father's hardness and determination. Michel knew that I had endorsed his appointment, and he also recognized that he would not be able to do his job without my continued support.

For my part, I knew that if I wanted to stay at Lazard, I had to help him succeed. Without giving it much thought, I began to work hand in hand with Michel.

During a long day at my beach cottage, we set the stage for Lazard's next decade. We were committed to running the firm as Mr. Meyer had shaped it—private, high-quality deals; low overhead; the David-Weill family and the heirs of André Meyer still maintaining their controlling interest. But to provide greater stability and balance, we decided the firm needed an asset management business to serve the needs of institutional investors. (This franchise within the firm now manages $1356 billion.) To help us continue to be aggressive, to regain our market share, and to attract able young people, we decided to hire more investment bankers. And we also realized we needed to weed out a number of people who had for some time not been productive. To accomplish all this, we moved rapidly, and rather ruthlessly.

These changes were necessary if Lazard was going to keep pace, albeit in its deliberately genteel fashion, with the monumental transformations in global finance and the structure of the American financial system that were taking place during the 1980s. The infusion of petrodollars—oil had jumped from $2 per barrel in the early 1970s to a $40 per barrel price by the end of the decade—had shocked the entire world economic system. A great deal of new money was in play, and many new international companies were prepared to spend and to invest. And as the global financial marketplace entered a new era, the investment banking business was also being reshaped.

A decade earlier Donaldson, Lufkin, and Jenrette (DLJ) had started the trend to public ownership, but now the finance industry was consolidating into bigger and bigger firms. Names that represented the pillars of American capitalism since the nineteenth century were acquired or disappeared. Emerging from this realignment were the firms of the future: Salomon Brothers; Goldman Sachs; Merrill Lynch, the dominant investment bank and brokerage house; and brash newcomers such as Drexel Burnham with its new financial invention, the junk bond.

The evolution of the investment banking industry was a direct result of what was happening to American business. It was changing rapidly. Institutional shareholdings had grown enormously, and this growth had created pressure on American companies to deliver value to their shareholders, rather than simply reward their managers. And as German and Japanese companies, riding the early wave of globalization, became more competitive, the pressure for American companies to increase their profits intensified. To accomplish this, one strategy was for boards of directors to remove top management and begin programs of drastic restructuring and downsizing. All through the 1980s and into the 1990s flagship companies such as General Motors, Eastman Kodak, American Express and Sears Roebuck dismissed their CEOs and went through painful layoffs. Another strategy, however, was to grow by buying new companies to put under the corporate umbrella.

These expansionist programs resulted in a wave of mergers and acquisitions. What distinguished these corporate deals from those of the previous decade, however, was the aggressive nature of many of these transactions, their almost previously unimaginable size, and the character of the new warrior bankers who, armed with an armory of new financial weapons, led the charge.

Until the 1960s, nearly all mergers or acquisitions were negotiated on a friendly basis. After all, senior management of the major American companies, for the most part, had gone to the same schools and came from the same class. Their lawyers and investment bankers were also largely cut from similar wholesome, Waspy cloth. It was as if all the principals in American corporations, despite their many differences, were members of the same country club. An attempt by a member to make a hostile takeover bid, it was well known, would be frowned on by the other members. In fact, most of the old-line investment banking houses would not participate in such unseemly business. Raiders such as Charles Bludhorn of Gulf-Western and James Ling of Ling-Temco-Vought were the much-criticized exceptions to these old school rules.

But in the 1970s, this unwritten "social contract" was ripped up by Morgan Stanley. This quintessential "establishment" investment house made a hostile bid on behalf of International Nickel, one of its longtime clients, for a battery maker. In the aftermath, all the old-line houses—with the exception of Goldman Sachs—followed. The rules had changed. And they had for us, too, at Lazard, at least somewhat. But I personally did not care for hostile takeovers, and would participate in such an activity solely on the behalf of a large, well-financed, longtime client of the firm and only after exploring all other possible alternatives. In a financial lifetime that included several hundred transactions, less than half a dozen of my deals involved my representing hostile bidders. Yet there was a new breed of combative, successful, high-profile investment bankers. Bob Greenhill of Morgan Stanley, the late Bruce Wasserstein of First Boston, the late Jim Glanville of Lehman Brothers, Marty Siegel of Kidder, Peabody—all would make celebrated, hard-driving deals, and fortunes for themselves and their firms.

As hostile takeovers grew to be a commonplace part of the industry, a new group of highly skilled lawyers came forward to service those involved. There were lawyers like the legendary Joseph Flom, a senior partner of Skadden Arps, who specialized in representing hostile bidders. And there were lawyers like Martin Lipton who specialized in defending against them. They were master tacticians, inventively using federal legislation and regulatory issues, turning litigation into a major component of the takeover process, and developing new, precedental legal techniques. Flom's "Saturday special" became a much-used takeover strategy; Lipton's "poison pill" became a standard defensive weapon.

There was also a new takeover instrument—the junk bond. This was the invention of Michael Milken, a brilliant young credit analyst at Drexel, Burnham. After studying the records of hundreds of second-tier bond issues, Milken had concluded that their failure rates were no greater than those of investment-grade bonds. Therefore, these allegedly riskier bonds with their significantly higher interest rates were actually not that much more of a risk. An investor would receive a larger return without taking any more of a gamble.

Large institutional investors saw the point of this logic—there was money to be made. They flocked to Milken. The junk bond was also particularly appealing to new entrepreneurs who previously would not have had access to the credit markets. William McGowan was able to launch MCI to compete with AT&T. Ted Turner was able to create Turner Broadcasting. Hundreds of millions of dollars were raised through the sale of junk bonds and used to build new companies.

And in the process, Milken and Drexel had made tens of millions of dollars placing the bonds with institutional investors. Almost single-handedly, Milken had turned Drexel—an old-line Philadelphia banking house, which had survived the NYSE crisis of the early 1970s only by merging with Burnham, a New York brokerage firm—into a powerhouse. With astonishing speed, Drexel had become a genuine competitor to the long-established investment banking firms.

But it was not only entrepreneurs who saw the financing potential in junk bonds. Corporate raiders realized that these instruments could give them the financial leverage they would need to
take over and break up much larger companies. And it would
be in the takeover field that Milken and Drexel would have their
greatest triumphs—as well as, in time, their downfall.

A key player in this financial tragedy was Ivan Boesky, the
king of the arbitrageurs. Arbitrage, a long-established investment
strategy, involved taking advantage of the difference in values of
two merging companies. The arbitrageur would buy the stock of
the company being acquired, and sell the stock of the acquirer. The
difference in the prices of the two stocks—the "spread"—would
be his profit. It was a time-tested, purposefully conservative investment strategy. If all went according to plan, the arbitrageur
would have taken a limited risk and made a small profit.

As the mergers and acquisitions business grew in the 1980s,
a new type of arbitrageur emerged—the "risk" arbitrageur.
Risk arbitrage involved only the purchase of the stock of the
company being acquired. There would be no hedging by selling
the stock of the company making the acquisition. The arbitrageur would make a bold investment, betting that a higher price
would ultimately be paid for the company "in play" either by
the original suitor or by a competitor. It was a strategy based
on an arbitrageur's conviction that he had correctly identified a
company about to be bought. If he was right, a fortune could be
made. If he was wrong, a fortune might be lost.

Boesky was the biggest of the risk arbitrageurs. He took the
business to an entirely different level. Boesky bought the stock
of a target company even *before* it knew it was about to be acquired. But this wasn't much of a gamble for him. He often had
inside information about pending deals.

It was a foolproof and very lucrative way of doing business. A raider would select a takeover target. Drexel would provide the raider, say with a letter stating that the firm was "highly confident" it could raise the necessary financing through the sale of junk bonds. Yet even before this letter was written, Boesky would have been informed of the potential takeover. He would quietly begin to acquire a significant number of shares of the target company's stock.

Once the takeover bid was announced, the stock's price would be destabilized. Arbitrageurs and other short-term holders would rush in with "buy" orders. By the time the dust settled, the target was either acquired by the raider or a higher bidder would have won. Either way, the stock price would have climbed significantly. And Boesky and Drexel would have made a large profit.

What was new in this scheme was that multibillion-dollar transactions would be set in motion by "highly confident" letters from Drexel, Burnham predicated on the anticipated sale of junk bonds. The players no longer needed to go to the old-line underwriting groups like Morgan Stanley or Goldman Sachs to obtain traditional financing commitments.

In the wake of Drexel's success, the entire financial industry tried to come up with ways to provide increased credit for clients. New instruments were invented. The short-term "bridge loan," for example, became common. This was an interim arrangement that allowed a company to complete a transaction without the permanent financing that would ultimately be required. The problem with bridge loans, however, was that sometimes the bridge was not long enough: if there was a downturn, the company might wind up in bankruptcy before the lenders of this interim financing would be reimbursed. It was a time of unprecedented competition among the lenders and investment bankers, and a time when greater financial risks were taken.

But there was more than tenuous inventiveness driving much of Drexel's deal making. Some of its deals were also illegal. The undisclosed partnership between Milken and Boesky, the manipulation of the market, and the pervasive use of insider information in these transactions—all this was not simply a new way of doing business. They were breaking the law.

Drexel and Boesky earned hundreds of millions from these illicit transactions. And with so much money to be made, with so much money to spread around, their conspiratorial web spread wide across Wall Street. Martin Siegel, for example, was a smart, hard-charging investment banker with movie star looks who worked for the old-line firm of Kidder, Peabody. I had done business with him in the course of a number of transactions and was so impressed that I had tried to hire him for Lazard. So I was stunned and disheartened after he was arrested. Siegel had been carrying a suitcase stuffed with $500,000 in cash, money paid by Boesky in return for inside information about the deals Kidder, Peabody was pursuing.

To my deep dismay, the greed that drove people to become involved in the burst of illegal insider trading was not limited to other investment banks. Lazard, too, was a victim.

One morning while I was having my breakfast, I happened to be reading an article in the *Wall Street Journal* about the SEC's and the U.S. attorney's investigation of Drexel. The article included a long list compiled by the SEC of transactions in which Drexel had participated and where insider trading was suspected. I started to read the list, and then discovered to my horror that Lazard had also been involved in possibly as many as ten of these deals.

As soon as I got to the office I called in Tom Mullarkey, our managing partner, and our lawyer, Marty Lipton. "We have a mole," I announced. It took us a few days to review the relevant phone records of every employee and partner who had anything to do with our merger activities during the periods when these deals were being put together. The telephone logs told a depressing story. A promising analyst who had already left the firm had been in regular phone contact with a senior official at Drexel. We turned this information over to the SEC, and subsequently the young man was indicted.

Nevertheless, my partners and I felt as if we had been raped. Lazard was a relatively small firm, and our main asset was our reputation. For an investment banking firm in the mergers and acquisitions business, nothing can be more damaging to relationships with clients than an apparent inability to maintain the confidentiality of their business dealings. Through the actions of a junior employee, Lazard had been caught up in the corrupt venality that was sweeping through Wall Street.

I was determined that this would not happen again. We established stricter internal standards to protect the confidentiality of our transactions. But in reality, there is no foolproof administrative way to prevent this kind of abuse. Ultimately, I came to realize, it all depended on the judgments we made about the people we hired and the ethical standards set by the firm and the ethics of the individuals themselves. I wanted the "culture" of Lazard to be one that valued honorable, conservative banking.

And so I spoke out strongly and publicly, in print and in television interviews, against junk bonds, excessive leverage, and the potential damage that these new, risky financial instruments could cause to capital markets. I viewed these practices as alien to the way investment banking should be conducted. But this was a difficult position to advocate, even at a genteel banking house like Lazard. After all, this was a time when activity in the trading and capital markets was growing rapidly. And this was business we wanted. When a number of our corporate clients began asking about leveraged buyouts (LBOs) and whether this business model would be suitable for them, I knew I would need to get the information that would allow me to advise them knowledgeably. Therefore, it was with some interest that, on separate occasions, I came to meet Mike Milken and Ivan Boesky.

It was Merv Adelson—the head of Lorimar, who had recently married our close friend Barbara Walters—who introduced me to Milken. This was in 1986, and my wife and I had flown to Los Angeles to attend Lew and Edie Wasserman's fiftieth anniversary party. It was a glamorous affair on the back lot of Universal Studios. Sets had been raised to celebrate many of the studio's famous movies, and many Hollywood stars attended. In the course of this happy evening, I found myself talking to Adelson. For years, Adelson had been telling me that Milken, who not only was his banker but also had been the best man at his wedding, was someone I should meet. Previously, I dismissed all these suggestions. I admired Milken's ingenuity and financial inventiveness, his ideas allowed small companies to have access to large sums of capital so that they could expand. However, this just wasn't my way of doing business. But this evening, when Adelson once again raised the possibility of my meeting Milken, I agreed.

It was arranged that my wife, Elizabeth, and I would attend a large party that Merv and Barbara would be hosting at their house in Malibu. Milken would be there. But it was understood that this would be a strictly social occasion. There would be no discussion about either the virtues or the dangers of junk bonds.

When I met Milken at the party in Malibu, he honored the terms of the arrangement I had made with our host. There was no talk of takeovers. Rather, I sat with an intense, courteous man in his forties, who clearly had a brilliant and knowledgeable mind, and we launched into a broad discussion about third world debt.

As a result of the inflation and the recession of the 1970s, many developing countries were reeling under heavy loads of debt. Mexico, in fact, seemed on the verge of bankruptcy. It was a looming problem for which the big international banks, the World Bank, and the IMF were trying to find a solution. It was also a situation that, if bankruptcy occurred, could create large troubles for American banks and the entire U.S. economy.

Milken had clearly given this problem of uncontrolled third world debt a good deal of thought. And that night he shared with me some insightful and innovative solutions. His ideas largely involved restoring market access for these struggling countries. It made sense, and I admired the breadth of his thinking.

But when he finished his analysis, I was taken by surprise. Why don't we work together and come up with a plan? he suggested. We can present it together to the countries that need help.

Although I found his ideas somewhat interesting, I was disturbed by the prospect of my being associated in any way with Drexel. And so, as politely as I could, I told Milken that I could not work with him. It was a prudent decision. Yet I have always had a great deal of respect for Milken. His financial insights helped provide struggling companies with capital, and after his release from prison, his philanthropic commitment to research on prostate cancer helped advance medical knowledge and treatment of the disease.

—

It wasn't long after the party in Malibu, a time when Milken was at the height of his power and influence, seemingly running the entire financial world from his celebrated X-shaped desk in his Beverly Hills office, that his coconspirator, Ivan Boesky asked to meet me.

I had made it a practice not to speak to arbitrageurs in general, and Boesky in particular. I did not want to be misquoted, to be misconstrued, or even to create a situation in which someone could imply that I was providing sensitive information. However, Lazard was a major participant in the mergers and acquisitions business, and members of my department would routinely talk to arbitrageurs to exchange information and get a sense of the markets.

Peter Jaquith, one of my partners, spoke occasionally with Boesky and had told me several times of Boesky's desire to meet. It was shortly after my return from California that Jaquith again brought up a possible meeting. He explained that Boesky simply wanted to discuss his philanthropic activities and the possibility of his doing public service work. There would be no mention of business. With those guidelines established, I agreed to a lunch.

I arrived on time at the Four Seasons restaurant for the 1 P.M. lunch. Boesky arrived half an hour later with a cell phone glued to his ear. He continued the phone conversation as he sat down. All I could do was stare in silence. He was a tall man, with a pinched, gloomy face. My first impression was that he reminded me of an undertaker.

When his phone call finally ended, he began our conversation by announcing that, as had been agreed, he did not want to discuss business. However, he went on without a pause, he wanted me to be aware of his interest in ITT. As a longtime director, perhaps I could give him some advice.

With firm and rather frosty directness, I responded that this was not a subject I wished to discuss. After all, I explained, Lazard still maintained a strong investment banking relationship with ITT. Further, it was my belief that Rand Araskog, the CEO, would be strongly opposed to any initiative by Boesky. And Lazard, of course, would support the company.

Breezily, Boesky dropped ITT and moved on. He said that

he admired the work I had done for New York as chairman of MAC. But he had heard rumors that, now that the city's financial crisis had stabilized, I was stepping down.

As for himself, Boesky explained as I listened with an increasing sense of dread, he had reached a stage in his life where money was no longer important. He was ready for public service. What would you think, he asked, about my succeeding you as chairman of MAC?

What did I think? MAC would ultimately issue more than $10 billion of outstanding bonds. The agency had gone through great struggles to regain the high credit ratings that it had temporarily lost. We needed to maintain billions of dollars in reserve funds, all of which were conservatively invested. For a long, unsettling moment I silently imagined these bonds and the billions of dollars in the hands of Ivan Boesky. I was literally speechless.

When I finally recovered, I managed to reply that I was not yet prepared to step down. However, I would, I continued with careful politeness, inform the governor of his willingness to serve.

After my terse dismissal of his suggestion, the meal meandered on tensely. Finally, Boesky explained that he needed to rush back to his office. Within minutes, our lunch came to a somewhat abrupt end. I never met with Boesky again.

❧

Throughout this period of increased activity in the financial marketplace, Lazard was growing. In the late 1970s, there were thirty partners and about 250 employees. Two decades later, there would be 1,000 people working at the firm and sixty-nine managing directors. We eventually moved from our comfortable but modest offices at 1 Rockefeller Plaza to a much larger space at 30 Rockefeller Plaza. I had previously been able to wander into and out of the offices of the people I worked with and get a feel for what was going on, what each was doing, what the tempo of the firm was like. Bill Hewlett, the cofounder of Hewlett Packard, had called this "walking-around management." Those days were over for me at Lazard.

Also troubling was the fact that the firm was venturing into areas for which I had little enthusiasm. Michel believed that a large markets activity was necessary to complement our successful mergers and acquisitions business and our relatively modest underwriting capability. At a meeting of our executive committee where we debated whether Lazard should take on an additional trading function, I had argued against it. But I was overruled. In time, the profitable, low-risk, non-capital-intensive advisory business of the firm would be subsidizing the high-risk, capital-intensive trading activities. And this discrepancy in our internal balance sheet would lead to tension within the firm.

As for me, I gradually reduced my interest in the firm. I wanted to set my compensation in a way that was obviously favorable to the firm and was not competitive with the other partners'. And all the while, as the marketplace went through transforming and too often disturbing changes, as the tension at Lazard grew more and more pronounced, I continued to do business.

Eighteen

The insistent ringing of the phone late at night is always disconcerting. It is a noise that immediately fills me with dread: someone is reaching out to me in the darkness with bad news. So it was with a measure of anxiety that, late one night in November 1987, I turned on the lamp on our bedroom table, leaned over toward the trilling phone, and picked up the receiver.

I was relieved to discover that the caller was my partner, Ira Harris. A gigantic man with an explosive temperament, Ira had dominated the investment banking business in Chicago as the resident partner of Salomon Brothers until I had succeeded in luring him to Lazard. The lateness of the hour, I knew, meant little to Ira; he was always doing business. I prepared myself for a report on some recent development that was too important to wait until morning.

"I've just spoken to Ross Johnson," he announced without even a pretense of an apology for the lateness of his call. "They want to meet us tomorrow for lunch in Atlanta."

I knew, of course, that Ross Johnson was the CEO of RJR Nabisco, the company that had been formed by the merger of R.J. Reynolds Tobacco, the world's second-largest cigarette manufacturer, and Nabisco, a major international grocery products company. But Johnson was neither a business nor a social acquaintance. And I was tired.

"Listen," I said with perhaps too much abruptness, "I don't know him or his company. Do you really want me to do this?"

"Absolutely," Ira nearly shouted. "The management wants to do an LBO. They want us and Dillon Read to advise the board. Can you meet me there?"

I just wanted to go back to sleep. "Ira—" I started.

"Let me know what flight you're on," he interrupted. "I'll have you picked up in Atlanta." Without waiting for me to respond, he hung up.

And so with that call I became one of the initial participants in a complex and hard-fought deal that would be the largest LBO ever. It would involve a crowd of Wall Street's most renowned bankers, lawyers, and public relations specialists. It was also a transaction that would, notoriously, symbolize the extravagant greed that energized and shaped the financial marketplace in the 1980s. And by the time it was concluded, I would almost be regretting that I had ever reached across my bed to answer the phone that late November night.

—

RJR Nabisco had lavish headquarters—a sprawling campus of enormous buildings gleaming like what seemed to be acres of polished marble. It had all been designed, I suspected, with the purpose of impressing visitors, and as I arrived at the meeting the next day I must admit that all the extravagance had the desired effect. I was impressed. Clearly, this was a very rich company, a conglomerate that had its own fleet of airplanes and sponsored golf and tennis tournaments with millions of dollars in prize money. But my banker's mind couldn't help wondering, How rich? On the plane ride down to Atlanta, I had worked out that at its present price of $55 a share, RJR was valued at about $16 billion. Yet not very long ago the stock had been trading at $76. The real market value price per share, I felt certain without even doing any due diligence, would be significantly higher. For the right price, the purchase of RJR Nabisco would be a very good investment. No wonder the Johnson group wanted to make a deal.

No sooner had I arrived at the headquarters then I was led into a meeting room. Charles Hugel, the chairman of RJR's executive committee, was sitting at the head of a long table. To his right, I recognized Peter Atkins, who was a senior partner at Skadden Arps, Meagher & Flom, and one of the profession's leading M&A lawyers. He was, I was told, acting as counsel to the executive committee. Ira and our colleagues from Dillion Read were also already seated.

Once I joined them, the meeting moved forward with surprising quickness. Hugel explained that the management of RJR, led by Ross Johnson, planned to propose an LBO of the company to the board of directors. The price was set at $75 a share, and Shearson Lehman Hutton, the investment bank advising the management, was confident that the financing could be arranged. A committee of independent directors, headed by Hugel, had been formed to review the fairness of this proposal. Lazard and Dillion Read would be the financial advisers to this special committee of the board; we would, assisted by Peter Atkins's legal advice, represent the shareholders's concerns.

Management, Hugel continued, was operating on a very tight timetable. But these top executives believed that the entire transaction could be swiftly concluded. After all, he pointed out, they were offering a premium of almost 40 percent over the current $55 share price. Of course, he concluded, there was undoubtedly some room for improving this initial bid. But there was every reason to believe that the special committee should be able to come to a prompt decision that was in the shareholders' best interest. Two weeks, he suggested breezily, and the deal should, largely, be concluded.

Dealings

I listened to Hugel and grew increasingly uncomfortable as he spoke. This would be one of the largest corporate transactions in the history of American business; certainly, it would be the biggest LBO. It was a deal in which management presumably would reap huge profits: a situation, I knew from past experience, that inevitably led to lawsuits from shareholders. In addition, a deal of this size involving a company whose products were household names would also attract the attention and scrutiny of the press. My every instinct was to be deliberate. Hugel's recitation struck me as too confident, too matter-of-fact. And the emphasis on speed made me extremely uneasy.

After conferring with Ira and the bankers from Dillon Read, I spoke. We would, I said, get to work immediately; a joint team was ready to begin doing due diligence. But, I emphasized, we would not guarantee that this process could be finished in the two weeks that had been suggested. Our responsibility was to see that the shareholders received the best price. Therefore, a thorough evaluation of the company and its components had to be done. And, since this was a transaction involving a potential purchase by insiders, we needed to provide sufficient opportunity for other bidders to step forward. Two weeks, I reiterated, was simply too little time.

Hugel seemed undisturbed by my reservations about his timetable. He just plowed on, showing us the press release describing management's purchase offer. It would be released immediately following the scheduled meeting later that day of the entire board. Then, he led us into the boardroom to meet with the special committee.

The boardroom, like everything at RJR, was gigantic. Seated around a table that looked nearly as long as the flight deck of an aircraft carrier were the members of the special committee. I had met many of these directors before. Martin Davis, chairman of Paramount, was a client of Ira's and mine; I knew him to be a tough, demanding, and difficult man. Bill Anderson, chairman of NCR; and John Macomber, chairman of Celanese, were close acquaintances of mine. Vernon Jordan was (and still is) everyone's friend and counselor. Juanita Kreps, the only woman on the committee, had been secretary of commerce in the Carter administration. John Medlin was chairman of Wachovia Bank. This was a sophisticated group; and I was buoyed by the certainty that no matter what pressures were put on us by management and Charlie Hugel, the committee members would not be intimidated. They would insist on an open and fair bidding process—and, if it was necessary, they would not allow their deliberations to be restricted to the proposed two-week timetable.

The directness of their questions reinforced my confidence. They wanted to know in great detail how we proposed to go about our task, and how often we would report to them. And they, too, expressed skepticism about a swift conclusion to the transaction.

When the committee members had finished with their questions, Peter Atkins spoke. With great deliberateness, he outlined the many legal issues involved in the transaction and the specific fiduciary responsibilities of the directors. He made it clear that management's participation in the equity of the new company would be disclosed not only to the board, but also to the public. In fact, he emphasized, to insulate the board members from litigation by stockholders, full disclosure in every aspect of this transaction was essential.

By the time I boarded the flight back to New York the next day, the press release detailing the management proposal led by Johnson had been distributed. When the plane landed, I called the office and learned that RJR stock had jumped nearly $17 in heavy volume. The company was now "in play."

Dealings

Leveraged buyouts—LBOs—were a popular financial strategy in the 1980s, and the theory behind them was quite simple. A publicly owned company with mediocre performance and a relatively low market value would prosper if it was privately owned, and management was part of the new ownership group. Only private ownership dominated by executives who knew the company, according to this financial logic, could take the necessary bold, long-term actions to improve business. There would be no pressure to report increased earnings each quarter, and costs could be cut by selectively selling or closing underperforming corporate units.

In a typical LBO, an investment group working with management would acquire the target company by providing its own capital and arranging for significant loans, often through junk bonds. The transaction would be highly leveraged; equity capital would generally be only 20 to 25 percent of the purchase price, and the large remaining portion would be debt. As assets were sold off, the proceeds would be used to pay down the debt to a more conventional amount. After two or three years, the company, now with a reduced debt and improved earnings, would return to the public markets at a significantly higher value for the underlying equity. And the LBO firm, the management-owners, and the holders of the junk bonds would stand to make a substantial profit on the relatively small sums they had invested.

The 1980s had seen an explosion in such transactions, with the deals steadily growing larger and larger. Beatrice Foods, General Instruments, Gulf Oil, Carnation, and Storer Broadcasting—all were acquired through LBOs. The two leading, and very competitive, companies engineering LBOs were KKR, a company formed by three former M&A executives at Bear Stearns—Henry Kravis, Jerome Kohlberg, and George Roberts—and Forstmann Little, an investment group headed by

Ted Forstmann, his brother Tony, and Brian Little. Drexel, with its proven ability to sell junk bonds to institutional investors, would often provide the debt financing. But no transaction the size of RJR had ever been attempted.

If Shearson Lehman, the bankers working with the Ross Johnson group, could engineer this deal, it would be a tremendous coup for the firm. Not only would Shearson reap a huge payday for its efforts—the fees alone on a deal of this size could total $200 million or more—but it would also be a direct challenge to KKR's and Forstmann's dominance.

I wanted to believe that Henry Kravis was too competitive a businessman to be content simply to read about the biggest LBO in history in the *Wall Street Journal*. In fact, I wanted him to make a competing bid. It was my responsibility to get the shareholders the best price possible, and without KKR's stepping into the fray I doubted that we could find another bidder.

Yet I also had genuine concerns about KKR's participation. Drexel had traditionally provided the firm's junk bond financing. However, Drexel was now in its death throes. The SEC and federal prosecutors were deep into their very public investigation of Drexel and Michael Milken for insider trading, stock manipulation, and fraud, among a variety of other violations of security law. The besieged firm was no longer capable of providing significant financing for Kravis, or, for that matter, anyone else.

Without KKR's coming in with a competing bid, we, acting on behalf of the shareholders, would be left with two options: either a recapitalization of RJR, or selling the company in several pieces. But both of these approaches were full of uncertainties. I felt we could push the RJR management–Shearson group to about $80 per share. To do better, however, we would need another bidder, and KKR seemed the only logical choice. But since Drexel could not provide the necessary debt financing, it was doubtful that KKR would step up. I was starting to think that maybe I had been wrong. Since there was only one bid, this transaction would, in fact, proceed as swiftly as Hugel had confidently predicted.

———

But even as I speculated anxiously about other bidders, I also knew we needed to begin our due diligence. On Saturday morning, the day after Ira and I arrived back in New York, our joint team set up a data room. If we were going to provide the shareholders with a value that would exceed management's bid of $75 per share, we needed to evaluate RJR on the basis of the sum of its parts. Would selling off some of the divisions and restructuring the company give the shareholders a combination of cash and stock that was worth more than $75? We also had to review all aspects of the RJR management bid, including, most important, the assurance that they could raise the necessary funds and the quality of their debt.

Lazard's members of the team included some of our best senior professionals: Bob Lovejoy would oversee the legal and regulatory aspects, while Luis Rinaldini and Josh Gotbaum would analyze the RJR numbers and derive values. Fritz Hobbs headed the Dillon Read group.

As we all gathered for the first time on that Saturday morning, what had started as an organizational meeting quickly turned into a valuation session. After only a few preliminaries, we began to speculate on what RJR was worth.

We all agreed: Shearson's $75 bid was a lowball offer. Ira and I, after just a cursory review of the numbers our people had gathered, believed that a valuation in the high $80s, or even as much as $90, could be achieved: that is, a sale price of $20 billion. Luis Rinaldini thought $100 per share was achievable, and possibly an even higher price.

Yet despite these lofty valuations, I remained discouraged. If there were no other suitors, the Johnson group would not be pressured to increase its initial offer. So, I considered corporate buyers. There were companies, such as Nestlé, Unilever, Philip Morris, and Coca-Cola, that certainly had the capability. However, I decided they would either be inhibited by antitrust concerns—Philip Morris was already bidding for Kraft—or be put off by the very real health issues raised by RJR's tobacco business. And once again, I thought about restructuring. But this still remained, I had to concede, a weak option. I doubted that the board would support such a risky plan.

Glumly, I began to imagine how all this would play out. We'd get the Johnson-Shearson team to improve its offer to perhaps $80 a share, and the board would have no choice but to accept that. Yet the shareholders would not get full value, and thousands of employees would be laid off as RJR subsidiary divisions were closed. It would be a terrific deal for the management; at that price they'd make a fortune. It would also be a terrific deal for Shearson, its banks, and its investment bankers; total fees would be about $500 million. And it was pretty much a done deal—unless there was another bidder.

I decided to call Henry Kravis.

Henry and I traveled in the same circles, and over the years we had done some business together. I respected him. He was bright, and he cultivated a careful, almost guarded reserve. I knew that trying to gauge his interest in bidding for RJR would be difficult; Henry was not a man to reveal his intentions. Yet I had no other choice. I made the call.

Henry, typically, did not give much away. With a tone of casual detachment, he disclaimed any interest in RJR. He was not ready, he said, to get into another bidding war, especially with a management group. He already had received, he complained, enough bad press. He did not want to be blamed once again for the employee layoffs that would be necessitated by an LBO.

Trying not to appear as if I were pressuring him, I responded with what I hoped sounded like cool reason. The best response to bad press, I suggested, was a successful deal—especially one that would fortify KKR's position as the leader in its industry. And I tried to assuage his concerns about the disadvantages involved in competing with management. We were specifically charged by the RJR board to seek the best result for the shareholders. We were prepared to provide any information he might seek.

Kravis listened without making any argument. Yet before we ended the conversation he conceded that if KKR decided to bid, it would want its bid to be the winning one. That gave me hope—but only small hope. I felt that even if Kravis were inclined to become involved, his partners—especially Jerry Kohlberg—would not want to proceed. They were famously risk-adverse. Ira Harris made a follow-up call. He, too, found Kravis cool, polite, and unrevealing. In the end, both Ira and I doubted that KKR would make a bid.

But Kravis, we later learned, had been following a well-crafted script in his conversations with us. Despite his coolly detached performance, he was seething. He felt betrayed by both Shearson and RJR. He had done a great deal of business with the investment bank, and had even previously discussed the possibility with Johnson of management's buying control of RJR. Their attempting to negotiate a deal behind his back left him outraged. But it was more than just a personal affront. Shearson was threatening his "franchise." It would be bad business to allow an interloper like Shearson to make the signature transaction of the decade, a deal three times the size of any previous LBO.

On Monday morning, before the opening of the stock market, the NYSE tape announced: "KKR to make $90 tender offer for RJR Nabisco."

—

Kravis was furious that KKR's intentions had been leaked to the press. Even more consequential, the leak set off a flurry of activity in the financial community. We were approached by a group led by the Pritzker family of Chicago and represented by First Boston. And the Johnson group was stunned. Shearson Lehman was then a subsidiary of American Express, and Jim Robinson, the chairman of AmEx, did not relish the prospect of going to war against Kravis. Suddenly, there were efforts to have Shearson and KKR submit a joint bid. But it quickly became clear that there were too many egos involved and that too much was at stake for even a pretense of cooperation. Peter Cohen, the CEO of Shearson, did not want to relinquish this opportunity to break into the LBO business in a spectacular way. Kravis, similarly, was unwilling to share leadership. And KKR's investment bankers—a group including Drexel, Wasserstein, and Morgan Stanley—were openly contemptuous of their upstart rival Shearson. The talks involving a joint bid soon broke up.

But Peter Cohen now realized that the LBO would not go as smoothly—or as cheaply—as he and the Johnson group had previously anticipated. Shearson would need a financial partner if it hoped to meet the capital requirements necessitated by a bidding war. He turned to Salomon Brothers.

Along with Goldman Sachs, Salomon shared the position of the largest trading firm in the marketplace. And John Gutfreund was Salomon's shrewd, autocratic boss. His photograph had recently been on the cover of *BusinessWeek* along with the headline "King of Wall Street." In a best-selling book about Salomon Brothers written by a former trader, Gutfreund would famously be revealed to have calmly played a single hand of liar's poker for $1 million. And in the aftermath of his recent marriage to a glamorous second wife, he had also became a well-publicized figure in New York society. I had known Gutfreund for many years and had a very high regard for his intelligence and integrity. By joining up with Salomon, Shearson had greatly increased its ability to make a winning bid. But I also had no doubt that Gutfreund's participation in the negotiations would add more fuel to the already blazing media fire.

And then there was another unexpected development. Forstmann Little entered the bidding. Teddy Forstmann was Henry Kravis's strongest rival and most severe critic. If they went head-to-head on RJR, I knew it would be an all-out war.

The two men, by both the nature of their personalities and the way they did business, were polar opposites. Henry Kravis was a small, slim, impeccably groomed man, a model of soft-spoken affability. Ted Forstmann was an athlete, a skilled tennis player, and defiantly outspoken. And while Kravis and his wife, Carolyne Roehm, like John and Susan Gutfreund and Jim and Linda Robinson, were what the newspapers called a "power couple," Forstmann was a bachelor who rarely appeared at charity benefits and rarely received a mention in the society pages. Yet what most differentiated these two competitors was the way they engineered LBOs.

Ted Forstmann opposed junk bonds with an almost religious fervor. His financing apparatuses involved straight subordinated debt, and this resulted in a more conservative structure for his management and his investors. Nevertheless, Forstmann Little's returns to its investors were remarkable, the equal of the KKR deals financed by Drexel and Milken's junk bonds.

It was Forstmann's distaste for junk bonds and for Drexel's way of doing business that ultimately had persuaded him to enter the bidding war for RJR. He was determined to derail

KKR's deal. And he wanted to demonstrate that the Forstmann Little formula was a winning one, a strategy whereby enlightened investment bankers could prevail over rivals who, financed by junk bonds, cavalierly bought old-line companies with the intention of breaking them up and laying off workers.

After securing Goldman Sachs's commitment to act as his investment bank, Forstmann then entered into discussions with the Shearson-Johnson group. He professed interest in joining their bid. Still, at the same time he was also negotiating with a consortium of large grocery companies. If his talks with the management team fell apart, Forstmann and the grocery companies would make their own competing offer.

The prospect of a bidding war—and a higher price for the shareholders—was, I was happily thinking, beginning to grow.

Nineteen

As the groups competing for RJR continued to gather information, I began a casual Saturday morning by reading the *New York Times*. I turned first, as was my habit, to the business section, and a headline caught my eye: "Nabisco Executives to Take Huge Gains on Their Buyout." Curious, I began reading the article.

I could not believe what I read. My friend Pete Peterson has an apt description for the shock I suddenly felt: an "Oh, shit! moment." This was one of the great "Oh, shit! moments." I realized at once that the story in the *Times* would make any transaction for RJR much more difficult—perhaps even, I feared, impossible.

The article revealed what would become famous as the "management agreement." Ross Johnson had apparently invented a new set of rules for this deal—all motivated by outrageous greed. First, Johnson had demanded control of the board; normally, ownership would maintain control. In addition, he had also demanded 20 percent of the equity for his group of eight to ten managers. Within five years, their share would be worth about $2.5 billion. Normally, the equity share would only be 10 to 15 percent, and that would be divided among a much larger management group.

Peter Cohen and his colleagues at Shearson, I later found out, had acquiesced in these unprecedented terms to keep the deal moving forward. Cohen knew the equity share would need to be renegotiated; he simply thought—or hoped?—it was something that could be dealt with in the final stages of the transaction. Gutfreund, too, had been shocked when, shortly after teaming up with Shearson, he heard of these demands. He was shrewd enough to anticipate the shareholders' anger that would accompany the announcement of such a staggering payday for Johnson and his team. But he, too, decided it was a point that could be resolved once the deal was farther along. As for my team and me, we had only recently begun our due diligence. We had not yet uncovered the "management agreement." But after it was mysteriously leaked to the *Times*, it was public knowledge.

The reaction was loud, widespread, and universally condemning. At a board meeting in Skadden's offices five days after the article appeared, the mood was tense. Vernon Jordan, Juanita Kreps, and John Medlin were bristling with anger. Their association with managers motivated by such excessive greed left them feeling publicly humiliated. Either they were willing accomplices in the avaricious Johnson group's LBO, or they had been dupes who had failed to scrutinize the terms of the deal. To disassociate themselves from management, the seething board members instructed us to proceed with the restructuring plan we had already begun preparing. It was clear to me that they now wanted to avoid making a deal with Ross Johnson.

Outside the boardroom, the reactions were no less enraged. The employees of RJR made it known that they were furious at being sold out, at seeing their jobs jeopardized, in a deal where a small group of the company's executives would split a $2.5 billion windfall. The chairman of the Federal Reserve, Alan Greenspan, sternly suggested that it was time for Congress to review the troubling questions raised by LBO transactions. Similarly, editorials throughout the nation not only railed against the proposed payout for the Johnson group, but also impugned the ethics of all LBOs. Were the fortunes made by a few business-men morally justifiable? After all, these colossal payouts would also result in thousands of employee layoffs, the restructuring of well-established companies, and the creation of destabilizing levels of corporate debt. *Business Week* put Kravis's photograph on its cover along with the headline "King Henry." The accom-panying article was scathing, criticizing LBOs in general and the RJR deal in particular. Kravis, who had always loathed public-ity, was incensed. He was, I was informed, seriously considering withdrawing from the bidding.

Yet as Kravis fumed and public outrage intensified, we had no choice but to proceed as if there would be three bidding groups: Johnson-Shearson-Salomon, KKR, and Forstmann Little. Peter Atkins and Skadden's lawyers dutifully constructed the bidding guidelines and had them distributed. It was decided that all the groups must agree to submit their offers by 5 P.M., Friday, No-vember 18.

The deadline was eleven days away. And each day seemed to bring new problems, new anxieties. The press leaks continued, and everyone involved in the process was left unsettled, unsure who could be trusted. The members of the Johnson-Shearson-Salomon group were fighting among themselves. Forstmann and Shearson were also growing increasingly antagonistic. And— perhaps our largest concern—the RJR executives were not disclosing fully to the bidders relevant information about the company. We, too, were in a similar predicament. We couldn't get the financial information that we, on behalf of the share-holders, needed. It was beginning to look as if only management would be able to formulate a truly informed analysis of the com-pany, and of its actual worth. And that was unacceptable.

Fortunately, a Nabisco executive, John Grenious, came forward to meet with us and the special committee. He was not part of the Johnson group. He carefully outlined areas where he felt certain major savings could be effected and profit margins increased.

At last we were beginning to have some confidence in the bidding process. The participants were getting factual information about the company that would allow them to justify a higher bid. Then, without warning, Forstmann Little dropped out. It no longer wanted to be a player in such an ugly and public dispute.

The battle for control of RJR had been reduced, I worried, to just a pair of rival groups. But as the deadline approached, two unexpected developments occurred that would dramatically affect the bidding.

—

First, the Pritzkers reentered the deal with renewed zeal. James Maher had taken control of First Boston's mergers and acquisitions activity after the departure of Bruce Wasserstein, and he was determined to show the financial community that even without the celebrated Wasserstein the bank was still a major player. The RJR deal, he decided, would be the perfect way to demonstrate this. And, even better, he had a plan. Maher had discovered an obscure tax regulation that could potentially save a buyer in the RJR deal as much as $3 billion in future taxes. That translated into a saving of $10 per share. Yet there was one very big catch: the IRS exemption expired on December 31, 1988—about one month from the bid date. It seemed impossible to close a deal as complicated as the sale of RJR in such a short time. In fact, Maher and his team had not even begun their due diligence. But armed with this theory about a possible game-changing exemption, they approached the Pritzkers and Citibank.

And so we were informed that the Pritzkers, working with

their new allies, might very well be making a bid. However, we never took this seriously. It was, after all, very late in the process for the entry of a new player. And to my mind, First Boston's exemption theory seemed more like wishful thinking than a feasible tax strategy.

—

As the deadline drew closer and closer, we had a new cause for concern: KKR began sending signals that it would not make a bid. During a week when KKR's team should have been focused on formulating a bid, Kravis announced that he was taking his family skiing in Vail, Colorado, for the Thanksgiving holiday. Dick Beattie, his lawyer, also acted as if KKR had lost interest in pursing this deal.

Trying to control my growing panic, I called Kravis. Once again, his performance was restrained. Maybe he would bid; maybe he wouldn't. He hadn't decided.

I was worried. If we were left with only one bidder, the Shearson-Johnson group, the stockholders would certainly not get the maximum possible price for their shares. So I disclosed to the press that it if we didn't get a higher bid, we would initiate a recapitalization of RJR that would yield no less than $100 per share to the stockholders.

Even as I conveyed this bit of news, I knew there were two problems with my strategy. The first was that it was only partially true. At this point in our research, I could not guarantee a yield of $100 per share through restructuring. I had used the figure of $100 in the hope of setting a floor for the bidders. But—and this was the second problem—there also was a real possibility that my floor would discourage bidders. The $100 price might be too steep, and a bidder would simply withdraw. But these were risks that, determined to strengthen the shareholders's position, I felt I had to take.

A similar logic led me to issue a pointed ultimatum to the bankers representing each group. We insisted on a "reset" provision in the bonds that would be issued. This meant that the interest rate on the bonds could be reset as of a certain date in the future; therefore, the value of the bonds would be maintained at 100 cents on the dollar. It was a mechanism that functioned like the adjustable rate on a home mortgage; when interest rates go up, the borrower has to pay more.

This provision, I understood full well, could be quite costly to the bidder. Interest rates often swing wildly; a commitment could cost the guarantor hundreds of millions of dollars. But Dillon Read and Lazard were representing the RJR shareholders. We were pushing for the reset to improve their position. Therefore, we insisted that it be part of the final deal. Drexel and KKR both agreed. Shearson and Salomon refused. And, truth be told, I could not blame Gutfreund for refusing to take such a huge risk.

———

At last, the bidding day arrived. Outside Skadden's midtown offices, a boisterous crowd of reporters and television camera crews assembled, calling out beseechingly to all the well-known players for an interview, or even just a comment, as they entered the lobby. Upstairs in the law firm's offices, there was an even larger assembly of bidders and their support teams of bankers and lawyers. The tension was palpable as the 5 P.M. deadline drew closer. The future of a great American company and its employees was about to be determined. And a investment of billions of dollars was about to be made.

The first two bids came in before 5 P.M. The Johnson-Shearson group bid $100 a share, or $23 billion; KKR bid $94 a share, or $21.6 billion. It seemed clear to me that the management group had won.

Then, just at the five o'clock deadline, First Boston submitted its bid. It did not offer a specific price. Rather, it said that, given some additional time, it could bid within a range of $105 to $118 per share. This would be a significantly higher offer than the two we had received. However, for the moment the offer was still unspecified. And it was predicated on a tax exemption that might not even be valid.

It was decided that the special committee would reconvene on Sunday to make a decision. On Saturday we would review the bids and evaluate the underlying securities.

The Saturday meetings were combative. The bidders had not been informed of their rivals' offers, and each bidder was trying to probe us for a clue. Kravis seemed particularly incensed. He claimed that KKR had been misinformed about key financial facts. As a result, he threatened, KKR might want to revise its bid.

The Sunday meeting brought new surprises. Atkins and his legal team announced that in view of First Boston's letter he recommended a postponement. The special committee, he advised, should call for another round of bidding in two weeks.

I was unhappy about this development, and so were Ira Harris and Fritz Hobbs, the head of the Dillon Read team. We all felt that the optimistic letter from First Boston would never result in a real bid. And—a more worrisome concern—the postponement would create an opportunity for the two bidders to confer and possibly offer lower bids. However, we were in no position to oppose the lawyers' recommendation; regardless of how the transaction was resolved, litigation was a certainty and our actions needed to be unimpeachable.

The meeting with the special committee was another tense, emotionally charged session. Charlie Hugel and Marty Davis were constantly sniping at each other. But when the vote was taken, the directors unanimously approved a ten-day postponement.

That afternoon, the wires carried the news of the postponement and the details of the actual bids. Johnson and his management group let it be known that they were furious. Johnson claimed that the postponement had been granted simply to revoke his winning bid. Kravis, too, was angry. But his mood seemed to change as he realized that his initial bid had been too low. Now he would have another chance. As for First Boston, it was delighted. It was now a player in the biggest bidding war in the history of American business.

The next day the new issue of *Time* magazine hit the stands, and I bought a copy and read it with a great deal of interest. Ross Johnson was on the cover beneath a banner that proclaimed, "A Game of Greed." "This man," *Time* reported, "could pocket $100 million from the largest corporate takeover in history. Has the buyout craze gone too far?"

Truth be told, I had begun asking myself that same question, too.

And then it was the day for the second round of bids. Once again there was the press scrum on the street, and the scurry of anxious bankers and lawyers moving about Skadden's floor of offices. One by one, we opened the bids. The Johnson-Shearson group offered $101; KKR came in with a stunning $106; First Boston's bid included some additional financing commitments but was still vague.

Atkins told the members of the First Boston group that we did not consider their offer a viable bid. They should, he said pointedly, leave. We then began trying to reach Kravis. It took a while, but we finally found him having dinner in a restaurant. We invited him and his group to come over.

The meeting with Kravis and his team was brief. We explained that, pending a review of the securities financing the offer, we were prepared to recommend his bid to the board. Kravis was ecstatic. And so were we. The price was beyond anything we had thought obtainable. The securities looked strong, and included reset provisions. This bid clearly was superior to the bid offered by the Johnson group. I felt that we not only had fulfilled our obligations to the shareholders but had gotten them top value for their shares. I thought my job was done.

I was wrong. The bidding was not over. In fact, it seemed as if there was nothing we could do to stop the process. There are no hard-and-fast rules that govern a bidding contest like this one. Generally, it's a simple auction: the best bid wins. However, if the loser comes back with a higher bid before the binding legal agreements are signed, there is no choice but to consider it. Further complicating the process was the fact that we were running a blind auction, not an open one. By not disclosing the offers, we had left a vacuum that the bidders tried to fill by feverishly searching for information. When any of us left the boardroom, whether it was to make a call in private or simply to use the washroom, we were intercepted by someone cajoling us for information.

The RJR board had no choice but to remain in session for the next twenty-four hours. And as the board reviewed the bids, a flurry of meetings were taking place in the offices around them. Bankers and lawyers from the two competing groups manned the phones searching for a crucial piece of information, and roamed the halls and the washrooms trying to corner members of the board and my team. Rumors and hard feelings exacerbated the suspicions between the two competing groups. Warlike contentiousness had become the tone of business. The situation had, I realized, spun out of control.

And, of course, the leaks continued. A news report flashed from Tokyo(!) divulged the broad details of KKR's bid. But, we would later learn, a member of the board had already phoned

Johnson and disclosed the specifics of that bid. All hell was breaking loose as the bidders asked for more time. It was crazy.

And it got crazier. We received a message that Ross Johnson wanted to address the board. I did not like this prospect at all. I did not know at the time that Johnson had knowledge of KKR's bid, but I was convinced he was more a salesman than a CEO. I had no doubt that since he was playing with other people's money, he would try to push Shearson and Solomon to the highest bid possible, even if it was not economically justifiable. Although KKR was, in my estimation, prepared to overpay, I was confident that it was also committed to running RJR competently. Yet there was no way we could prevent Johnson, a director of RJR, from addressing the board. And so we distracted the Kravis people with some new questions, a tactic that we hoped would keep them too busy to notice that Johnson was going in to speak with the board.

Johnson's speech was brief. He announced a new bid: $108 per share. But we still had to determine its true value, and that would take time. Kravis, however, felt he had given us sufficient opportunity to evaluate his bid. To assuage him, we agreed to reimburse KKR $45 million if it granted us an extra hour to negotiate. Bids were reaching ridiculously high levels, and yet, I worried, we had less and less time to evaluate their true value.

The board members were drained. Yet in spite of their fatigue, the sniping and bursts of temper between them raged on. The time had come, I decided, to demand that each side submit its final bid.

Now, KKR declared that it would remain at $106. The KKR team members had seen a Dow Jones report that management had upped its offer to $108. However, they knew we were comfortable with their securities, which included a reset provision. They also believed, with ample reason, that the board had become hostile to Johnson. With only $2 per share separating the bids, they were confident we would choose them.

But then the Johnson group came in with a new offer: $112 per share. I was surprised by this development. But I also knew we would need more time to analyze this bid, focusing particularly on the strength of the underlying financing securities.

Knowing I was in for a battle, I went off with Harris and Atkins to meet with Kravis and his advisers. When I asked once again for more time, they adamantly refused. But, perhaps predictably, they raised their bid, to $108 per share.

We left to return to the board and review the situation. On its face, the Johnson group had made the higher bid. But to determine accurately the relative value of the two bids, we needed to analyze the value of the paper. The KKR bonds provided, as I had requested, a critical adjustment mechanism to protect their value. The Shearson-Salomon bonds did not have this reset provision; Gutfreund and Cohen simply refused to consider it. Yet without a reset clause, Shearson's $112 bid was not worth $112. Its actual value was not significantly higher than KKR's offer of $108.

The RJR board, logically, asked us to try to negotiate a reset with the Shearson group. We traipsed out of the room, huddled with the Shearson-Salomon bankers, and tried to change their minds. They refused. When we reported this to the board members, they asked us to try again. We did, and once again their answer was an unconditional "no."

Meanwhile, the members of KKR's team could not help noticing our conferences with their rivals. They became incensed. As their anger and frustration escalated, I began to imagine KKR's withdrawing its offer and the group's walking off in a huff. I went in to talk to Kravis and Roberts, hoping to somehow assuage them.

We need a little more time, I pleaded. We just need to clarify some aspects of the Shearson bid. Reluctantly, they agreed to give us another half hour.

I hurried back to meet with my team and the Dillon Read group. After a brief discussion, we all came to the same conclusion: without a reset provision in the management offer, the bidding was too close to call.

Now I went in to address the board. Speaking on behalf of Dillon Read and Lazard, I announced, "Neither firm was willing to give an opinion that the management offer was superior."

The board members conferred. Then they asked us to attempt for the third time that night to negotiate a reset clause with Shearson. So we tried, and once again we failed.

The time now had come to conclude the process. Just as we were heading off to talk to Kravis and his team, John Medlin, the senior financial executive on the RJR board, gave us one final instruction: "Tell them we need another dollar in cash to tilt to their direction."

It was a difficult meeting. We all were tired and frustrated. We told Kravis's people that this was their chance to make a final bid, but I doubted that they believed us. "Final bids" had been made and then dismissed throughout the long night. At last, we left them alone to caucus.

It did not take long before Beattie appeared and asked Atkins and me to come in. I wasn't sure what I was about to hear. Would they raise their bid? Perhaps they would even withdraw. The process had been riddled with confusion and bad feelings, and I had come to expect that anything was possible.

I was informed they were raising their bid to $109. And if the merger agreement was not signed within the next half hour, they would cancel their offer.

—

I conferred with the Dillon Read and Lazard teams. We quickly agreed on the presentation I would make. I then spoke to the board.

"Both bids," I stated, "are between $108 and $109. When you get that close, when you're dealing with securities in amounts that have never been dealt in before—in my business judgment, these offers are essentially equivalent."

I knew the board members wanted a clear opinion about the better offer. But, regardless, I was determined to tell them what I believed was the objective reality of the situation, and to give them an opinion that would not be reversed by litigation. I went on: "Both bids are fair from a financial point of view. They are close enough that we can't tell you one is clearly superior to the other."

The lawyers spoke next. In view of the financial equivalence of the bids, they advised that the directors could use other standards to make their decisions. As this was being explained, I studied the directors' weary faces and believed I knew what they were thinking: if we can find valid reasons to vote for KKR, we will. It was clear to me that Johnson had become anathema to many on the board.

I once again had the floor. I began to list the main differences between the two bids. The KKR bonds had a reset provision, but the Johnson group's did not; KKR left 25 percent of the stock with the shareholders, but Johnson left only 15 percent; Kravis intended to sell just 20 percent of Nabisco, but Johnson would sell the entire company.

After I listed these differences, the directors spoke. Many were persuaded that the reset clause was crucial; it had to be part of the deal. Bill Anderson, a director, spoke with considerable passion, as he had done throughout the process, about what he called "stakeholder" issues—the treatment of employees, customers, and company communities. The fact that considerably more employees would have job protection under KKR's ownership was, he said, a valid reason to vote in support of its offer.

When the vote was taken, it was unanimous: KKR's bid won.

I left that night after the contracts were signed, feeling totally exhausted. We had successfully completed the biggest LBO in history. We had gotten a high, previously almost unimagined price for the stockholders. But I felt little exhilaration. Greed had run rampant. The process had gotten out of control. I knew we would be attacked by Shearson and Salomon, which would claim that we had unfairly penalized their offer. I knew we would be sued. And I feared that the Johnson group would try to enjoin the board's decision. These fears escalated when I received a call at home that evening from John Gutfreund. I listened as he went through a litany of complaints about the process and how his bid had been unfairly evaluated. When he finished, I spoke from the heart. "John," I said, "We acted professionally. Looking back at it all, I still would not change anything I did."

Yet there is a bittersweet coda to this story. By 1990, the $4 billion in RJR bonds which carried the reset provision were selling at a deep discount. The cost of a true reset would be billions of dollars. Gutfreund's and Cohen's evaluation had been correct: the reset clause had been an unacceptable risk. It had turned into a debt that could shatter the company. I began to fear that I would be called before a judge in bankruptcy court to explain why I had so fiercely insisted that the clause be included as a provision in the securities.

But RJR and I were saved: KKR rushed to the rescue by refinancing the company with a $7 billion package that included buying back the junk bonds. As a result, the deal turned out to be a mediocre investment. In the end, it became a blot on KKR's balance sheet. The firm had, in my estimation, overpaid by between $4 billion and $5 billion simply for the glory of triumphing in the bidding war for the biggest LBO in history.

As for me, the RJR deal was a defining moment in my evolving thoughts about American business. In the aftermath, it became clear to me that despite the famous assertion that "greed is good" in the movie *Wall Street*, the raging avarice of the 1980s was a pernicious force that would undermine the marketplace. I am a capitalist and I believe in making a profit. However, the experience with RJR had caused me to rethink my traditional banker's calculus. The bottom line was no longer simply the bottom line—the ultimate cost of the profit had to be considered. The issues Bill Anderson had raised at RJR's board meetings about laid-off employees, damaged communities, and cutbacks in employee benefits necessitated by higher corporate debt needed to be addressed. If market capitalism was going to continue to be an effective and revitalizing force in American business, it would need to focus not simply on executive paydays but also on the widespread consequences of its actions. Executives could be winners without workers becoming losers. Business was not a zero-sum game. For America to prosper, the marketplace needed to be fair and democratic.

Twenty

In business, as in life, you often find yourself following a circuitous route; and at the end, you arrive at an unexpected destination with a good measure of surprise. So it was with the twisting progression of deals, would-be deals, and alliances that ultimately led me to become involved in one of the key transactions that changed the face of the entertainment industry—RCA's merger with GE. My participation in this epic union was set in motion by, of all things, my helping to thwart the hostile takeover of a relatively small theme park company.

Sea World, my client, was under siege. The powerful movie and television studio MCA had its sights set on this aquatic playland company; both Lew Wasserman, the legendary chairman and CEO of MCA, and Sidney Sheinberg, the company's president, were convinced that ownership of Sea World would facilitate their growing ambitions in the theme park business. Sea World, however, did not want to be controlled by MCA. I worked with it to prevent a takeover, and we prevailed.

Not long after this aborted takeover, I received a call from MCA saying that Wasserman and Sheinberg would like to meet with me. I expected it would be a bitter, accusatory session, a recitation of all the alleged injustices that had been inflicted on their company in the course of the unsuccessful transaction. I considered finding some excuse that would politely allow me to turn down the invitation. But, truth be told, my hesitation was only momentary. Lew Wasserman was "Mr. Hollywood," a former talent agent who had negotiated the personal contracts of dozens of the biggest movie stars, and then had gone on to help create the modern television and film industry. He was the respected voice of the entertainment business, the man who spoke to Congress and to presidents. And I was a banker who had done significant business in this industry, and hoped to do more. If Lew Wasserman wanted to meet, even if only to upbraid me, I would go.

The conversation did not go as I had expected. I had been sitting across from Wasserman, a tall, white-haired man with a hawklike face, when he leaned toward me and announced, "If we can't beat you, we want you to join us." He explained that he wanted me to serve on MCA's board of directors.

I was not only surprised but flattered—and very interested. Part of the attraction was the chance to work with Wasserman. Another was the opportunity to cement my relationships with two of the country's leading political wise men. Robert Strauss, the influential Washington lawyer who had served as chairman of the Democratic Party, and Howard Baker, a former Republican leader in the Senate, were both board members. And although still a busy deal-making banker, I had also begun to think seriously about public policy issues. I was convinced that hard money and low taxes, combined with heavy investment and higher productivity, would result in increased growth without inflation. I had presented this theory in articles in the *Wall Street Journal* and the *New York Review*. But I also had not totally abandoned the prospect of serving in government. I liked and respected both Strauss and Baker, and perhaps it could be beneficial to have further opportunities to develop my acquaintance with them.

Still, as I made clear to Wasserman and Sheinberg, I had a long-standing relationship with Steve Ross at Warner Brothers.

I was not prepared to walk away from my friend, or his company. Only if Ross was willing to allow me to serve on the MCA board and also represent him would I accept the directorship.

Fortunately, Ross had no objections, and I joined the MCA board.

—

It was a period of dramatic change in the entertainment industry. Cable television and satellite channels were eroding the networks' domination of the airwaves. At the same time, syndication rules protected the studios by keeping television networks from owning the series that ran on the network stations. And alliances were being forged between the studios and pay channels. I would play a significant role in the merger of Time Inc. with Warner Brothers, and it exemplified the entertainment industry's business model for the future: movie studios, television production companies, and cable stations with pay subscribers would all be consolidated under one corporate roof.

It was during this hectic, inventive period of transformations and acquisitions in the business that Wasserman missed what was arguably one of the greatest opportunities of his career. And I, MCA's new director, encouraged and reinforced this wrongheaded move. On my advice, he turned down an opportunity to merge with Disney.

In 1984, Disney was reeling. It had disappointed the investment community with lackluster earnings and, as a result, seemed a prime target for a takeover. In fact, Saul Steinberg, a corporate raider who had failed in his attempt to gain control of Chemical Bank, already had his sights on Disney. As he began to accumulate stock, Disney's anxious management began to look for a more appealing alternative.

Joe Flom, a senior partner at Skadden Arps, represented Disney. He approached Wasserman with the suggestion that MCA merge with Disney. Even in this early discussion, it was made clear that while the deal would be presented to the Hollywood community as a "merger of equals," MCA's management would control the new company.

I met with Wasserman and Sheinberg at Lew's palatial Beverly Hills home to discuss the proposed merger. The two men had deep concerns about the structure of management, the composition of the board, and how these would affect their ability to make forceful decisions in the new, combined company. They also believed that Disney's low valuation in the financial markets would have a profoundly negative effect on the trading price of the new company's shares. It would most likely be a number well below MCA's current stock price.

I disagreed—somewhat. I told them that I had no doubts about their ability to control the new company. Lew's status in the industry was unchallengeable; "wherever you sat," I said, "would be the head of the table." He would be the decision maker.

However, I shared their view about the low price that would be put on the shares of the merged company. And this conservative valuation was one of the greatest mistakes of my career. All that had been necessary, I realized only later, was to have added $1 to the admission price at Disney's theme parks, and the price-earnings ratio would have become very reasonable. Instead, we turned the deal down.

The Bass family wound up taking control of Disney. The Basses brought in Michael Eisner and Frank Wells to run the company. And, among other shrewd moves, they raised the admission price. Their investment in Disney was a great success. Yet, looking at the proposal from the all-knowing perspective of hindsight, I now believe that if Wasserman and I had been a bit more imaginative, an even more profitable merger could have taken place.

Not long after we had walked away from Disney, another ultimately doomed attempt to merge with MCA began to be played out. Thornton Bradshaw, the CEO of RCA, felt he could strengthen both the parent company and its NBC television network by acquiring MCA. And I was in a particularly good position to observe these discussions: not only was I on the MCA board, but for more than two decades I had been an adviser to RCA and the Sarnoff family.

Following General David Sarnoff's retirement in 1970 as chairman of RCA, the company did not flourish. In 1981, though, the frustrated RCA board turned to Thornton Bradshaw, the highly regarded president of Atlantic Richfield, a large energy company.

Bradshaw moved quickly to get rid of many of RCA's extraneous operations. But it still remained an unwieldy and struggling conglomerate. Its flagship network, NBC, was a weak number two to CBS. Innovative Japanese and Korean firms were putting strong pressure on its consumer electronics business. Its position in the defense electronics industry was strong, but certainly not dominant. The company seemed vulnerable to a takeover. And Bradshaw's inspired preventive strategy was to acquire MCA.

For Bradshaw, the deal made good economic sense. The regulations prohibiting the cross-ownership of studios and networks were being eased. Here was an alliance, he was convinced, that would allow NBC to avoid having to pay outside studios huge fees for producing network programming. Billions of dollars could be saved.

Wasserman, too, was intrigued by a merger with a network. The potential synergy with the films and television shows MCA produced was very appealing. Yet in the end, Lew did not want his entertainment company to be under the control of what he felt was basically a defense electronics concern. The two cultures were too different for the marriage to be successful. He ended the discussions.

In their aftermath, however, a disappointed Bradshaw was even more committed to making a suitable alliance. And now that I knew RCA wanted to protect itself with a merger, I was determined to find it a corporate partner.

Twenty-One

The sharks were swimming around RCA. The company's performance, driven by a reinvigorated NBC, had been improving rapidly. But despite an increase in revenue and earnings, its stock price remained flat. This was precisely the sort of financial paradox that suggested an undervalued company. Of course, the corporate raiders couldn't help noticing. And the word went out on Wall Street: RCA was an appealing takeover target.

Irwin Jacobs, a raider in Minneapolis, bought a large block of RCA stock and went hunting for more. Lazard stepped in to discourage him. We let it be known that Thornton Bradshaw, the CEO of RCA, was unwilling to do business with him. Not looking for a prolonged fight, Jacobs kept his position as an investment, but gave up any hope of controlling the company.

The Bendix Corporation was a more serious, and more tenacious, suitor. Headed by William Agee, a hard-charging executive, Bendix was a major automotive and defense industry company. It had quietly begun buying RCA stock. But when it had accumulated slightly over 5 percent, Bendix, under SEC regulations, had no choice but to announce its stake in RCA. Bradshaw was furious, and concerned. He didn't see himself working with Agee; they were men of very different temperaments. So before Bendix could increase its percentage, Bradshaw retained Marty Lipton, an attorney who had made a celebrated career out of defending companies from hostile takeovers, to represent RCA.

I met with Lipton and Bradshaw shortly after the announcement that Bendix had acquired more than 5 percent of RCA. It was Lipton's advice that we go for the jugular.

Agee's name had recently been in the headlines, in both the financial press and the tabloids, because of his extramarital relationship with Mary Cunningham. She was a financial executive whom he had summarily promoted to be his chief adviser, and the press was enjoying its exploration of her meteoric rise in the company. Journalists had reported plenty of salacious facts, and then had gone on to offer a slew of even more provocative rumors and innuendos.

Lipton's strategy was to use Agee's troubles to get rid of our own. He drafted a statement: "We question the wisdom of turning RCA's affairs over to Mr. Agee; he seems to have problems taking care of his own."

When I read this I was aghast. I was uncomfortable about our making such a personal attack. I feared not only that was it unseemly, but that it could backfire: an infuriated Agee would be a dangerous adversary. But Marty and Bradshaw dismissed my squeamishness. The statement was released to the press.

And they were proved right. The tough (snide, actually) tone of the statement gave notice to Agee that an attempted hostile takeover of RCA would be a no-holds-barred fight. He immediately understood that the battle, with all its freewheeling litigation and lawyers' discovery depositions, would focus a probing spotlight not just on Bendix, but on him. The prospect of such scrutiny, and the headlines that would follow, was too disturbing. He abandoned his designs on RCA, and focused on trying to get control of Martin Marietta instead. Yet this new ambition backfired. Allied Signal, led by its own aggressive CEO, Ed Hennessy, swooped in to take over Bendix.

So, RCA had escaped—but perhaps only for the time being. Now Michael Eisner, the CEO of Disney, wanted to acquire the company. And he came to Bradshaw with a plan that had much to recommend it.

Disney's proposal involved acquiring NBC for Disney stock, which would then be distributed to RCA's shareholders. The price of the RCA shares, even without NBC's being part of the valuation, when combined with the allotted Disney shares would give RCA's stockholders a return significantly higher than the present price of RCA. Or so went Eisner's logical and reasonable projection.

Additionally, a deal with Disney would solve a problem that had been one of Bradshaw's major preoccupations—his successor. Bradshaw had recruited Bob Frederick from GE three years earlier, planning that Frederick would eventually run RCA, and had even gone so far as to announce this. But by 1985, Bradshaw had concluded that Frederick, whose expertise was in engineering, was the wrong person to lead a restructured RCA. Now, NBC accounted for almost three-quarters of the RCA profits. And television was a talent business predicated on relationships with people in the entertainment industry; an engineer's intelligence would not be likely to grasp its nuances.

Adding to Bradshaw's misgivings was the fact that Grant Tinker, the executive who had guided NBC's remarkable turnaround, was about to retire. The search for someone to replace Tinker had so far been futile; and the prospect of Frederick, who was basically a nuts-and-bolts guy, attempting to fill that vacuum, too, left Bradshaw even more troubled.

The solution to these problems, Bradshaw became convinced, was Disney. Michael Eisner, the chairman of Disney, had been a senior programming executive at ABC. Bradshaw felt comfortable with Eisner's ability to understand NBC's programming needs, to recruit talent, and to run the network.

But as Bradshaw, Lipton, and I discussed the possible deal, it gradually became clear to us that this was impractical. Splitting RCA in two would be a long, complicated process. And the resulting value of RCA without its flagship network was, despite Eisner's optimistic projection, an uncertainty. Even with the Disney stock added to the package, the valuation could very well be much lower than RCA's current share price. Another concern was that while NBC was being publicly disentangled from RCA, a raider could swoop in and buy large blocks of stock, and Bradshaw and his board could lose control of the process. As our misgivings took hold, the talks with Disney eventually drifted to an end.

—

The discussions with MCA and Disney, however, had made it clear to Bradshaw that his differences with Frederick were fundamental. He was convinced that NBC, especially after Tinker's retirement, could not prosper with Frederick running the parent company. Yet it was too late for Bradshaw to recommend another president for RCA; he had, after all, already publicly announced that Frederick would have the job. The only real solution, Bradshaw confided to me, was the sale or merger of RCA with another company.

But which one? As I thought about it, I realized that, even in theory, there were not many candidates. The ideal partner had to be a big (i.e., Fortune 50) company, with a management and a culture that could deal with RCA's hardware business (the defense and electronics divisions) and software business (NBC). It had to be willing to pay a substantial premium over RCA's depressed market price. And it had to be able to move quickly; if there were protracted merger discussions, the inevitable leaks would attract a slew of corporate raiders who could disrupt the process.

The huge Japanese companies like Sony and Matsushita were aggressively searching for American acquisitions. However, we could not do business with them. A merger with a Japanese corporation would have been impossible because of both RCA's military defense business and the prohibition against foreign ownership of television stations.

The big U.S. communications companies were also not attractive partners. They were giant bureaucracies. A freewheeling, individualistic entertainment company like NBC would have its creativity smothered in such a restrictive corporate atmosphere. And my concerns were not simply intellectual, but pragmatic. It was this creative energy, after all, that was creating nearly three-quarters of RCA's entire annual profit.

In the end, I decided there was only one logical candidate—General Electric. Jack Welch was chairman and CEO of GE, and after just five years of running the company his determination and success had become legendary. He had made it his goal that GE should be in only those businesses where it was either number one or number two in the field, and he had succeeded. Under his leadership, GE's flagging divisions had turned around. The entire company was now prospering. And there was something else: Bill Paley, the CEO of CBS, had told me that Welch had approached him about acquiring the network.

I told Bradshaw that I wanted to talk to Welch. Bradshaw was intrigued, but he was also cautious. He knew that Frederick, who was a losing candidate when Welch had been picked by the GE board, would be vehemently opposed to the deal. And he was also nervous about some of the board members; he was uncertain of their support. Negotiations, Bradshaw insisted, had to be conducted quickly and covertly.

It was decided that I would offer Welch a proposition: if he was interested, he would need to make an offer at a price the board could not ignore. And we required secrecy; there could be only a limited number of people in the loop. If Welch was comfortable with these conditions, then I was authorized to arrange for a meeting with Bradshaw.

With these instructions as my guide, I went off to call Jack Welch.

⸺

"I'm interested," Welch blurted out.

As soon as I mentioned RCA and the purpose of my call, Welch did not hesitate to share his enthusiasm for a prospective merger. He explained that RCA was on the list of promising acquisition targets for GE and he already knew a great deal about the company. Therefore, the possibility of a friendly merger, he said, was particularly appealing.

I then felt it was necessary to explain that while the interest in a merger had a good deal of support at RCA, there might also be a few discordant voices on the board. Frederick, I went on candidly, would no doubt oppose a deal with GE and try to persuade other directors. Welch listened without comment, and I decided that this was a good sign; I knew he was famously opposed to hostile transactions. Finally, I suggested that if he were serious, he should meet with Bradshaw to see if the two of them were compatible. After they talked, we could decide on the next steps.

Let's meet, he agreed.

⸺

The meeting was held on a cold November evening in 1985 at my Fifth Avenue apartment. It had been decided that this location would allow the two CEOs to meet in secret and to talk with candor. I led them into my library, and they settled into armchairs that offered a nighttime view across Central Park toward the illuminated apartment towers on the West Side of

Manhattan. Bradshaw was on his way to a Navy League dinner and wore a tuxedo. Welch teased him about dressing up for the occasion, and that got the meeting off to a friendly, light-spirited start.

The talk was wide-ranging. They discussed the threat from increased foreign competition, changes in the entertainment industry, consumer and defense electronics, the Reagan administration. They seemed to discuss everything but the subject that had brought them together.

Still, over the years I had attended many of these "first date" meetings, and I thought the atmosphere at this one was convivial and promising. They were very different men; however, each possessed the confidence to respect and understand the other's point of view. Bradshaw was an intellectual, a former professor and social liberal who also paid attention to the bottom line. Welch was a hard-driving street fighter, an ebullient force who also realized that to run a business that included NBC would require a more subtle and sophisticated approach.

It was not until the end of their one-hour discussion that a problem—of sorts—surfaced. Bradshaw rose from his armchair, and I saw to my dismay that his tuxedo was covered in white cat hairs. I should have remembered that the chair was a favorite resting place for Figaro, my wife's black-and-white cat. While I muttered embarrassed apologies, Elizabeth, my resourceful wife, rushed into the room to save the day (and perhaps even keep the merger on track). She produced a cylindrical device and began rubbing it vigorously over Bradshaw's dinner jacket. As if by magic, the cat hairs disappeared from the tuxedo. And in the process, everyone enjoyed a good, laugh.

The next day I spoke with both men and emphasized that it was now necessary to move quickly, and in secret. I also, for the first time, gave Welch an indication of what sort of share price we were looking for. That November, RCA's stock was very depressed, fluctuating between $45 and $50 per share. Most analysts, however, agreed this was much too low; and some were even willing to put a $90 per share valuation on the stock. I told Welch that the price would need to be a significant premium over the market. It should start with a "seven," I suggested coyly.

Welch did not comment on the price. He simply said that he had ordered a study team to be formed under the leadership of Mike Carpenter, his director of planning. He would be ready to give us his preliminary analysis of the team's findings in two weeks.

We waited with anticipation. Bradshaw talked to no one other than Lipton and myself about a possible merger with GE. Yet the more we discussed it among ourselves, the more we were convinced the two companies would be a good fit. Then two weeks passed and Welch, true to his word, called.

⸺

Welch asked to meet again with Bradshaw, and this time I thought they should have their discussion without my being present. It turned out to be a friendly conversation, but also a somewhat disappointing one.

Welch announced that he wished to acquire RCA. He said he felt confident about the fit between the two companies. There would be no rush to sell any of RCA's businesses. And he insisted that NBC would be treated no differently from how it always had been. It would be, he said, "an independent company with independent management." These were all encouraging remarks. However, in a moment the mood of the discussion abruptly changed.

Welch stated he was prepared to offer only $61 per share. He realized that this was not the price Bradshaw was anticipating, but, nevertheless, he hoped RCA would consider the offer.

Bradshaw conceded that he was disappointed; the price was too low. But he would nevertheless present it to his board.

I spoke with Bradshaw after the meeting and did my best to rein in his disappointment. I said that this was just Welch's opening bid; that I believed we could push him to between $65 and $70 per share; and that even at $61, we were coming to the board with an offer that was nearly 25 percent over the current market price of RCA stock. Further, this was a friendly bid from a rich and powerful company. The likelihood of negotiating benefits for senior management and key employees was strong; and I could guarantee that this would not be the case in a hostile takeover. Somewhat assuaged, Bradshaw called a special board meeting for the following Sunday.

⟡

We had gone into this board meeting prepared for a difficult, contentious session. The fact that GE was the suitor gave us a good deal of credibility. However, there were other large problems. Directors and senior managers would, I expected, be offended that they had not been included in prior discussions. There was the risk that they would now use every opportunity to criticize a deal that had been worked out behind their backs. Or they might even argue for a full auction of the company to the highest bidder. Compounding the problem was that Bradshaw, although he was a successful CEO, was not an insider at RCA; he had been recruited from outside the company and therefore didn't have any well-established alliances on the board.

The board meeting lived up to all our anxious expectations. Many of the members were livid that things had gone so far without their being informed. John Petty, head of Marine Midland Bank, had strong reservations about the deal. Bob Cizik, chairman of Koppers Industries, also expressed doubts. And Frederick, as we had anticipated, was fiercely opposed. There was a discussion about running an open auction, but Bradshaw was able to persuade the directors that such a course would be long, chaotic, and in the end disastrous for the company. For hours, the angry debate swirled around the room; and I listened with growing doubts about the prospects for this board to endorse a deal that had been initiated without its knowledge.

Finally, it was proposed that a vote be taken: could Bradshaw and Frederick receive authorization to represent RCA in further discussions with GE? Frederick voted "no." Cizik abstained. Petty, meanwhile, had left for the airport to catch a flight to Moscow. In this shaky, rather tentative manner, the resolution was approved. Talks between the two companies could move officially forward. And I was authorized to talk to my friend John Weinberg, cochairman of Goldman Sachs, GE's investment banker.

———

My negotiations with Weinberg progressed quickly and without incident. After all, we both knew that our clients wanted to make this deal. And we also knew that if we allowed our discussions to drag on, leaks would be likely to occur, bringing a flock of other interested parties into the process. I was aiming for a price in the high sixties. Weinberg wanted to pay only about $65 per share. In three days we settled on a price of $66.50. At a total purchase price of $6.28 billion, this would be the largest industrial transaction in history.

The RCA board meeting the next day included the company's senior executives and was another tense, suspicious affair. But Bradshaw handled it well, speaking candidly and with conviction about the benefits of the merger. Frederick, perhaps realizing it was too late to stop the deal, gave it his support, too.

Still, the next few months before the merger was finalized were a rocky time. As soon as the deal was announced in the press, I received calls from companies wanting to bid. Martin Davis of Gulf and Western was one of the first, and he immediately offered to pay more than the $66.50 share price GE had agreed on. I told him the same as I told the other suitors: it was too late; Bradshaw would not hear any new bids.

There was also growing dissent among many of RCA's employees, especially those at NBC. They feared that GE's bottom-line culture would be too narrow-minded to support the creative (and often expensive) decisions that help to make a network successful. These concerns lingered even after the merger, until Welch made a bold and shrewd move. He appointed Bob Wright, head of GE Finance and a former executive vice president of cable operations at Cox Communications, to replace the retiring Grant Tinker. This was an inspired choice, one that was endorsed by Bradshaw and NBC's employees; and it effectively assuaged many suspicions at the network about the new parent company.

But before that calm came about, there was one last crisis. I was in Hawaii with my wife for the Christmas holidays when I received a call from a worried Welch. He had talked to Bradshaw, he told me, and what he had heard made him very nervous. One or two RCA directors were trying to instigate an internal revolt that would remove Bradshaw and cancel the merger with GE. I listened, and now I was nervous, too.

From Hawaii, I got Marty Lipton and Bradshaw on the phone. It was Lipton's advice that we needed to confront the instigators directly in a board meeting—and that this meeting should take place as soon as possible.

During the first week of the New Year, we convened a special meeting of the board. Bradshaw took the floor, and he was masterful. He persuaded the majority of the board to rally behind him, and in the end even the instigators went reluctantly along. The $6 billion merger went forward.

—

A word about Jack Welch. Along with Harold Geneen, he was the most impressive CEO I had ever worked with in my long career. While Geneen was a brilliant manager of numbers, Welch was a similarly brilliant manager of people. He was a creative force, perpetually full of energy, and he expected those around him to have the same traits. He could be a stern and demanding taskmaster, but to my mind he was always fair. He also recognized and appreciated talent; his appointments to key positions were inspired.

Of course, like any businessman, Welch paid attention to the bottom line. He turned GE Capital, a huge operation that financed everything from airplanes to refrigerators, into a moneymaking machine. And the consistent growth in his company's earnings was remarkable.

Yet he did make mistakes. One of his few strategic misjudgments grew out of his fascination with the investment banking business. He was determined to acquire one of the major firms. And he wanted my help.

It was shortly after the RCA deal had been concluded and he was in my office having a cup of coffee, when he abruptly stopped the conversation. He put down his cup, turned to me, and then announced, "I want to buy Lazard."

I had already told him a number of times that I thought purchasing an investment banking firm was a terrible idea. Now I decided to give him some visible proof. I got up from my desk and said, "Jack, let me show you something."

I walked him around the floor, leading him into one after another of the many offices filled with Lazard's bankers. When we had completed this circuit and returned to my office, I posed a single question. "How would you," I asked, "like to have spent a billion dollars for this firm and the next day discover that the offices were empty? That everyone had left for another job?"

But when Welch had an idea in his head, he was a hard man to discourage. He didn't pursue Lazard. Instead, he ultimately acquired Kidder, Peabody. Kidder was an old-line firm that had become immersed in the scandals involving Ivan Boesky. Welch believed he could turn it around. Its problems, however, continued under GE Capital's ownership; accounting irregularities by one of its traders threatened the entire firm. To rescue Kidder, a merger was engineered with Paine Webber, a very successful brokerage house. Welch was able to extricate himself with some Paine Webber stock that was worth only a small portion of his company's original investment in Kidder. Perhaps, I thought, he had at last learned the lessons I had been trying to teach him about the pitfalls of owning a financial concern.

But Jack Welch had the last laugh. When UBS paid a colossal price to take over Paine Webber, he made an enormous profit on the stock he was holding. And I was wrong once again.

Twenty-Two

"Would you like to meet Mike Ovitz?"

The caller on the telephone that September day in 1990, asking me this question was Mort Janklow, one of New York's premier literary agents and a longtime friend. Mort didn't, of course, need to identify Ovitz. I knew he was the head of the Creative Artists Agency, the Hollywood superagent who not only held an impressive list of clients—stars, directors, and screenwriters—but had also represented Sony in its 1988 acquisition of Columbia Pictures. What I didn't know, however, was whether Mort was initiating a social engagement or a business meeting.

When Mort suggested we meet at the Four Seasons for lunch, I had my answer. At lunch, the spacious, light-filled barroom of the Four Seasons is not simply a place to enjoy a good meal. Seated across from one another on the oval, leather-tufted banquettes are many of New York's most prominent figures in finance, real estate, the arts, and publishing. And they share a tacit understanding: lunchtime is also time for business. The meal, while always delicious at the Four Seasons, is only an excuse for another agenda.

And so when I met the two men at the restaurant a week later, I was not too surprised that Mort, after just a few minutes of small talk, rose from the table. I'll leave you two to get better acquainted, he said, and then left.

What did Ovitz want? I wondered. I knew I would find out in due course, so I let the conversation ramble. But at the same time, I also suspected that even our seemingly casual discussion was being steered according to Ovitz's prearranged plan. My first impression was that he was a very precise man. His sentences, his tightly knotted tie, his black hair brushed flat against his scalp—everything about Ovitz seemed to have been arranged with deliberate, almost meticulous care.

It was not an accident, I understood, that we had begun talking about our experiences working with the Japanese. I had represented Sumitomo Bank in its acquiring of a minority interest in Goldman Sachs, and he pretended to be fascinated by my thoughts about the differences between American and Japanese executives. I listened as he chatted amicably about Sony and his role in the Columbia Pictures deal.

Then, as if he were simply making casual lunchtime conversation, Ovitz happened to mention that he now represented another large Japanese electronics company, which was hoping to acquire an American entertainment company. He went on breezily, taking bites of his salad as he enumerated all the reasons for the Japanese company's interest: the supposed synergy between hardware and software; the recycling of Japanese capital; the growing dominance of Japanese electronics companies; and the innovative role Japanese scientists would play in shaping the future of both communications and entertainment.

Yet all the time he was talking, my mind was churning. Was he representing Matsushita or NEC? And what was the target? Time Inc. and Warner Brothers had recently merged; GE had acquired NBC in its deal for RCA; Murdoch owned Fox; Sony had acquired Columbia. That left either Paramount or MCA. Which of those two studios had Ovitz come to talk about?

I didn't have to wait long to find out. Once again in his seemingly absent way, he let our chat drift to some reminiscences about his early career as an agent at William Morris. Then he segued into some earnest pronouncements about his admiration and respect for Lew Wasserman. Wasserman had also started out as an agent, but, Ovitz exclaimed, he had gone on to do much more. Finally, the conversation arrived at the destination he had been guiding it to from the moment we had sat down at the table. "But, of course, you know Lew," he said. "You're a director of MCA."

I now understood why I had been invited for lunch: the target was MCA. And with this revelation, Ovitz's talk, to my relief, became much more direct.

For more than a year, he explained, he had been working with Matsushita to devise a business strategy for this giant company's future. The alliance had led to a series of secret meetings in Hawaii between himself, a team of his colleagues from Creative Artists, and a group of Matsushita's executives. It had been decided in Hawaii that MCA's mix of businesses—motion pictures, records, and theme parks—could fit logically and successfully into Matsushita's plans for long-term growth. A presentation was made in Japan to the senior managers of the company, and they began to consider the idea. Recently a decision had been made at the highest levels of the company, Ovitz announced with a rather grave formality. Matsushita wanted to acquire MCA.

He went on to assure me that the Japanese company respected Wasserman and his standing in the industry. Matsushita was interested only in a "friendly" takeover; it would not pursue a deal unless the deal was supported by MCA's management and board. And, Ovitz added with what struck me as genuine concern, it was essential that Matsushita's interest in MCA remain secret; if any news of a pending deal leaked, the Japanese would peremptorily end the negotiations.

As Ovitz talked, I mentally ran through what little I knew

about Matsushita. Based in Osaka, it was one of Japan's oldest and most conservative companies. Few, if any, American businessmen or bankers had contact with its CEO, or even with its senior officers. Unlike Sony—which was run by a pro-American CEO, Akio Morita—Matsushita was a bit of a mystery to the U.S. business community.

Yet I did know enough to have little doubt that Matsushita, with more than $35 billion in annual sales, had the resources to acquire MCA, a company with $3 billion in sales and a $5 billion market value. I also knew that Lew Wasserman was fearful that MCA did not have the resources to compete on its own in a changing industry; his talks with RCA's Thornton Bradshaw had convinced me of that. He was not in principle opposed to a merger.

Still, I couldn't help wondering if MCA would fit as neatly into Matsushita as Ovitz confidently predicted. The cultural challenges involved in merging a very Jewish, very Hollywood, very inbred organization into a private, well-established, hierarchical Japanese company would be enormous. But I also realized I was getting ahead of myself. It would be foolish to give this any serious thought until it had been presented to Lew Wasserman.

"Have you discussed this with Lew?" I asked Ovitz.

No, he answered. Then he rambled a bit, trying to give the impression that he had been too intimidated to bring up the issue directly with Wasserman. In fact, Ovitz said sheepishly, he was unsure whether Wasserman, knowing the purpose of the discussion, would see him. He wanted my help in arranging a meeting.

This, I realized, was nonsense. Ovitz was well aware that Wasserman would see him, if only to turn down the proposal. However, by asking me to arrange a meeting to discuss the acquisition of MCA, Ovitz would implicitly signal to Wasserman that I was supportive of at least the possibility of this transaction. Further, since I was a director of MCA, my involvement in setting up the initial discussion would mean that I had a fiduciary obligation to give his proposal a fair hearing.

Nevertheless, I told Ovitz that I would call Wasserman; I was certain Lew would listen to his proposal. But before I contacted Lew, Ovitz needed to give me some idea of what price the Japanese had in mind. It would be a waste of everyone's time if all they were planning to offer was a number close to the present $55 share price, I warned. Additionally, I was sure Wasserman would want an assurance that Matsushita would not attempt a hostile bid if MCA rejected its approach.

Ovitz replied that their studies had put a valuation of between $75 to $90 on MCA's shares. This valuation, he added warily, was predicated on due diligence confirming their research.

It was a wide price range, but after all, this was a very preliminary discussion. There would be ample time to negotiate a satisfactory price—if the discussions got that far. Without making a comment about the numbers he had thrown out, I asked if Matsushita's senior executives were prepared to come to the United States to meet with Wasserman.

Secrecy, Ovitz emphasized once again, was a key issue. Yes, senior company officials would be willing to meet, perhaps in Hawaii, perhaps in Los Angeles. But all talks must be kept strictly confidential; nothing must be made public. It was unlikely, he conceded, that Akio Tanii, Matsushita's CEO, would directly involve himself in the discussion.

With that, our lunch ended. I returned to my office at Rockefeller Plaza to call Lew Wasserman. It was only as I was placing the call that I realized I was hungry. I had been so busy focusing on the conversation that I had only nibbled on the meal I had ordered.

As soon as I got Lew Wasserman on the phone and started my report, he insisted I stop. He wanted Sid Sheinberg, MCA's president, to hear this, too. Sid got on an extension, and both men were amused as I described Ovitz's meandering approach. But they were also convinced he was conveying a realistic offer. It was decided that it would be prudent to inform Marty Lipton, the company's outside counsel, of what had happened. And Lew agreed to meet with Ovitz.

I waited a day or so to call Ovitz; in business, it is never wise to appear too eager. I told him that Lew and Sid would see him, but they had agreed to the meeting only contingent on the proposed purchase price of $75 to $90.

Ovitz did not answer directly. He simply said that he had brought in Allen & Company, a powerful and respected investment bank that had long experience in the entertainment industry, to advise Matsushita.

I responded with only a perfunctory comment. But once again I found myself appreciating Ovitz's strategic thinking. He knew that my fellow board member Bob Strauss was a close friend of Herb Allen, the head of Allen. By bringing Allen and Co. in to work with Matsushita, Ovitz had very wisely engineered a point of contact with another board member besides myself. And he had also created, if necessary, another approach to Wasserman.

Not long after ending the conversation with Ovitz, I called Bob Strauss. Even before I had learned of Herb Allen's involvement, Wasserman had instructed me to call Strauss. Bob had been the U.S. trade representative in Japan and he had strong relationships there. He also was a former chairman of the Democratic National Committee and continued to have extraordinary contacts in the federal government. Lew respected Bob, and wanted me to get not just his thoughts on what cultural problems might arise in a merger with a Japanese company, but also his feelings about Washington's reaction.

Bob, in his steady, reasonable way, acknowledged that there would be problems. The different management styles of the two companies would inevitably result in friction. However, it was the likely reaction in Washington that troubled him more. There was genuine anguish in official circles about selling America's cultural heritage to foreigners. Sony owned Columbia. Rupert Murdoch's Australian News Corporation controlled Fox. Giancarlo Parretti, an Italian, had purchased MGM/UA. Only four American-owned studios remained: Warner, Paramount, Disney, and MCA-Universal. And now the Japanese were setting their sights on MCA, the studio that had produced *Jaws, Born on the Fourth of July, ET,* and dozens of other iconic American movies. Its television division had produced such classic series as *Columbo; Magnum, P.I.;* and *The Rockford Files.* The prospect of putting this company, one of the nation's great cultural resources, under foreign control would, Strauss suggested, make influential people in Washington very nervous.

But, Bob said as we concluded our talk, he felt that all the problems in management and in government could be overcome—if Matsushita was willing to offer a reasonable price.

I hung up the phone, and my thoughts, too, turned to a fair price. Ovitz's low number, $75 a share, would, I thought be reasonable. The $90 price would be a great coup. And what would be MCA's alternatives if a merger with Matsushita failed? I knew that raiders had already been accumulating MCA shares. After the stock market crash of October 1987, MCA's shares had skidded to the mid-thirties, and the raiders had first begun to make their moves. My next-door neighbor in Sun Valley, Steve Wynn, the owner of the Mirage and other casinos in Las Vegas, went on a buying spree. Unknown to us, he had acquired 4.9 percent of MCA's stock, and at that point he had sent his friend Merv Adelson to meet with Wasserman. Adelson had a proposition: Wynn wanted Lew's blessing to increase his interest to 20 percent. Lew responded by having me call Wynn. Acting on Lew's instructions, I informed Wynn that his stock purchases were not welcomed by the company. In fact, if he bought one more share, I explained with rigid politeness, we would go to the attorney general of Nevada and demand an investigation of his stock acquisitions, while at the same time our attorneys would litigate his purchases. Wynn eventually sold his MCA shares.

No deal, I had learned too well over the years, comes without its problems. And the more I thought about it, the more I started to believe that a friendly acquisition by Matsushita might offer the least problems and the best future for MCA.

In time, however, I would find myself rethinking this optimistic appraisal. My doubts would soon grow.

Twenty-Three

W
as Matsushita serious? Was there still genuine interest in acquiring MCA? I found myself asking these questions with mounting concern as the weeks after my initial conversation with Ovitz passed, and yet nothing substantive happened. I heard reports that the Japanese had teams of lawyers and financial people scurrying about Creative Artists' offices on Wilshire Boulevard. But the promised meeting with Matsushita's senior executives still remained little more than a promise; the arrangements, Ovitz explained vaguely, were difficult. Then, finally, in mid-October a date was scheduled for Wasserman and Sheinberg to have a discussion with Masahiko Hirata and Keiya Toyonaga, both vice presidents of Matsushita.

In anticipation of this meeting, Wasserman, without intending to do so, did something that quickly energized the long, lumbering process. He called David Geffen.

After Lew Wasserman, Geffen was MCA's second-largest individual shareholder. He owned 10 million shares, with a market value of $550 million. And I had helped him make the deal that had earned him this fortune.

In the early 1970s, Geffen had started a record company in a partnership with Steve Ross and Warner Brothers. But it was a rocky relationship, and when Geffen had a cancer scare, he simply withdrew from the business. He eventually returned, however, and helped lead his company to new prosperity. He released hit after hit.

By 1988, though, Geffen wanted to sell his company and asked me to represent him. I listened; and at the end of our conversation I was still not sure whether his coming to me was nothing more than a strategy to get Ross to rush in with a pre-emptive offer. However, after making sure that Warner and MCA had no objections, I agreed to represent Geffen.

We started with EMI, the British music company, but these talks ended quickly. The discussions with Paramount were more substantive; Martin Davis, Paramount's CEO, wanted to acquire a record company to complement his motion picture and publishing divisions. However, the two men were never able to agree on a management structure that would give Geffen the independence he wanted. And then I got a call from Sid Sheinberg.

"Felix," he began, "you represent Geffen. Right?"

"Yes," I said.

"Is there any reason why we should not buy his business?"

"I can't think of a single one," I answered truthfully.

When I spoke to Geffen, he was immediately enthusiastic: MCA was a powerhouse in the entertainment industry and would have the ability and the resources to promote and distribute his records. But what Geffen, a very canny businessman, also found appealing was the fact that MCA's stock price was relatively depressed. A payoff in company stock would very likely be worth significantly more in the future; the share price, he felt, was certain someday to climb.

I told Wasserman and Sheinberg that we wanted something in the range of $600 million to $700 million. In the end, we made a deal for MCA stock that was worth $550 million. But Geffen's shrewd prediction could soon be proved accurate. If MCA was acquired by Matsushita for even the lowest price that

Ovitz had suggested—$75 per share—Geffen's holdings would increase in value by an additional $200 million.

—

Wasserman had some trouble reaching Geffen but finally found his company's second-biggest shareholder cruising on a yacht off the coast of Greece. Lew detailed Matsushita's interest and the scheduled meeting, and Geffen declared that he was very supportive of a merger. As the call was ending, Lew added that Geffen must not speak to anyone about the pending talks between the two companies. The Japanese were adamant about this; their obsession with secrecy was extraordinary. I understand, said Geffen. No problem.

The next day a story in the *Wall Street Journal* reported Matsushita's interest in MCA. Hollywood was stunned; the match of a stolid manufacturer of consumer electronics with a movie studio was seen by many as neither natural nor propitious. Wall Street, however, was enthusiastic: in a single day MCA's stock climbed from the mid-fifties to a closing price of more than $63.

Ovitz was furious, and I feared with good reason. I suspected that now, with secrecy no longer possible, the Japanese would put an end to any discussion before it had truly started. I was wrong.

The leak had a positive effect on Matsushita. Rather than walking away, the company publicly confirmed its interest in MCA. And now that the secret was out, Matsushita decided to move forward with newfound speed. Ovitz was instructed to proceed with the planned meeting between Matsushita's two vice presidents and Wasserman and Sheinberg.

I spoke with Wasserman after his face-to-face discussion with the two Japanese executives, and he told me it had gone quite well. To my surprise, he said he even felt comfortable with the two Matsushita officials. There had been no discussion of terms. But a time and place had been set to begin negotiations in earnest: we would meet on November 18 in New York.

In anticipation of these discussions, both sides set up their teams. Matsushita would be represented by Ovitz, Allen, Hirata, and Toyonaga. I recruited Luis Rinaldini and Bob Lovejoy from Lazard to assist me. As we prepared, I realized we would be in for a battle. Because MCA's recent earnings had spiraled downward and its theme parks and real estate holdings were continuing to underperform, I believed that $90 per share was out of the question. In fact, I predicted that we would have difficulty getting Matsushita to honor the lower limit, $75.

Before the hard-nosed negotiations began, however, a dinner was arranged so that we could get to know one another. We gathered on Sunday night, November 18, in a private dining room at the Hotel Plaza Athénée, just a short walk from my apartment in Manhattan. Seated at the table in the ornate, dimly lit room were Wasserman, Sheinberg, Hirata, Toyonaga, Ovitz, myself, and two sets of interpreters. It was the oddest, most uncomfortable dinner I have ever had to sit through.

Wasserman rose to make an opening statement welcoming the Japanese executives. We waited as this was translated.

Then it was Hirata's turn to speak. Next he waited as his remarks, too, were translated.

Silence followed. And more silence. Finally, Sheinberg spoke. He pointed his fork at the first course—melon and prosciutto—and remarked, "I hear you have very good melons in Japan."

We waited while this was translated. Then came more silence. At last Hirata had formed an appropriate response in his mind. He replied, "Yes, we have wonderful melons because we have electronically heated hothouses."

And so the meal dragged on and awkwardly on for the next three hours. I walked back to my apartment filled with grim misgivings. If we could not communicate in any meaningful way across a dinner table, how were representatives from the two companies going to be able to work together to run a movie and television studio? Perhaps, I began to speculate, this merger was not a good idea.

But the next day's meeting at Sid Sheinberg's apartment was more reassuring. The Japanese volunteered that they wanted Wasserman and Sheinberg and MCA's other senior executives to operate with considerable autonomy. They agreed to support MCA's capital needs. They also revealed a plan to engineer Matsushita's developing CD, videotape, and laser disc technology so that it would support the films and television shows produced by MCA. The goal, they explained with impressive precision, was to create an integrated global software-hardware company. All this made a great deal of sense, and, encouraged, we agreed to meet that afternoon at the offices at Wachtell Lipton to discuss terms.

Two hours later I walked into a room filled with at least twenty young Japanese men, each dressed in a dark suit, and each armed with a calculator. Hirata and Toyonaga were in charge, but Ovitz did the talking. Without preliminaries, he announced that Matsushita was prepared to offer a price of $60 a share.

I was not too surprised; for weeks he had been suggesting to me that MCA would need to lower its expectations. I simply listened, deliberately silent, as he explained that his team had been shocked to discover the actual weakness of MCA's business. I let him go on in this disparaging way uninterrupted for what seemed to me to be quite a while.

When he was done, I spoke. This offer, I said with what I hoped sounded like steely resolve, was too far away from his original price range of $75 to $90. It smelled of bad faith. I suggested he get authorization from Osaka to make a significantly higher bid. In the meantime, I said as I began gathering up my papers and putting them into my briefcase, we were too far apart to have a meaningful discussion. With a polite "Good afternoon," I then left.

The next day Ovitz upped the offer to $64. I told him we were still far apart and left to meet with Wasserman, Sheinberg, and Strauss at MCA's offices on Park Avenue. I was not happy with the way the negotiations had developed. I felt that Ovitz had railroaded us, and that Lew and Sid would be unable to work in a productive way with Matsushita's executives. I told Lew that as MCA's financial adviser I would have to confirm that $64 per share was a fair offer. However, it was my feeling and business judgment that he was not under any obligation to sell the company. If he thought MCA could do better on its own, I would support that position.

Lew disagreed. He wanted to sell, but at a better price. It was decided that Strauss would meet with Allen to see if it was possible to get the Japanese to increase their offer. But before Strauss left, Lew spoke with Hirata. He informed the Matsushita official that he would convene a conference-call board meeting the next day, Thanksgiving. He would put the $64 offer to the board; however, he would recommend against it.

The next day we gathered at Lipton's offices to initiate the telephone calls to the board members. But before the first call was placed, Allen contacted us. A final offer would be coming from Matsushita. He asked us to postpone the board meeting, and we did.

Hirata and Toyonaga arrived within the hour. Their new offer was $66 a share. The deal could not include their controlling WOR-TV, MCA's independent New York television station; U.S. law prohibited foreign ownership. However, rather than their selling off WOR-TV, Matsushita proposed that the stock of the station would be distributed to MCA's shareholders as an additional compensation. The station's shares were each worth between $5 and $6, and this brought the total value of the deal to about $72. This was close enough to our price objective. We instructed the lawyers to prepare final papers.

But before there could be a deal, the MCA board had to give its approval. The meeting took place on Sunday, November 25, and it was long and contentious. Many of the directors were firmly against the merger. Some thought the price was low. Others worried about the political reaction; the sale of one of America's great cultural forces to foreigners would, they felt, provoke criticism. And there was concern over the fact that Akio Tanii, Matsushita's CEO, had not come to Los Angeles to meet with Wasserman; this was a tacit message, several board members felt, that MCA would always be treated as a humbled, ineffectual partner.

I informed the board members that in my opinion the price was fair. And I reminded them that it had been public knowledge for the past two months that MCA was considering a sale. In this time, no other bidder had stepped forward. If the board wanted to sell, this offer might be the best we could ever get.

At the end of a long day, the board voted to accept Matsushita's offer. The $6.6 billion deal was the largest nonindustrial acquisition in American history.

—

Yet I was not happy. The next morning Ovitz hosted a lavish champagne breakfast to celebrate. Dozens of people came up to me to offer their congratulations. This deal, I was told, was one more huge success for me and for Lazard. But I could not help feeling that it would not work out. The personalities and cultures were too different to work together smoothly.

The next day brought further intimations that my instincts would prove correct. At a press conference in Osaka, Akio Tanii,

Matsushita's CEO, was asked whether Universal would be allowed to produce an anti-Japanese film. He responded, "Something like that should not emerge. Filmmakers must create films that are inspirational, that will be enjoyable for everyone."

Universal's creative people were incensed. They feared that a group of electronics manufacturers in Osaka would soon be censoring their films. Tanii was forced to issue a mollifying statement. But suspicions lingered.

The relationship between the two companies never worked. Wasserman and Sheinberg were treated without respect. One example: When they attempted to acquire a 25 percent interest in CBS, the two men were summoned to Osaka. They were left waiting for hours before they were ushered into the offices of a senior executive. Then, without even the pretense of a discussion, their proposal was abruptly rejected.

In April 1997, Matsushita, without any prior discussions with the MCA management, announced that it was selling MCA to Seagram, a company owned by the Bronfman family. Once again Ovitz had negotiated this transaction. He waited until a mere fifteen minutes before the public announcement of the sale to inform Wasserman. "A confidentiality agreement," he explained to Lew, had left him no choice but to keep silent. Wasserman never spoke to him again.

As Seagram's deal became public, I discovered without any satisfaction that I, in a small way, had helped make it possible. Edgar Bronfman, Jr., was fascinated with the entertainment business, and he had agreed to acquire MCA from Matsushita for nearly $6 billion in cash. To raise this colossal sum, Seagram had to dispose of one of its main assets—its 26 percent interest in du Pont. I had been instrumental back in 1981 in Seagram's acquisition of that company.

Du Pont had been a spectacularly profitable investment for Seagram. And now I felt it was a mistake to dispose of this stable asset, a company paying growing dividends, in order to acquire a risky entertainment company that used up more capital than it produced. In time, I would be proved right.

Yet the entire MCA saga would help to teach me an important business lesson. Wasserman was driven to make his deal by looking largely at the bottom line. The price Matsushita was offering had persuaded him to ignore the differences between the two companies. Bronfman, on the other hand, seemingly ignored bottom line considerations. He made a deal because he was determined to be in the entertainment business. For a merger to be successful, I had come to realize, a delicate but well-balanced mix was required. The numbers had to add up; and the people doing the addition had to be able to work together.

Twenty-Four

The 1990s moved forward as a hard fought yet also productive and profitable decade for me. In the wake of our role in the $14 billion Time-Warner merger, I went to war alongside my Lazard team as Viacom struggled to gain control of Paramount, Comcast took over a reluctant QVC, CBS held off a hostile bid from QVC, and Dreyfus was sold to Mellon Bank. I was also active politically, one of the many voices urging, without success, that Mario Cuomo run for president in 1992. And I was still chairman of MAC.

Nevertheless, as the decade moved closer toward the start of a new century and I moved deeper into my sixties, I began to think that the time had come to make some changes in my life. I had a lifetime contract at Lazard, but I now thought seriously about retirement. Part of my reason was that Lazard no longer resembled the firm where I had worked for my entire professional life. It had grown not simply bigger, but also more cumbersome. It was no longer the rarefied and collegial investment bank that André Meyer had envisioned. Now there were separate and competing fiefdoms as our business expanded beyond investment banking into other aspects of financial management, and the possibility loomed of a potentially contentious merger that would further increase our size. I had also decided I needed to do something different with my own life. Over the past five decades I had done enough deals. I did not want to be only an investment banker.

But what should I do next? Once again, fate led me on a cir-cuitous route; a journey of opportunities and disappointments. Yet when I finally reached my destination, it was as gratifying as it was unexpected.

—

It was the winter of 1996, and my wife and I were in the Aus-trian village of Zurs for a few days of skiing and relaxation, when opportunity struck. I had just returned from the slopes and was hoping to get some rest before dinner when the phone rang. It was Roger Altman, then deputy secretary of the trea-sury. Lew Preston, the president of the World Bank, he told me, had an advancing cancer and was forced to resign. President Clinton wanted to know if I would be interested in the job.

It was tempting. For two days, instead of skiing, Elizabeth and I spent our vacation mulling over the offer. The World Bank is one of the great financial institutions, and the president of the World Bank can potentially serve as an important agent for global economic transformation. However, Lew and Patsy Pres-ton were close friends of ours. Elizabeth knew from Patsy about the peripatetic, demanding life the CEO of the World Bank was required to lead. My business activities and my involvement with New York City had already placed burdens on our family life over the years of our marriage. And when I telephoned Lew for advice, he candidly told me, as one old friend to another, "You would hate it, and Liz would hate it." The bureaucracy was massive and entrenched, and the bank's ability to effect real change was frustrating, if not impossible. At the end of the second day of Elizabeth's and my discussions, I called Altman. "I appreciate the compliment," I said. "But I do not wish to be considered."

Then came the disappointment. In late 1996, when I was at the White House as a participant in a fiscal policy conference, Dr. Laura Tyson, President Clinton's chief economic adviser, asked me to stay behind for a few minutes. There was a vacancy at the Fed, she told me as we huddled, and she'd like some suggestions for the position. I agreed that I would think about some names. But in the next moment I impetuously set in motion a process I would soon find myself regretting. According to stories I had read in the press, I told Tyson, Alan Blinder, the vice chairman of the Fed, was considering stepping down. If he did, I volunteered, I might be interested in that job. I added that the possibility of my pushing for a more rapid economic growth policy was very appealing. Tyson seemed surprised, but said she would let the president know about our conversation.

When I returned to New York and discussed what had happened with my wife, Elizabeth said I had made a tremendous mistake. The vice chairman of the Fed, she said, was a non-job. Alan Greenspan's authority was total; any other opinion would be irrelevant. "How would you have liked it," Elizabeth asked pointedly, "if Mario Cuomo had appointed Alan Greenspan as vice chairman while you were still chairman of MAC?" And she offered some loving advice: "You don't need to do this simply to have a reason to leave Lazard. You should have left some time ago. All you have to do is retire."

I should have listened to my wife. But I had the arrogance and the innocence to think that because I had the right credentials and the right relationships the prestigious job would be mine. I was wrong.

Events, though, started out encouragingly. After Alan Blinder announced his retirement, the *Wall Street Journal* reported that I would be named vice chairman. The leak, I understood, had to have come from the White House. And the day brought additional reason to be optimistic. Mack McLarty, the former White House chief of staff who remained a presidential counselor, called to tell me he was in charge of my nomination process. The White House, he announced to my delight, did not foresee any problems.

But over the next several weeks there were problems—and then more problems. I was being attacked, but I did not even know who was doing the attacking. Unattributed negative comments kept appearing in the press, alleging inaccurately that I was for cheap money and a weak dollar, and that I had irresponsible views on growth. I began to hear that Alan Greenspan at the Fed and Bob Rubin at Treasury were unwilling to support my appointment. Then the *Washington Post* reported that Leon Panetta, the White House chief of staff, was convinced there was not a single Republican vote in the Senate in support of my nomination.

The article, I assumed, had been leaked by the White House and that the president had no desire to fight for my appointment. I decided there was little point in trying to join a club where even your friends don't want to admit you.

In my letter to the president withdrawing my name from the appointment process, I tried to confront my anonymous critics by clearly articulating my economic philosophy. I wrote that I had long stood for principles of "financial integrity, strong credit, balanced budgets, a strong currency, and low inflation." I believed in the "need for higher rates of economic growth, as well as a role for government in order to deal with the social and economic problems created by globalization of the economy and rapid technological change. I make no apologies for these views."

What I did not mention, however, was the sense of disappointment I felt at not getting the job—and at finding my nomination opposed by people I thought would support it.

There is also a coda to this story. At the time my nomination was still being considered, Greenspan had told the *Washington Post* that aiming for a higher targeted economic growth rate would result in inflation, and a columnist wrote in the *New York Times* that I was "living with a delightful fairy tale." But the Fed's policy soon changed. Alan Greenspan became a strong proponent of the idea that advances in American technology could promote higher growth without inflation. The economy, in fact, did grow at 4 to 5 percent annually without an increase in either interest rates or inflation.

—

I returned to Lazard and went about my work. Yet I was restless, still uncertain about what I should do next. Then dinner with a friend in Paris set in motion an opportunity that would change the course of my life.

Twenty-Five

Pamela Harriman was angry. My wife and I were in Paris shortly before Thanksgiving 1996, and we had invited Pamela to dinner. She was the American ambassador to France, but the tone of her conversation that evening was decidedly undiplomatic. More troublesome, the brunt of her rage was directed at my wife Elizabeth.

A recent biography detailing Pamela's marriages to Randolph Churchill and Averell Harriman as well as her romances with the fabulously wealthy Aly Khan, Gianni Agnelli, and Elie De Rothschild had left her feeling demeaned and slandered. And compounding her anger over what she felt were scurrilous allegations was the author's recent appearance at a forum at the New York Public Library. My wife, Elizabeth, was chairman of the Library; Pamela was now arguing that Elizabeth should not have allowed the reading to occur.

"This happened on your watch," Pamela snapped. "It was your responsibility to prevent this from happening. You should not allow yellow journalism at the library."

Elizabeth was taken aback by the fury of our friend's attack, but her response was firm: "We do not censor the authors who read from their books at the library." Besides, Elizabeth pointed out, the publicity generated by a cancellation would surely have been more damaging than the reading; it would have put the book on the front page of the *New York Times*.

Pamela, however, refused to be mollified. Cautiously, I stepped into the fray. What about the expulsion from France of several members of the embassy's CIA station? I asked, referring to an incident that had created recent headlines. Their controversial activities occurred "on your watch." Nevertheless, I suggested, it would be absurd to believe that Pamela had condoned, or for that matter had prior knowledge, of their actions.

My argument apparently was persuasive; and as she let it sink in, her temper downshifted. By dessert we were once more three friends having a rich, indulgent meal in a candlelit restaurant on the Right Bank, and enjoying each other's company.

Caught up in this comfortable, affable mood, Pamela, as we finished our bottle of wine, asked me for a favor. Would I accompany her tomorrow on a visit to Edouard Balladur? She wanted my help in trying to convince Balladur, a former prime minister and President Jacques Chirac's main conservative rival, that the U.S. government was not involved in a sinister covert plot to drive down the dollar against the franc and subvert the euro. I agreed to go with her; but I was not sanguine that reason would prevail.

The next day's discussion with Balladur was a courteous, tactful affair. Pamela, with a diplomat's practicality, seemed to think that this was victory enough. And she suggested that during his forthcoming trip to New York Balladur might want to attend a lunch with a group of American CEOs of my choosing. Both the former prime minister and I politely agreed that such a luncheon would be beneficial; although neither of us, I suspect, had much hope that anyone would leave the meal with changed opinions.

When we returned to the embassy, Pamela's often mercurial moods now found a somber pitch. Her words had the earnest gravity of a heartfelt confession.

I have decided not to seek reappointment, she revealed. She

needed to get back to Washington. Numerous legal problems with the Harriman family involving the settlement of her late husband's estate needed to be addressed. Anyway, Pamela went on, she had done everything she had wanted to do in Paris. All that concerned her now was her successor. It was important that someone with a European background be appointed as ambassador.

I listened attentively, but I was not sure where the conversation was leading, or if there was a specific reason Pamela was sharing her thoughts with me. In the next moment, though, I found out, to my surprise.

"It should be someone like you," she said. "Would you be interested? I have to see Clinton next week and make my recommendations."

I had never before thought about being an ambassador. I did not know much about the job, but what I had observed on my visits to the embassy gave me pause: a world of rigid protocol and constant social engagements. Yet I had been planning to leave Lazard, and I had been looking for a substantive alternative, especially after my unsuccessful attempt to be appointed to the Fed. Becoming the American ambassador to France would be a great honor. And it was a job I felt I could do well. I had lived in France as a child. I spoke the language fluently. France had always been an essential part of my life: I had a network of French friends, family, and business and political relationships. Also, the most crucial issues facing France at this time arguably were economic. This was an arena in which I had both experience and a confident philosophy. France was, I felt, a country where I could make a difference.

"I'm flattered," I told Pamela. But before I could respond further, I said I would need to have a discussion with Elizabeth. I told Pamela that if the ambassadorship was something we both wanted, I then would ask her to suggest my name to President Clinton.

—

Elizabeth was not delighted by the prospect. She was happy with our life in New York, her work as chairman of the New York Public Library, and being able to spend time with her grandchild. She had no doubt that the role of an ambassador's wife would be demanding, as well as a challenge. Yet, as always, she was also sympathetic to my wishes. She knew I wanted to redirect my life away from investment banking. And she was aware of how deeply France and its politics and culture had remained a part of my being.

I had escaped from Nazi-occupied France as a twelve-year-old Jewish immigrant from Austria in 1940. I became a proud and loyal American; in my new homeland I made my life, married, and raised my sons. But I had never lost my ties to France, or my involvement in the country.

Lazard had always played a major role in French investment banking. André Meyer, in fact, had been one of the most powerful men in the country and he had introduced me to the French business and political establishment.

Beginning in the mid-1960s, I had assisted Pechiney, a large French aluminum company, to acquire Howmet, an American aluminum fabricator and manufacturer of jet engine parts. In the 1970s, I had helped Renault, France's nationalized auto company, acquire control of American Motors and Mack Truck and was appointed to its board. As a result, I began to meet French government officials.

I worked closely with Bernard Vernier-Palliez, the very British-sounding chairman of Renault, and our friendship continued after he was appointed French ambassador to the United States. However, the most significant relationship I had was with Jean Riboud.

A man of charm, intelligence, and culture, Riboud was CEO of Schlumberger, the world's largest oil service company. He was France's leading socialist business figure, a survivor of Buchenwald and a close friend of François Mitterrand, the leader of the French socialist party. I had started working with Jean on Schlumberger business, and our discussions moved on to politics; he was, in reality, more of a Social Democrat than a socialist. In time, Jean asked me to join his board and handle the company's banking relationship with Lazard.

When François Mitterrand was elected president of France in 1981, defeating the conservative Valéry Giscard d'Estaing in a close election, the American reaction was one of concern. Mitterrand had included communist ministers in his government and proceeded to nationalize a large portion of France's industrial and financial sectors. In response, President Ronald Reagan had appointed Evan Galbraith, a highly conservative, fiercely anticommunist Republican, as ambassador to France. It was during this period of tension and suspicion between the two nations that Riboud first introduced me to Mitterrand.

Riboud and I were received in an ornate salon at the Élysée Palace by Jacques Attali, the president's chief of staff. A prolific writer, historian, playwright, and economist, Attali was one of the many intellectuals in Mitterrand's inner circle. When Attali brought us into Mitterrand's small office, I immediately thought of a mandarin. With his long-fingered hands steepled beneath his chin, he spoke in a quiet, almost hushed voice. An economic summit was about to take place in Ottawa, and he wanted my impressions of Ronald Reagan—or, as Mitterrand referred to him, "the movie actor turned president."

To Mitterrand and his socialist colleagues, I must have been a unique American: a capitalist with a liberal conscience; an investment banker who voted democratic; an American who spoke their language and knew their country. My economic views were far to the right of the socialists, but when I was compared with the Republican officials from the Reagan administration they routinely encountered, I was seen, I suspect, as one of their own.

Mitterrand asked a few questions about the American president, and then the conversation turned to New York. How had we managed, he wondered with what struck me as genuine astonishment, to get the municipal labor unions to agree to make sacrifices? How had we been able to get unions and businesses to work together on a plan to rescue the city? How had we handled strikes? What about the intervention from the state and the federal government? And how was it that I, a Jewish millionaire investment banker, had been acceptable to both labor and capital?

I explained that I had attempted to model my response to New York's economic crisis on the actions of Jean Monnet. Monnet's determination to get unions and businesses working together during the reconstruction of Europe during the 1950s had been my inspiration.

"You must come to France and do for us what you did for New York," Mitterrand said. "We have many similar problems."

I explained that while I was flattered by the suggestion, I was uncertain whether what had worked in New York could work in France. I added, "I was able to do what I did, Mr. President, because I am a New Yorker and I live there. I was working in my hometown."

"Never mind that," said Mitterrand, "We have brought other people to France to help us. We make them cardinals. We will make you a cardinal."

I replied that this was an almost irresistible offer for a Jewish boy whose great-grandfather had been a rabbi in a Polish shtetl.

Mitterrand never appointed me a cardinal, but we became

friends. Over the years I saw him regularly—at the Élysée Palace; at his modest house on the Left Bank; at his country home in southwest France; and at Jean Riboud's house near Lyon. He appointed me to the board of directors of Pechiney when the aluminum producer was under government ownership. And he twice awarded me decorations at the Élysée Palace, elevating me to the rank of Commander of the Legion of Honor and Elizabeth to the rank of Officer.

Now I was being asked if I wanted to be considered as a candidate for the American ambassadorship to France. As Elizabeth and I discussed Pamela Harriman's offer, we both soon came to the same conclusion: this was an opportunity I could not turn down.

I called Pamela and told her that if she was prepared to recommend me to the president, I was prepared to throw myself into the appointment process.

Pamela sounded delighted.

After we returned from our trip to France, I made it my business to go to Washington. I wanted to speak with my friend Vernon Jordan. Jordan was not simply an adviser to the president; he was Bill Clinton's close friend. He would be able to give me an accurate appraisal of whether there was a realistic hope that I could become the ambassador.

Vernon confirmed that Pamela was not going to be reappointed. He was also enthusiastic about my replacing her. It would be, he said, an excellent opportunity for me, as well as an excellent appointment for the president. He added that Clinton still felt bad about the fiasco surrounding my stillborn appointment to the Fed.

A few days after our conversation, Jordan called. He had talked to the president, and he believed the nomination would happen. "Don't do anything else," he instructed. "They will take care of it from the White House."

I thanked him and went to tell Elizabeth. But I also could not help recalling that Mack McLarty, the White House counsel, had been confident when he had first called me about the vice chairman's job at the Fed.

Twenty-Six

Weeks passed, and I heard nothing more about the ambassadorship. But I was not overly concerned. Clinton had just been elected to a second term, and there was a new cabinet to appoint. Then I received a phone call from France. And after that conversation, I was not only concerned but unnerved. I felt let down.

The caller was someone who worked closely, I knew, with Pamela Harriman at the embassy. However, the caller (and years later I still feel that discretion requires that I do not reveal the name) made it clear that she was telephoning me from outside the embassy; she did not want a record of our conversation. Her call was a warning: Pamela was trying to torpedo my nomination.

Apparently, Pamela now wanted Frank Wisner, a career diplomat who was the ambassador to India, to succeed her. Further, the caller believed that this effort to get Wisner the post would be successful. Pamela had already gotten support for her new candidate from allies in the State Department and the White House, including such influential officials as Deputy Secretary of State Strobe Talbott, Undersecretary of State Peter Tarnoff, and National Security Adviser Sandy Berger. "You're not going to get the post," the caller concluded. "You should try for another ambassadorship. Perhaps London."

I thanked the caller, and hung up the phone. My mind was

reeling from the devious machinations in which I had become entangled. I felt betrayed—lied to!—by a friend. Wisner was a first-rate diplomat; I was sure he would do a fine job in France. I certainly was not prepared to attack him. I was also not going to try to obtain the ambassadorship at another embassy. France was where I could do the best job. I quickly decided I would not meekly surrender my chance to represent my country in France. I would not simply walk away from the battles that loomed in Washington. I would fight to get the post.

My first move was to call Vernon Jordan. He was surprised by my news, and promised to find out if it was accurate. Vernon managed to track down Strobe Talbott, who was on a cruise in the Caribbean, and Talbott confirmed the gist of what I had already reported. Tarnoff, Berger, and he were in agreement: Wisner should be appointed. However, Talbott candidly added, the president had not yet made up his mind. Vernon ended the conversation by informing Talbott that his own choice was unchanged: Rohatyn should become ambassador to France.

In the weeks that followed, Pamela, now back in Washington, stepped up her efforts to undermine me. She spoke about how my "relationship" with Edouard Balladur would cause problems for Clinton; Jacques Chirac had, she pointed out, narrowly defeated Balladur in the 1995 French presidential election, and the two men remained bitter rivals.

This accusation was particularly infuriating. My so-called "relationship" with Balladur consisted of a single lunch I had hosted for him in New York with American CEOs—at the request of Pamela Harriman. She had even written me a note to thank me for arranging the luncheon. I passed on her letter to Vernon Jordan, and that was the last I heard of my "relationship" with Balladur. However, I had little doubts that Pamela was whispering the same maliciously inflated accusation to members of Chirac's circle, in the hope that they would work from Paris to stop my nomination.

Inevitably, the newspapers got hold of the debate within the administration involving who should be appointed ambassador to France. I did not enjoy being caught up once again in a public controversy involving my assuming a government position.

I also knew Wisner had many loyal friends and supporters both in and out of government. His father was one of the founders of the CIA; his mother was part of Washington's social establishment. So I was not totally surprised when Assistant Secretary of State Dick Holbrooke advised me to try to get appointed to London. It would be a mistake, he said, to try to succeed Pamela in Paris, because she had been "our best ambassador to France since Thomas Jefferson."

As the controversy continued to swirl, I could not help wondering if this process would inevitably play out like my nomination to the Federal Reserve—a disappointing failure. I called Vernon and asked whether I should withdraw.

I'm still on your side, Vernon announced. So is Erskine Bowles, the president's chief of staff. And, most important, he said, President Clinton is determined that you should go to Paris.

So, I waited. And then in February 1997, Pamela Harriman died. She died while swimming her daily laps in the basement pool at the Ritz Hotel, not far from the embassy in Paris. There was one memorial service in Paris, at which her life and career were praised by France's political establishment, and another similarly grand ceremony at the National Cathedral in Washington, attended by President Clinton.

Yet even after her death, the debate surrounding who should succeed her continued. The diplomats supported Wisner. Jordan and Bowles stuck by me. If this prolonged debate continued much longer, even winning might be an embarrassment. Elizabeth and I made a plan: we would go to London for a long weekend, and if there was still no decision by our return, then I would officially withdraw.

At about 10:30 the night before our departure for London, Vernon Jordan called. I immediately detected hesitancy in his usually effusive voice. Finally, he blurted it out. "There is still no decision on Paris," he said. And then rather sheepishly he added, "But the president wants you to go to Tokyo."

I was stunned. There had been six months of discussions about Paris, and now the president thought I should become ambassador to Japan? It made no sense. I started to explain this to Vernon, but he cut me off. You should speak with Bowles, he suggested.

Bowles was direct. "Felix," he said, "the president thinks you could make an enormous contribution by representing us in Tokyo. Japan is in terrible financial condition. They need help. They know you, and would listen to you. If you say you are willing to go, I am authorized to tell you that the president will offer you the nomination to Tokyo tomorrow."

"Erskine," I responded, all the time trying to control my building frustration, "I have spent a fifty-year career in finance. In all those years, I have not spent more than a total of two weeks in Japan. Of the three hundred or so mergers that I have negotiated, at most only five have involved Japanese companies. I do not speak a word of Japanese. I have practically no relationships there. I have little knowledge of Japanese history. I am utterly unqualified and would embarrass myself as well as the president at a confirmation hearing."

I let that sink in, and then I asked, "And what about Tom Foley?" I had heard that Foley, the Democratic speaker of the House, had been scheduled to go to Tokyo.

Bowles did not respond to my arguments. Instead, his comments remained both terse and matter-of-fact. "The president thinks you can do the job. No commitment has been made to Tom Foley."

"What about Paris?" I asked, sounding, I realized, a bit desperate.

"Paris is very complicated," Bowles answered. "It is still a possibility, but it is a long shot. Tokyo is yours for the asking."

It was almost ludicrous. I felt that the State Department was being run the way the army was during my time in the service. If you've been a chef as a civilian, the army assigns you to the motor pool. If you know France, the State Department sends you to Japan. I told Bowles that I would consider the president's request, but if he needed an immediate answer, my response was "no." I also added that I might very well withdraw from any consideration; the process was simply too frustrating. I ended the call by saying I would call Monday, on my return from London.

When I got back to New York, one of the first calls I received was from my friend Dick Beattie. Over the weekend, he had learned that Frank Wisner would retire from the Foreign Service to become vice chairman of AIG, the giant insurance company. The competition for Paris, I decided, was quite possibly over.

I also now had a clearer understanding of what had happened in Washington. To persuade Wisner not to retire, his supporters at the State Department had no doubt told him Paris was his for the asking. And to make that a reality, they had to tell the president I would willingly accept another assignment—the Tokyo post. The machinations in Washington, I was beginning to appreciate, were even more complicated than those in business.

When I called Bowles later that day, I decided not to reveal that I knew about Wisner's withdrawal; I, too, after all, could

Felix Rohatyn

play a strategic game. I merely informed him that I was still interested in the Paris post. If it opened up in the next few days,
I would gladly accept the nomination. If not, I would want my
name withdrawn.

About a week later, in April 1997, Sandy Berger called: the
president was officially nominating me to be ambassador to
France.

—⁓—

I chose Dick Beattie and Lloyd Cutler to represent me as my attorneys and advisers at my Senate confirmation hearings. The
process was scheduled to be on a fast track; there had been no
American ambassador to France since January. It was hoped
that I could be approved before the August congressional re-
cess and take up residence in Paris before September. Yet from
the start, we anticipated a difficult time. Senator Jesse Helms of
North Carolina was chairman of the Senate Foreign Relations
Committee, and the committee had not confirmed a single political appointee in some time.

A right-wing Republican who vehemently opposed the Clinton administration, Helms refused to schedule hearings. And
the administration, embarrassed by a succession of fund-raising
scandals, including overnight stays by big contributors in the
Lincoln bedroom and foreign contributions, was reluctant to
press for a public forum that would allow Helms to unearth
new dirt.

I also suspected that Helms would relish an opportunity to
lead an attack against my nomination. I had never met him, but
I had contributed modestly to the campaign of one of his oppo-
nents. And I could imagine his knee-jerk reaction against an active liberal, an important contributor to the Democratic Party,
and, not least, a New Yorker.

But I was wrong. When my friend Senator Chris Dodd of

Connecticut spoke to Helms about my confirmation, Helms said he admired my record and my accomplishments. And his actions proved it.

I was confirmed in time to arrive in Paris at the tail end of summer.

Twenty-Seven

As our car approached 41 rue du Faubourg Saint-Honoré, the residence of the U.S. ambassador, a pair of huge, heavy doors opened slowly. We drove under a tall archway into the cobbled courtyard of our new home—one of the most splendid *hôtels particuliers* in Paris.

We stepped into a grand entrance hall built in the mid-nineteenth century and designed by Louis Visconti, the same architect who had built the Louvre. The first-floor reception rooms were both elaborate and enormous, and seemed to glitter under the glow of great crystal chandeliers. It was like entering a palace, and we could not help feeling daunted by the magnificence. With almost gleeful excitement, we made our way up a sweeping marble staircase to the third floor apartment where we would live.

Yet the next day my official duties began sadly. On our first night in the residence, after Elizabeth and I went to bed exhausted, only to be awakened by a tremendous noise. It sounded as if a bomb had gone off. This was followed by the harsh wail of sirens. All through the night, the sirens continued, loud and insistent. It sounded as if Paris was under attack.

In the morning, I was awakened by my assistant and given my first diplomatic assignment. I was to deliver a letter from President Clinton to the British ambassador to France offering his condolences on the death of Princess Diana.

Unfortunately, the sad circumstances surrounding my posting continued. Within a few months Elizabeth was diagnosed with cancer. Dr. Paul Marks—our friend, and the president of the Memorial Sloan-Kettering Cancer Center in Manhattan—advised that she move back to New York for her treatment. She did; and every weekend I flew back and forth between Paris and New York to be with her.

It was an anxious, difficult time. I relied on Bob Pearson, my deputy chief of mission, and his wife, Maggie, the embassy's press attaché, to help me with both my duties and the running of an embassy that had more than 1,000 employees, including about 700 French citizens. Bob, a former navy man, had a true gift for getting things done despite the often plodding State Department bureaucracy. And Maggie was adroit at handling the media. They both were extraordinarily competent; and they also grew to be our close friends.

By late spring, Elizabeth was on the mend, and to my great joy, she was judged by her doctors fit enough to return to Paris and take up her official duties. We celebrated her return by hosting a Casablanca-themed party. It was a wonderful night, and I felt as if my ambassadorship could now at last truly begin.

—

The French, as well as many other Europeans, have conflicted thoughts about their own reformed version of market capitalism. The conservatives are suspicious of the markets; the socialists are suspicious of wealth. Yet both the political right and the political left insist on a significant role for government in their economy and a guaranteed high level of economic security for all citizens. And both political wings were in nearly unanimous agreement about American capitalism: it was a force to be viewed with great suspicion.

I decided to incorporate into my official and social duties

an explanation of our form of "popular capitalism." I wanted to be a champion of American economic life, its opportunities, and its accomplishments. I wanted to try to erase many of the theories some of the French had about the way our economy was manipulated and how the marketplace catered only to the rich. I went throughout France, meeting with mayors, prefects, and businessmen, and I always tried to educate them about the democratic power in our American marketplace.

Elizabeth would often accompany me on these official trips around the country. While I was meeting with representatives from the local government or businesses, she would usually be given a tour of the town's museum. As chairman of the New York Public Library, she had been immersed in cultural issues; she supervised programs that reached out across the city to schools, museums, and neighborhood libraries. Now, as she traveled around France, she began to envision creating a formalized relationship between regional French museums and their American counterparts—a cultural diplomacy project that could exchange resources and museum staff members, as well as sponsor exhibitions.

Working with Bill Barrett, my assistant, Elizabeth devised a preliminary proposal for this art exchange program. Then I put both of them in touch with John Bryan, chairman of Sara Lee in Chicago. Bryan oversaw one of the world's great corporate art collections and dealt regularly with museums, and he suggested they talk with Dr. Richard Brettell.

Brettell, former curator of European painting at the Art Institute of Chicago, former director of the Dallas Museum of Art, and an expert on the French impressionists, was in Lyon to return an important Pissaro that had been on loan to the Chicago museum. Elizabeth met with him and asked his help in establishing a network connecting regional French and American museums.

Dealings

In November 1998, the Musée des Beaux-Arts of Lyon hosted a meeting of eighteen regional art museums: nine from France, and nine from the United States. The result was FRAME—the French Regional and American Museum Exchange. It grew to include twenty-five museums, a network visited on a typical day by hundreds of thousands of people. These cultural connections also helped to reinforce trade and economic alliances between French and American cities; and local mayors and prefects were eager for their cities to join. Another benefit: since French mayors were members of parliament, we now had strategic access to this powerful governing body, too.

The success of FRAME in the regions beyond Paris suggested that what worked for culture could work for commerce. I knew from my decades of business dealings in France that the true engines of the country's economic development and progress were its large regional cites. I was determined that our diplomatic mission would not ignore these bustling, innovative business centers.

Therefore, we established seven American Presence Posts (APPs) as (in a sense) mini-consulates in Lyon, Bordeaux, Rennes, Grenoble, Lille, and Toulouse. Trade relationships between businesses in the regions across France and American cities were facilitated. And, no less gratifying, we were able to convince previously hostile senators and congressmen of the value of the APP offices and exchange programs.

In fact, when I went to Washington for a series of meetings to discuss, among other issues, my APP plan with a supportive Secretary of State Albright and President Clinton, I also scheduled a meeting with Senator Jesse Helms of North Carolina, the chairman of the Senate Foreign Relations Committee. Although Helms had surprised me by supporting my confirmation as ambassador, I went in to see him with some trepidation; he was still a far-right Republican who, according to legend, did not even have a passport. I assumed he would be skeptical about a plan by a liberal New Yorker to expand the United States' French mission.

"So, Felix," the senator began after we had exchanged a few pleasantries, "tell me about these little teller windows you want to put all over France."

I responded by immediately pointing out that it would not add to our operating costs. And in the process, we would be able to reach a great number of French people who had no previous access to America's diplomatic mission.

"This is a smart plan," Helms decided when I had finished. "I will support it every way I can."

And, true to his word, he did.

Both Elizabeth and I were decorated by the French government for these two programs. It was an honor we were proud to accept.

I also knew from my years as a banker that there was surprisingly little dialogue, and only rather limited partnerships, between French and American companies. I thought I would try to change this, and when I spoke to officials in the State Department and the White House, they responded with enthusiasm.

I began to call the chairmen of both American and French companies, many of them friends. The result was the French American Business Council (FABC).

The first FABC conference was held in June 1998, in the ornate Treaty Room of the Old Executive Office Building adjacent to the White House. President Clinton addressed the large group of executives and spoke about the huge commercial potential of transatlantic business partnerships. In her excellent French, Secretary of State Madeleine Albright also addressed the CEOs.

The next year's meeting in Paris, hosted by the Banque de France, attracted an even larger number of participants. Annual meetings continued during the next few years, but then tapered off. However, plans are presently under way to revive the FABC. Cooperation between American and French companies has grown significantly and I believe that FABC played a part in the renewed economic growth that has taken place between France and the United States.

And then, after I had served nearly four active and enjoyable years as ambassador, a new American president was elected. George Bush, of course, wanted to appoint his own representative to France. Shortly before Christmas 2000, Elizabeth and I returned to our home in New York.

Epilogue

There had been warnings throughout the summer, intimations of the disaster that was looming. For months I had noted the succession of telltale signs; each bit of news was about another financial structure certain to break apart. Nevertheless, when it finally happened I was still shocked. I picked up the *New York Times* as I sipped my coffee on the morning of September 15, 2008, and read a banner headline that once would have seemed unimaginable: "Lehman Files for Bankruptcy."

I sat in stunned silence at the breakfast table, unable to do much more than look out my apartment windows and gaze at the wide, leafy canopy of Central Park's trees stretching into the distance. Autumn had arrived. And Lehman Brothers—one of Wall Street's iconic firms for more than 150 years; an international investment company with $600 billion in assets and 25,000 employees in offices all over the world; a firm I had known and respected throughout my career in finance—had, for all practical purposes, ceased to exist overnight. Lehman had suffered such massive, unprecedented losses from its speculation in mortgage-based securities that it was now forced to file for Chapter 11 bankruptcy protection. This was the largest bankruptcy filing in U.S. history.

I struggled with the unsettling news. I had returned home in 2000 after my nearly four years as ambassador in France to find a changing financial marketplace. And what I observed filled me with concern.

A booming stock market had sent executive compensation soaring, but there was little accountability for performance. Deregulation, an easy monetary policy, and media-driven hype of new information technologies had created essentially "free money" and astronomical stock values. Thousands of stockholders were wiped out and companies ruined when the dot-com bubble burst, but nevertheless little changed. Nonprofit organizations such as colleges, hospitals, and churches saw their endowments crippled and their income reduced to a fraction. The basic requirements of market capitalism—transparency and fairness—were not reinstituted. To the contrary, deregulation gained new political appeal.

The repeal of the Glass-Steagall Act had enabled banks to reenter the securities field for the first time since the Great Depression. One result was that the marketing and manipulation of vast sums of capital had become for some a surefire way to make a profit. Investing, using capital in innovative ways to build a better America, manufacturing reliable products that people needed and would want to purchase—these had become secondary ambitions for many twenty-first-century capitalists.

The financial services business—once very personal, a dialogue between individuals—more and more evolved into an electronic game. Staring at their computer screens, traders would deal with people they never met, buying and selling highly leveraged financial packages throughout the world with a click of a mouse. The only measure of performance was the day's profit or loss. Fortunes were made almost in an instant, and the media roared their approval. Financial wheeler-dealers became heroes, replacing the visionary businessmen who had built America. And neither the SEC, nor the Federal Reserve, nor Congress tried to slow down the wild, freewheeling party.

Dealings

Of course it all had to come to an end. Wall Street's greed, its devising arcane technological methods for packaging and re-packaging ways to make money simply for the sake of profit, its reckless shoveling of enormous amounts of capital into companies whose assets existed largely as a result of inventive account-ing—the consequences were inevitable.

I had denounced the highly leveraged derivatives flooding the marketplace. In a speech at Harvard's Kennedy School in April 2005, I had said that "greed had become one of the main engines of American market capitalism and speculation." "A global fi-nancial crisis," I had suggested, "could very well happen as a re-sult of our present fiscal policies."

And mine was not a solitary voice urging prudence. There were admonitory cautions from such respected personages as Warren Buffett, arguably the nation's most astute investor; from Paul Krugman, the *New York Times* columnist who won a Nobel Prize in economics; and from many others.

As I recalled all the warnings that had gone unheeded, I had little doubt that this disaster could have been avoided. Un-like other economic upheavals, this crisis was not a result of cataclysmic events like wars, natural disasters, or shortages of resources. Rather, the causes of the present collapse were self-inflicted. The nation's economic well-being had been victimized by wrongheaded government policies and avaricious corporate mind-sets. The inevitable product of these two toxic patterns of behavior was a wildly speculative, loosely regulated, grossly un-fair, runaway version of market capitalism: that is, an economic crisis in the making.

More daunting was a fact I knew too well: Lehman's implosion would reverberate with sinister effects throughout an intertwined global economy. Sitting at my breakfast table I grappled with re-ported estimates of the potential worldwide damages: somewhere between $2 trillion and $4 trillion in wealth would be lost.

Even more heartbreaking would be the human consequences, the loss of jobs and personal savings, of foreclosed homes and the economic moorings that had held them in place. Families, suddenly without personal resources or significant government support, would be left to an uncertain future.

In the end, though, my reaction to the news in the morning's paper was personal. About two years earlier I had received a call from Richard Fuld, the chairman of Lehman Brothers, asking if I'd like to play a role as a consultant in its European investment business. At the time, I had been working in semiretirement from the Park Avenue offices I shared with my son Nicky. My days were spent happily, and busily: I researched and wrote *Bold Endeavors*, my book that chose ten episodes from U.S. history to demonstrate how large-scale public investments by tenacious leaders helped to create a better America; I wrote essays for the *New York Review of Books* voicing concern about the nation's deteriorating infrastructure and the gathering economic storm; I headed a commission with former Senator Warren Rudman of New Hampshire that worked on a bill advocating the creation of an Infrastructure Development Bank; and I was still a banker. I regularly advised some of my old clients and a few new ones, and I served on the board of two large European-based companies.

Nevertheless, when Dick Fuld called. I felt confident that the corporate relationships I had in this country and overseas could help Lehman's business in Europe. I told my small personal staff that we would be moving a few blocks uptown to Lehman's sleek office tower on Seventh Avenue.

Now, sitting with my wife at our breakfast table just about two years later, holding the *New York Times* with its incredible banner headline in front of me, I realized I would need to phone my staff and ask them to find cartons. There was packing to do. We'd be leaving Lehman Brothers. The firm was going out of business.

Dealings

Later that morning at Lehman, I watched as all around me people were packing up to leave. The halls and offices were busy with grim activity, and a series of troubling questions filled my mind: When had the seeds of America's present economic crisis been planted? At what point had we, as bankers, as capitalists, as American businessmen, gone so wrong? And what would we need to do to make things right?

I had entered investment banking in a simpler time. My job was to facilitate the vision of businessmen in creating companies that would have the resources to deliver services to consumers and profits to shareholders. Over the decades, however, sound financial principles were trampled by rampant greed. A merger became simply a deal, an abstract financial transaction. It was of little consequence what the businesses "in play" actually did, what they produced, or, for that matter, what would ultimately happen to them. It was irrelevant to the deal makers if thousands of jobs would be lost, if communities would be devastated when companies were shuttered. All that seemed to matter was the astounding wealth that a few people could make in the process.

I witnessed the creation of a new corporate culture. The RJR-Nabisco merger set the tone: huge deals were what mattered, while consequences for employees and communities were too often overlooked. This was the era of highly leveraged speculation—LBOs, junk bonds. Bankers weren't investing in companies as much as churning them. It was an era that created practices and mind-sets, ways of looking at the world and manipulating the marketplace, that led directly to our current economic crisis. Bundles of mortgage-based financial derivatives, the speculative instruments that brought down Lehman, are the stepchildren of junk bonds. The astounding paydays that managers pocketed during successful LBOs are the progenitors of today's huge Wall Street bonuses.

If we are to find a way out of the current crisis, the speculative aspects of our markets need to be addressed. We must follow the advice of Paul Volcker and return to many of the principles of the Glass-Steagall Act to rein in rampant speculation. We must direct capital into productive uses, into businesses that manufacture and produce. And we must deal with the inequalities of lavish paydays for the few in an era of 10 percent unemployment.

Similarly my experiences at the New York Stock Exchange and at MAC had taught me that financial mismanagement and wishful accounting practices were causes of economic disaster. Financial regulations need to be in place and—more important—enforced if market capitalism is going to succeed and government is going to be able to deliver essential services to its citizens. And there must be basic protections for investors, financial safety nets that will offer basic security in rough times.

A no less important lesson I learned from my years dealing with New York City's problems is that in a deteriorating financial situation, sacrifices will have to be made. Yet inexplicably, the Bush administration reduced taxes during wartime, the first government ever to do so. The financial crisis at home, the risks to our banks, and the increasing needs for defense have created a current budget deficit of $1.4 trillion. This deficit is projected to rise over the next decade to $9 trillion. If we are going to move into the future with a strong dollar, if we are going to be able to offer all our citizens the benefits of adequate health care and education, if America is to regain its position as a land of opportunities, then we will need to deal with these deficits in a responsible, programmatic way.

Yet I remain a capitalist. I believe that market capitalism is the best economic system ever invented. But it must be fair; it must be regulated; and it must be ethical. That is the fundamental lesson I had learned in my fifty years in finance and politics.

And that day as my boxes were packed, I found reassurance in these principles. Yet I could not help wondering, what would be the next adventure in my life?

—

And then, as throughout my life and career, a chance moment brought a new and propitious opportunity. I was standing next to my friend Vernon Jordan in Rockefeller Center as we waited for an elevator when he turned to me and, with a seemingly off-handed nonchalance, asked, "Why don't you join us?"

I was stunned. Vernon, a director of Lazard, was asking me to return to the investment banking firm where I had started my career and had worked for nearly half a century. Without any hesitation, I answered.

"I'd be delighted," I said. Still, I told Vernon, I had to wonder if the firm's other partners would be interested in having an eighty-one-year-old investment banker join them. If they were, though, I'd be very happy to have a discussion with them.

Vernon called later that afternoon. He had spoken to Kenneth Jacobs, the new CEO of Lazard who had been appointed in the aftermath of the recent sudden and tragic death of Bruce Wasserstein, and to Antonio Weiss, the head of the firm's global investment banking division. Both men thought my coming back to Lazard was, he said, "a very good idea."

I thought so, too. It would bring my career in banking full-circle—a return to the firm where I had first learned my trade. And I believed I could make a contribution to Lazard. At a time when the marketplace was besieged with doubts and uncertainties, I hoped that I could work with my new colleagues to help the firm through these difficult and demanding circumstances.

Certainly, I could not pretend that I had real expertise in the new financial technologies that were shaping large segments of the investment industry. These are the domain of a younger generation.

The financial services industry is at a turning point. If it is going to help companies and investors during a decade when doubts continue to undermine the marketplace, if it is going to help businesses to provide jobs and services—then, I believe, it needs to return to the values and practices that were first instilled in me by André Meyer. Investment banking is not a business; it is a personal service where bankers work hand in hand with their clients. And it is a service that must not simply be about making bigger and bigger deals that reap rewards for only a small group of executives. It should aim to create new partnerships that result in stronger, more innovative companies able to provide new jobs and better services. These are the fundamental beliefs that guided me in the past. And they will once again guide me in the future.

So, as I finish this memoir, I am returning to where I had started. It is, however, not simply a return to something that came before. As I enter my ninth decade, these new challenges are my future, too. With great anticipation, I look forward to what lies ahead.

Acknowledgments

First and foremost, I would like to thank my wife, Elizabeth, who is always my wisest counsel.

I owe a great debt of thanks to Howard Blum, whose skillful editing enabled me to refine and improve my original manuscript. I was also fortunate to have the insight of a legendary editor, Alice Mayhew, and without the efforts of my agent, Lynn Nesbit, this book probably would still be a large stack of handwritten pages. I am grateful as well to Roger Labrie and Victoria Meyer at Simon & Schuster for their expertise and support.

I would also like to thank Bill Barrett for his suggestions and help in editing the manuscript, particularly its later chapters. My assistant, Liz Davies, also provided important editorial assistance and made certain that the book was factually correct. Alexandra Truitt's excellent photo researching was also greatly appreciated, as were the efforts of Marie-Noelle Knowlton in assisting with the text edits.

Photo Credits

All photos are from the author's private collection with the following exceptions:

7: © Bettmann/Corbis

8: © Philippe Lesage/Elipsa/Sygma/Corbis

9: From *TIME* 9/8/1967, © 1967 TIME, Inc. All rights reserved. Used by permission and protected by the Copyright Laws of the United States. The printing, copying, redistribution, or retransmission of the Material without express written permission is prohibited.

10: © Bettmann/Corbis

11: © Martha Holmes/Time Life Pictures/Getty Images

12: © Paul Conklin/Pix Inc./Time Life Pictures/Getty Images

13: Courtesy of GE

14: © RED/dqcartoons/NewsCom.com

15: © NY Daily News Archive via Getty Images

16: From *Newsweek* 5/4/1981, © 1981 Newsweek, Inc. All rights reserved. Used by permission and protected by the Copyright Laws of the United States. The printing, copying, redistribution, or retransmission of the Material without express written permission is prohibited. Cover photos; © Henri Dauman, © Bill Ray.

18: © NY Daily News Archive via Getty Images

19: © Bettmann/Corbis

21: © NY Daily News Archive via Getty Images

22: © STF/AFP/Getty Images

24: © Star Black

25: Presidence de la Republique Francaise, Service Photographique

26: Official White House Photograph

30: Photo by Mark Ribaud

Index

Index

Index

Index

Index

Index

Index

Index

About the Author

Felix Rohatyn, a frequent contributor to the *New York Review of Books,* was a managing director at the investment banking firm Lazard Frères and served as the U.S. ambassador to France. From 1975 to 1993, Mr. Rohatyn was chairman of the Municipal Assistance Corporation of the State of New York, managing the negotiations that enabled New York City to resolve its financial crisis.